# THE
# POWER
# OF THE
# POWERLESS

# The Power
# of the Powerless

Citizens against the state in central-
eastern Europe

Václav Havel *et al.*

Introduction by Steven Lukes

*Edited by John Keane*

**M. E. Sharpe, Inc.**

Armonk, New York

Copyright © Palach Press, 1985

**Library of Congress Cataloging-in-Publication Data**

Main entry title:

The Power of the powerless.

"Published simultaneously as vol. XV, no. 3-4, of International journal of politics"—T.p. verso.
    Contents: The Power of the powerless / Václav Havel — Spiritual values, independent initiatives, and politics / Rudolf Battěk — Catholicism and politics / Václav Benda — [etc.]
    1. Europe, Eastern—Politics and government—1945-    —Addresses, essays, lectures. 2. Civil rights—Europe, Eastern—Addresses, essays, lectures. I. Havel, Václav. II. Keane, John, 1949-

DJK50.P68    1985    323.4'0947    85-24978
ISBN 0-87332-370-X (cloth) ISBN 0-87332-761-6 (paper)

Printed in the United States of America

MV (c) 10  9  8  7  6  5  4  3  2  1
MV (p) 10  9  8  7  6  5  4

# Contents

6 *The Power of the Powerless*

# Editor's preface

## John Keane

Books of great political insight and novelty always outlive their time of birth, and this one is no exception. Written shortly after the formation of Charter 77 and just prior to the birth of Solidarność, it is among the most original and compelling pieces of political writing to have emerged from central and eastern Europe during the whole of the post-war period. It is centrally concerned with explaining the anti-democratic features, as well as the limits, of Soviet-type 'totalitarian' systems of power. For some time now, it is true, the concept of totalitarianism has been in relative disfavour in the West, certainly when compared with the years of the 1940s and 1950s. That period saw not only the popularization of the term, first as an element in the struggle against fascism and, later, as an anti-communist slogan of the Cold War; it also spawned the 'classic' intellectual writings against the Stalinist and Nazi forms of totalitarian rule, such as Hannah Arendt's *The Origins of Totalitarianism*, Max Horkheimer and Theodor Adorno's *Dialectic of Enlightenment*, Arthur Koestler's *Darkness at Noon*, and George Orwell's *Nineteen Eighty-Four*.

Since those years, serious analyses of the twentieth-century problem of totalitarianism have been relatively scarce in the West. This can be attributed to various connected factors. These include the virtual monopoly exercised by the conservative Right over the public criticism of Soviet-type totalitarianism, as well as the consequent unease and embarrassment of many on the Left about the disturbing implications of this totalitarianism for the whole ideal of socialism. The validity of 'totalitarianism' as a theoretical concept was also challenged, on the grounds that a perfectly totalitarian regime has nowhere ever been established (a wholly unconvincing objection, considering that every concept we employ to analyse large-scale political phenomena necessarily has no perfect empirical equivalent). Finally, the decline in popularity of the concept of totalitarianism also stemmed in part from the growing awareness that some things have changed in Soviet-type regimes, that the brutal and monstrous delirium of 'classical' totalitarianism has, since the death of Stalin, given way to regimes of power whose systematic repressiveness is less openly brutal and more calculated.

*The Power of the Powerless* is a welcome reaction against this recent Western silence about the problem of totalitarian forms of power. Writing mostly from a highly original democratic socialist standpoint, its authors draw attention to the depressing *novelty* of contemporary Soviet-type regimes such as Czechoslovakia. These neo-totalitarian regimes, as they might be called, are, like their Stalinist predecessors, systems of state control of all areas of human life. These systems can only function by extinguishing civil society in its entirety and, thus, by denying any difference between the orders of power, law and publically circulated opinion and information. Consequently, no citizen is innocent before the state; in effect, each citizen is subject to a form of permanent interference. Public opposition of any kind is always regarded by the State authorities as seditious, which is also why 'dissidents' are to be found not only among the intellectuals, but also in every café, street queue, factory and church.

Compared with their 'classical' counterparts, the authors of this book suggest, neo-totalitarian regimes nevertheless exhibit some decidedly novel characteristics. Brutal repression and government by fear continue, but in more anonymous, selective and calculated form. Moreover, while the party-dominated state continues its attempts to smother public life by constructing and reproducing a wholly fictitious image of the past, present and future world, almost no one (probably not even senior party apparatchiks) believes any longer in its pantomime of empty, ritualized claims. The utter disregard for efficiency characteristic of the delirium of the Stalin period has also been abandoned. Finally, no longer do these regimes strive to control fully the bodies and souls of their subjects, to embrace everything in depth, to bring everyone together so as to produce a single will, crystallized in the caesarist leader. Contemporary totalitarianism demands precisely the opposite of its populations: passivity, opportunism, mediocrity, cynicism, an exclusive concern with cultivating such 'private' concerns as career and family life. The regime of 'real socialism' is content with the regulation and control of *apparent* behaviour; so long as its subjects conform and only disagree silently, they are probably safe.

This is why all attempts to democratically resist the pressure of the neo-totalitarian system have their essential beginnings in the extra-state areas of civil society. Here a different life – a kind of anti-political politics – can be lived, and the self-sustaining aspects of the system, its presence within each individual, can be shaken off. The history of *The Power of the Powerless* is an exemplary case of this democratic form of civil resistance. This book is the fruit of a 1978 initiative of Czechoslovak and Polish citizens committed to the defence of civil rights. In that year they prepared a joint seminar on the aims, problems and possibilities of their respective democratic movements. The written contributions to the seminar were to be published in a joint Czechoslovak–Polish collection. However, the original venture was jeopardized by the arrest, in May 1979, of ten members of *VONS* (the Czechoslovak Committee for the Defence of the Unjustly Prosecuted), of whom four are contributors to this somewhat selected and shortened English edition of the original collection. As a consequence of this state interference, the original project had to be hurried forward, and it was decided by the authors to publish the Czechoslovak contributions separately. This original volume, entitled *On Freedom and Power*, was introduced by an extensive essay by Václav Havel, who had earlier agreed to write a kind of discussion paper for the seminar participants. This very fine and innovative essay by Havel, reproduced here in full, was subsequently made available to the other contributors, who in turn responded to the many questions raised by Havel about the potential power of the powerless under neo-totalitarian conditions.

The enthusiastic and committed efforts of the following people made possible this English edition of the original Czechoslovak collection: Jan Kavan of Palach Press; Steven Lukes and Zdena Tomin; A. G. Brain and Paul Wilson, who translated the essays; and Hutchinson University Library editors, Sarah Conibear and Claire L'Enfant.

John Keane
*London*
*January 1985*

# Introduction

## Steven Lukes

This remarkable collection of essays has for some time deserved translation and a wider readership for two sorts of reasons. On the one hand, these essays are important historical documents. They are evidence of great interest to the historian and observer of contemporary communism in Czechoslovakia and within the Soviet bloc as a whole. More importantly, they are valuable texts in their own right. They are essays of interpretation, argument and analysis that shed light not only upon the nature of contemporary communism but, more widely, on some basic political questions that arise in the West no less than in the East. Moreover, they address these questions in a fresh and challenging way.

### I

As historical documents, they are to be seen as the product and expression of the Czechoslovak experience of 'real socialism' at a moment when the opposition to it crystallized and coalesced in a peculiarly dramatic way. They represent the first flowering of theoretical reflection on the part of a wide variety of intellectuals in the period between the founding of the Charter in 1977 (see Appendix) and the subsequent persecution of its signatories and supporters. The history of that persecution can be glimpsed in the Biographical notes.

One of the first instances of such reflection was Václav Benda's essay, 'The Parallel Polis' (written in May 1978 and circulated in *samizdat* in Czechoslovakia).[1]* This argued powerfully for the growth of a whole range of 'parallel' cultural, educational, economic, even political structures. Benda sought in this way to

---

* Superior figures refer to the Notes at the end of each chapter.

transform an 'abstract moral attitude' into a unifying factor and source of dynamism, which would thus have a field of activity and a positive goal: the creation of a 'parallel society'. Benda had in mind the cultural underground, especially rock music (decisive in the very beginnings of the Charter itself), and graphic art, alternative theatrical performances, unofficial publishing, unofficial education, both for children and adults, parallel information services, the 'creation of conditions for political discussion and the formulation of political opinions', a parallel 'foreign policy' and co-operation with parallel movements inside the eastern bloc. Benda's essay led to much discussion, some of it continued in these essays (see especially Uhl's and Hejdánek's). Indeed, most of them were written in an atmosphere created by discussions that Benda's essay helped to create.

No less important was Václav Havel's 'The Power of the Powerless'. Like his plays (notably *The Garden Party*, *The Memorandum*, *The Increased Difficulty of Concentration*, and *The Interview*), this gives a striking and penetrating portrayal of the distinctive bureaucratic structure of domination in eastern Europe today and its complex roots in, and impact on, the relationships of ordinary life. Havel's essay made a great impression and formed the centrepiece to a collection of eighteen essays published in 1979 in *samizdat*, of which ten are republished here.

The 1979 collection, originally entitled *On Freedom and Power*, was intended as a joint Czechoslovak-Polish venture, the beginnings of a projected collaboration across frontiers. This project met with harassment and persecution in Czechoslovakia and, with the rise of Solidarity in Poland, it has assumed different forms. The Poles were from the start much impressed by what Havel and the others were saying. For instance, the Warsaw Solidarity leader, Zbygniew Bujak, commented in 1981 that Havel's essay 'gave us theoretical backing, a theoretical basis for our actions. He enabled us to believe in their effectiveness. Until I read his text I was full of doubts'.[2] Paradoxically, at that time (1978–80) there was significantly greater space for a parallel *polis* and developing the power of the powerless in Poland than there ever was in Czechoslovakia. Unofficial publishing, for example, had reached immense proportions and the 'Flying University' was significantly more extensive and organized than the underground 'Patočka University' in Czechoslovakia. More important still was the growth of independent, 'parallel' unions in the Baltic ports and the links between intellectuals and workers, notably through the 'Workers' Defence Committee' (*KOR*). One central reason for this difference was, of course, the protective existence, and sometimes assistance, of the Catholic Church in Poland. The Poles, in a sense, saw the Czechoslovaks as helping to develop the theory for their emerging practice – and the debate was continued by Adam Michnik and others in Poland. Most of the essays in *On Freedom and Power* were published in Polish *samizdat* periodicals soon after they were written and they were widely discussed and commented upon. Such comments and responses appeared as individual articles in Polish *samizdat* magazines, not, as originally intended, in a second volume of *On Freedom and Power*. A more active and mutual collaboration was temporarily postponed with arrests and trials in Czechoslovakia and the eruption of Solidarity in Poland in late 1980. Nevertheless, the Czechoslovak-Polish discussion has continued and developed out of this early and formative discussion.

*On Freedom and Power*, and the discussions flowing from it, can be seen as the latest Czechoslovak link in the chain of indigenous oppositional movements that reaches back to East Germany in 1953, Poland and Hungary in 1956, and Yugoslavia and Czechoslovakia itself in the mid 1960s, and forward to events in Poland. And indeed these essays look both backwards and forwards. The ghosts of 'reform communism', 'Dubčekism', 'socialism with a human face' (and, behind them, of all the earlier 'revisionist' attempts to 'humanize' east European Marxism) stalk some of these pages. These essays also appeal, variously, to Czech national traditions, notably its suppressed literary heritage (mourned by Černý) and the ethical teachings of Jan Patočka, to non-Marxist social democracy, to Catholicism, Woytilla-style, to lay protestantism, and to a kind of transplanted Trotskyism. They all, however, share a commitment to the rule of law and the restoration of civic virtue, the official commitment to, and betrayal of, which, they all unite in exposing. This was and remains the meaning of Charter 77, of which all our authors are signatories.

They also look forward, though with less agreement and less certainty, to innovative forms of opposition, alternative ways of acting and living, new ways of turning moral gestures into political activity. The overwhelming problem was, and remains, how to convert the tiny minority of Chartists into a significant social and political force, how to make connections with the concerns and interests of the silent, or rather *silenced*, majority. It was clear from an early stage that the programme of the Charter could not achieve this. As Kusý puts it succinctly here, the claim that the Charter could make it possible for people to live in truth and justice and for decency and legality to prevail within the existing framework was unconvincing:

If we understand this defence as an exclusively moral appeal, it is utopian; if we take it to be a tactical confrontation with the powers that be, it is Švejkian;* if we see it as a political program, it is inconsistent, half-hearted and toothless.

This problem raised by Kusý runs like a thread through all these essays and subsequent Charter discussions. In Poland, for fifteen extraordinary months, this problem at least seemed to be solved.

One may even venture the thought that this collection may turn out to have been one of the last remnants of recognizably socialist dissent in the Soviet bloc. None of these essays is explicitly unfriendly to the socialist idea or socialist principles. None advocates a return to capitalism or even liberal democracy; and none is touched by the various forms of free market ideology that have since become dominant in the Anglo-Saxon West. Most engage in the 'immanent critique' of so-called 'real socialism' for failing to live up to its principles, which none explicitly rejects. With the exception of Uhl, and in a different way Hájek, these authors have no particular attachment to the *Marxian* socialist tradition, but they do not reject it either (though Havel suggests that there was in its origins a 'genetic disposition to the monstrous alienation characteristic of its subsequent development'); some explicitly adhere to democratic, non-Marxist socialist traditions. The socialist tradition, in one form or another, still haunts these essays.

Recent events in Poland have already marked a decisive move away from this position. I vividly recall talking to Jacek Kuroń in Warsaw in 1980 (six months before Solidarity) and asking him whether he thought contemporary Poland or western capitalist

---

* *Editor's note*: The term Švejkian refers here and throughout to the ironic and naïve, but earnest adoption of official regulations and commands, as if they were always appropriate and genuine guides to action. The term derives from the main character of Jaroslav Hašek's humorous and satiric novel, *The Good Soldier Švejk*. Švejk was an infantry man who, in the Austro-Hungarian army during the First World War, exploited his apparent stupidity to survive military life.

democracies were nearer to socialism. His response was instructive. We could not, he said, discuss my question any longer in such terms. 'What we have here', he said, gesturing around him '*is* socialism.' We must use other vocabulary and talk, for example, of 'democratizing the state apparatus'. The language and indeed the very conceptual structure of socialism was, for Kuroń then, hopelessly compromised.[3] And it is noteworthy that Solidarity, the largest popular revolution (albeit initially 'self-limiting' and eventually aborted) against communist rule ever to have erupted was a remarkable amalgam of the ethical teachings of Catholicism, of Polish nationalism, of liberal democratic values and of a basic egalitarianism. But this last feature was not dominant and it had no particular links with socialism, even with a human face.

There are many reasons why the Czechoslovaks did not and could not follow the Poles (nor are either likely to follow the Hungarians into a kind of semi-affluent consumerism). But in one respect at least they are all at one. The aspirations of 'socialism with a human face' à la Dubček (now called reform communism) now seem hopelessly antiquated, above all in Czechoslovakia. There is a felt need for a new framework that is at once morally, intellectually and politically compelling. Hence the appeal of Christianity, especially Catholicism (increasingly popular and increasingly repressed), nationalism and the various varieties of contemporary conservatism, some highly reactionary (the very word 'progressive' is contaminated). Some voices in Charter circles may still speak the language of democratic socialism. Yet it seems possible that one of the long-term achievements of 'real socialism' in the Soviet bloc may turn out to be the extinction there of the entire socialist tradition as a theoretical system worthy of serious consideration, let alone allegiance, wherever it is practised. (It has not exactly helped the prospects of socialism in the West either.) These essays help explain and partially resist that ironic and tragic development.

## II

These essays are not, however, merely symptomatic. They attempt to explain and interpret the Czechoslovak and more generally the east European system and the nature of, and prospects for, opposition within it. As such, they greatly repay attention and reflection.

Taken together, they constitute a wide spectrum of approaches to

Christian and Marxist influences, and the need to separate civil society and the state and democratize both.

There are also, however, notable continuities. All agree that the age of ideological socialist commitment and enthusiasm is long past, and that the present system rests upon what Vohryzek calls 'a total vacuum of civic will, a *perpetuum silentium*, passivity and quiescence': 'quiet disagreement is one of the pillars' of what Vohryzek persists in seeing as 'totalitarian power'. All see this vacuum or silence as the central problem of interpretation and the overwhelming obstacle to be overcome. What is the meaning of that silence? Or rather, what is the political meaning of all the various activities of everyday life - the greengrocer's slogan, the general retreat into privacy and withdrawal from public concerns, the turn to consumer values (stressed by a number of our authors), graft, corruption and skiving on a mass scale, pushing up the value of labour, the telling of jokes - on which the entire system depends? To what extent, and when, can they be seen as forms of *resistance* rather than quiescence?

Of course, the system is also a massive system of control and coercion. Behind it - the obvious sometimes needs to restated - stands the Red Army, without which the system would not survive for a moment. Central to such control, as Vohryzek argues, is the officially proclaimed 'right to work' which, ironically enough, is invoked in threatening and punishing dissenting intellectuals and professionals and their children with *manual labour*. Fulfilling, identity-conferring work becomes a privilege within this system; manual work (especially of the unproductive variety) a punishment. Once more, a brief look at this book's biographical notes (p. 222) makes the point better than I can.

Yet, as Vohryzek also notes, the silence is one of 'silent disagreement'. This profoundly important point indicates another common theme of these essays: that the term 'dissident' is misleading in suggesting that those, such as the authors printed here, who speak out are a small and isolated minority *who think differently from the rest*. The point, rather, is that they are few and isolated just because they speak aloud, and reflect upon, what everyone thinks.

## III

The interest of these essays, seen as explanatory and interpretative texts, reaches, however, beyond the confines of central and eastern Europe and the analysis of contemporary communist systems. There is rich material here for reflection upon the mechanics of power, the nature and effects of ideology, the meaning of a public sphere, the point and justification of civil disobedience, and the links between morality and politics. Such classical questions are addressed, Czechoslovak-style, in the form of *feuilletons*, 'published' originally in *samizdat*, and combine hard thinking with literary flair, and both with a pressing sense of immediacy and sometimes danger. There is, as a matter of fact, little idle small-talk (although there is much rich humour) among Czechoslovak intellectuals. There is also scant reason and little opportunity for scholasticism, erudition and idle flights of fancy for their own sakes. These essays are, in my view, examples of applied political theory at its best: reflections upon fundamental moral and political questions that link (in C. Wright Mills's phrase) public issues and private troubles, and thereby reach to the heart of things.

Students of power can derive much from Havel's essay and students of ideology much from Kusý's; and students of both much from reading them together. I know of few subtler and more thought-provoking discussions of the way in which power becomes impersonal and anonymous, a feature of the system in which individuals are caught up, such that they become 'agents of its automatism . . . petty instruments of social autototality'. Also worthy of particular note is Havel's distinction between 'the post-totalitarian system' and 'classical dictatorships', in which the line of conflict between rulers and ruled can still be drawn according to social class. In the post-totalitarian system,

this line runs *de facto* through each person, for everyone in his or her own way is both a victim and a supporter of the system. What we understand by the system is not, therefore, a social order imposed by one group upon another, but rather something which permeates the entire society and is a factor in shaping it. . . .

As for ideology, Havel treats it as 'an increasingly important component of power, a pillar providing it with both excusatory legitimacy and an inner coherence'. By giving individuals 'the illusion of an identity, of dignity and of morality while making it easier for them to *part* with them', enabling them 'to deceive their conscience and conceal their true position and their inglorious *modus vivendi*, both from the world and from themselves', it creates a 'bridge of excuses between the system and the individual' spanning 'the abyss between the aims of the system and the aims of life'. As I have suggested above, Kusý's essay is a fascinating further exploration of this theme. His concept of the ideology of 'as if' (echoing Vaihinger's *Philosophy of 'As If'*) is a neat and subtle variation upon a familiar Orwellian theme:

those who preach it behave *as if* the ideological kingdom of real socialism existed in 'what we have here now', *as if* they had, in all earnestness, convinced the nation of its existence; the nation behaves *as if* it believed it, *as if* it were convinced that it lived in accordance with this ideologically real socialism.

This, too, is a rich idea worthy of further development and applications to other ideological systems. To what extent, for example, does it capture the present 'revival' of Islam? To what extent, in our own society, are 'belief' and 'commitment' to various causes sustained in such inglorious ways?

All these essays bear eloquent witness to the manifold consequences of the lack of a public sphere, an arena in which collective concerns and interests may be articulated and public policy debated and formulated openly. Equally, they all exemplify – as do the lives of their authors (as I write, Rudolf Battěk is still in prison) – the case for resistance through the reasoned and principled gesture in defiance of unjust laws, directed at the conscience of one's fellow-citizens – in other words, civil disobedience. Yet such resistance requires there to be a minimal public sphere to make its point and achieve its results. Draft resistance in the United States during the Vietnam War, Gandhi's campaigns against the British in India, and various law-breaking activities of western peace movements precisely rely upon the possibility that rulers will respond to such appeals to the *public* conscience. What many east Europeans have often held (and not always unjustly) against certain sections of the western peace movement is that they, and others in the west, have sometimes failed to understand that just this possibility is absent in the East. Ironically, it is precisely those laws that have extinguished public life in Czechoslovakia that render the typical activities of Chartists – such as unofficial publishing, lectures and seminars, the circulation of banned books and manuscripts, underground cultural activities – illegal. Indeed, pursuit of the very activities banned in the East is a necessary condition for the occasional effectiveness of civil disobedience in the West.

What could render it more effective in the East? One answer is: far greater responsiveness and support from the west. For, as recent Polish events have demonstrated, even if a direct, indeed revolutionary confrontation with the ruling powers must fail in such systems, they may be amenable to well-judged western pressure, especially in the context of economic adversity. The moral is, perhaps, that the 'parallel *polis*' should be seen as not merely a potentiality within central and eastern Europe, but in the form of international solidarity outside it. This moral was suggested in Benda's original essay. It is implicit in various recent developments, notably the regular visits by western philosophers and others to Prague seminars, and the opening up of a dialogue between the Charter and sections of the western peace movement.[4]

Finally, these essays are all, in different ways, reflections upon the links between morality and politics. All see a line between morality and politics, though they draw it in different places. All distrust mere *moralizing* and the falsely reassuring thought that taking a moral stand is enough, under present conditions, to make such a stand political. All are critical of the narrow conception of, and the vastly extended scope of, official political life in contemporary Czechoslovakia. What are the political conditions for a morally healthy society? When they do not obtain, what forms of political action are morally appropriate and which are to be ruled out? In a system where political life is universally seen as involving deceit, manipulation and opportunism, as an 'as if' game in which all the participants have 'dirty hands', how can a sense of morality in public life be rediscovered? These are fundamental and urgent questions and the experience of central and eastern Europe poses them in a peculiarly acute form.

## Notes

1  Translated into English by Palach Press and published in *Palach Press Bulletin* (London 1979).
2  *Krytyka*, no. 8 (Warsaw 1981), and reprinted in *Aneks* (London 1982), p. 35.
3  According to the Czechoslavak writer Milan Šimečka, 'existing

socialism' has turned 'a movement totally geared to the future into a self-satisfied present. It has thus stolen from socialism any future it might have had. There can be no other way of understanding the term; indeed that is how it is officially interpreted. What it says is that socialism as a model for a just and ever-changing order of society has ceased to exist: socialism is neither more nor less than the system we have in the Soviet Union and the countries of eastern Europe. Miroslav Kusý has accurately described this as an 'ostensive' definition, typical of a time of ideological desperation. When asked to define socialism, they point their finger and say: this is socialism. The finger is never quite sure whether it should also point in the direction of Yugoslavia, China, or even Albania. But what it does say quite clearly is that only the actually existing systems of socialism can be taken seriously – everything else, above all Euro-communism, is poppycock designed to deceive public opinion. Democratic socialism is just such poppycock, and the worst of all was the ludicrous and short-lived socialism with a human face in Czechoslovakia'. (Milan Šimečka, *The Restoration of Order: The Normalization of Czechoslovakia* (London 1984).)

4  See *Voices From Prague. Czechoslovakia, Human Rights and the Peace Movement*, edited by Jan Kavan and Zdena Tomin, and published by European Nuclear Disarmament and Palach Press (London 1983). Also relevant here is a recent Charter document which states: 'We consider the emergence of the independent peace movement in the West to be a major watershed . . . for our strivings to obtain more democratic and freer conditions in our part of Europe', while insisting that 'peace and democracy are indivisible, that it is naïve to consider building peace on the ruins of civil liberties and democratic rights'. (Charter Document no. 14/84: *Open Letter to the Third Conference on European Nuclear Disarmament*, translated by Palach Press, London 1984.) On his release from prison, Havel gave an interview in which he said:

I consider these young, long-haired people who keep demonstrating for peace in various western cities and whom I saw almost daily when I was in jail, where we were forced to watch the TV news, to be my brothers and sisters: they aren't indifferent to the fate of the world and they voluntarily take upon themselves a responsibility outside the sphere of their own personal well-being, and that – though in more difficult circumstances – is exactly what we are doing. (*Voices from Prague*, p. 42)

# THE
# POWER
# OF THE
# POWERLESS

# 1   The power of the powerless*

## Václav Havel

*To the memory of Jan Patočka*


I

A spectre is haunting eastern Europe: the spectre of what in the West is called 'dissent'. This spectre has not appeared out of thin air. It is a natural and inevitable consequence of the present historical phase of the system it is haunting. It was born at a time when this system, for a thousand reasons, can no longer base itself on the unadulterated, brutal, and arbitrary application of power, eliminating all expressions of nonconformity. What is more, the system has become so ossified politically that there is practically no way for such nonconformity to be implemented within its official structures.

Who are these so-called 'dissidents'? Where does their point of view come from, and what importance does it have? What is the significance of the 'independent initiatives' in which 'dissidents' collaborate, and what real chances do such initiatives have of success? Is it appropriate to refer to 'dissidents' as an opposition? If so, what exactly is such an opposition within the framework of this system? What does it do? What role does it play in society? What are its hopes and on what are they based? Is it within the power of the 'dissidents' – as a category of subcitizen outside the power establishment – to have any influence at all on society and the social system? Can they actually change anything?

I think that an examination of these questions – an examination of the potential of the 'powerless' – can only begin with an examination of the nature of power in the circumstances in which these powerless people operate.

---

* Translated by Paul Wilson.

II

Our system is most frequently characterized as a dictatorship or, more precisely, as the dictatorship of a political bureaucracy over a society which has undergone economic and social levelling. I am afraid that the term 'dictatorship', regardless of how intelligible it may otherwise be, tends to obscure rather than clarify the real nature of power in this system. We usually associate the term with the notion of a small group of people who take over the government of a given country by force; their power is wielded openly, using the direct instruments of power at their disposal, and they are easily distinguished socially from the majority over whom they rule. One of the essential aspects of this traditional or classical notion of dictatorship is the assumption that it is temporary, ephemeral, lacking historical roots. Its existence seems to be bound up with the lives of those who established it. It is usually local in extent and significance, and regardless of the ideology it utilizes to grant itself legitimacy, its power derives ultimately from the numbers and the armed might of its soldiers and police. The principal threat to its existence is felt to be the possibility that someone better equipped in this sense might appear and overthrow it.

Even this very superficial overview should make it clear that the system in which we live has very little in common with a classical dictatorship. In the first place, our system is not limited in a local, geographical sense; rather it holds sway over a huge power bloc controlled by one of the two superpowers. And although it quite naturally exhibits a number of local and historical variations, the range of these variations is fundamentally circumscribed by a single, unifying framework throughout the power bloc. Not only is the dictatorship everywhere based on the same principles and structured in the same way (that is, in the way evolved by the ruling superpower), but each country has been completely penetrated by a network of manipulatory instruments controlled by the superpower centre and totally subordinated to its interests. In the stalemated world of nuclear parity, of course, that circumstance endows the system with an unprecedented degree of external stability compared with classical dictatorships. Many local crises which, in an isolated state, would lead to a change in the system, can be resolved through direct intervention by the armed forces of the rest of the bloc.

In the second place, if a feature of classical dictatorships is their lack of historical roots (frequently they appear to be no more than historical freaks, the fortuitous consequence of fortuitous social processes or of human and mob tendencies), the same cannot be said so facilely about our system. For even though our dictatorship has long since alienated itself completely from the social movements that gave birth to it, the authenticity of these movements (and I am thinking of the proletarian and socialist movements of the nineteenth century) give it undeniable historicity. These origins provided a solid foundation of sorts on which it could build until it became the utterly new social and political reality it is today, which has become so inextricably a part of the structure of the modern world. A feature of those historical origins was the 'correct understanding' of social conflicts in the period from which those original movements emerged. The fact that at the very core of this 'correct understanding' there was a genetic disposition toward the monstrous alienation characteristic of its subsequent development is not essential here. And in any case, this element also grew organically from the climate of that time and therefore can be said to have its origin there as well.

One legacy of that original 'correct understanding' is a third peculiarity that makes our system different from other modern dictatorships: it commands an incomparably more precise, logically structured, generally comprehensible and, in essence, extremely flexible ideology that, in its elaborateness and completeness, is almost a secularized religion. It offers a ready answer to any question whatsoever; it can scarcely be accepted only in part, and accepting it has profound implications for human life. In an era when metaphysical and existential certainties are in a state of crisis, when people are being uprooted and alienated and are losing their sense of what this world means, this ideology inevitably has a certain hypnotic charm. To wandering humankind it offers an immediately available home: all one has to do is accept it, and suddenly everything becomes clear once more, life takes on new meaning, and all mysteries, unanswered questions, anxiety, and loneliness vanish. Of course, one pays dearly for this low-rent home: the price is abdication of one's own reason, conscience, and responsibility, for an essential aspect of this ideology is the consignment of reason and conscience to a higher authority. The principle involved here is that the centre of power is identical with the centre of truth. (In our case, the connection with Byzantine theocracy is direct: the highest secular authority is identical with the highest spiritual authority.) It is true of course that, all this aside, ideology no longer has any great influence on people, at least within our bloc (with the possible exception of Russia, where the serf mentality, with its blind, fatalistic respect for rulers and its automatic acceptance of all their claims, is still dominant and combined with a superpower patriotism which traditionally places the interests of empire higher than the interests of humanity). But this is not important, because ideology plays its role in our system very well (an issue to which I will return) precisely because it is what it is.

Fourth, the technique of exercising power in traditional dictatorships contains a necessary element of improvisation. The mechanisms for wielding power are for the most part not established firmly, and there is considerable room for accident and for the arbitrary and unregulated application of power. Socially, psychologically, and physically conditions still exist for the expression of some form of opposition. In short, there are many seams on the surface which can split apart before the entire power structure has managed to stabilize. Our system, on the other hand, has been developing in the Soviet Union for over sixty years, and for approximately thirty years in eastern Europe; moreover, several of its long-established structural features are derived from Czarist absolutism. In terms of the physical aspects of power, this has led to the creation of such intricate and well-developed mechanisms for the direct and indirect manipulation of the entire population that, as a physical power base, it represents something radically new. At the same time, let us not forget that the system is made significantly more effective by state ownership and central direction of all the means of production. This gives the power structure an unprecedented and uncontrollable capacity to invest in itself (in the areas of the bureaucracy and the police, for example) and makes it easier for that structure, as the sole employer, to manipulate the day-to-day existence of all citizens.

Finally, if an atmosphere of revolutionary excitement, heroism, dedication, and boisterous violence on all sides characterizes classical dictatorships, then the last traces of such an atmosphere have vanished from the Soviet bloc. For some time now this bloc has ceased to be a kind of enclave, isolated from the rest of the developed world and immune to processes occurring in it. To the contrary, the Soviet bloc is an integral part of that larger world, and it shares and shapes the world's destiny. This means in concrete terms that the hierarchy of values existing in the developed countries of the West has, in essence, appeared in our society (the long period of coexistence with the West has only hastened this process). In other words, what we have here is simply another form of the consumer and industrial society, with all its concomitant social, intellectual, and psychological consequences. It is impossible to understand the nature of power in our system properly without taking this into account.

The profound difference between our system – in terms of the nature of power – and what we traditionally understand by dictatorship, a difference I hope is clear even from this quite superficial comparison, has caused me to search for some term appropriate for our system, purely for the purposes of this essay. If I refer to it henceforth as a *post-totalitarian* system, I am fully aware that this is perhaps not the most precise term, but I am unable to think of a better one. I do not wish to imply by the prefix 'post-' that the system is no longer totalitarian; on the contrary, I mean that it is totalitarian in a way fundamentally different from classical dictatorships, different from totalitarianism as we usually understand it.

The circumstances I have mentioned, however, form only a circle of conditional factors and a kind of phenomenal framework for the actual composition of power in the post-totalitarian system, several aspects of which I shall now attempt to identify.


## III

The manager of a fruit and vegetable shop places in his window, among the onions and carrots, the slogan: 'Workers of the World, Unite!' Why does he do it? What is he trying to communicate to the world? Is he genuinely enthusiastic about the idea of unity among the workers of the world? Is his enthusiasm so great that he feels an irrepressible impulse to acquaint the public with his ideals? Has he really given more than a moment's thought to how such a unification might occur and what it would mean?

I think it can safely be assumed that the overwhelming majority of shopkeepers never think about the slogans they put in their windows, nor do they use them to express their real opinions. That poster was delivered to our greengrocer from the enterprise headquarters along with the onions and carrots. He put them all into the window simply because it has been done that way for years, because everyone does it, and because that is the way it has to be. If he were to refuse, there could be trouble. He could be reproached for not having the proper 'decoration' in his window; someone might even accuse him of disloyalty. He does it because these things must be done if one is to get along in life. It is one of the thousands of details that guarantee him a relatively tranquil life 'in harmony with society', as they say.

Obviously the greengrocer is indifferent to the semantic content of the slogan on exhibit; he does not put the slogan in his window from any personal desire to acquaint the public with the ideal it expresses. This, of course, does not mean that his action has no motive or significance at all, or that the slogan communicates nothing to anyone. The slogan is really a *sign*, and as such it contains a subliminal but very definite message. Verbally, it might be expressed this way: 'I, the greengrocer XY, live here and I know what I must do. I behave in the manner expected of me. I can be depended upon and am beyond reproach. I am obedient and therefore I have the right to be left in peace.' This message, of course, has an addressee: it is directed above, to the greengrocer's superior, and at the same time it is a shield that protects the greengrocer from potential informers. The slogan's real meaning, therefore, is rooted firmly in the greengrocer's existence. It reflects his vital interests. But what are those vital interests?

Let us take note: if the greengrocer had been instructed to display the slogan, 'I am afraid and therefore unquestioningly obedient', he would not be nearly as indifferent to its semantics, even though the statement would reflect the truth. The greengrocer would be embarrassed and ashamed to put such an unequivocal statement of his own degradation in the shop window, and quite naturally so, for he is a human being and thus has a sense of his own dignity. To overcome this complication, his expression of loyalty must take the form of a sign which, at least on its textual surface, indicates a level of disinterested conviction. It must allow the greengrocer to say, 'What's wrong with the workers of the world uniting?' Thus the sign helps the greengrocer to conceal from himself the low foundations of his obedience, at the same time concealing the low foundations of power. It hides them behind the façade of something high. And that something is *ideology*.

Ideology is a specious way of relating to the world. It offers human beings the illusion of an identity, of dignity, and of morality while making it easier for them to *part* with them. As the repository of something 'supra-personal' and objective, it enables people to deceive their conscience and conceal their true position and their inglorious *modus vivendi*, both from the world and from themselves. It is a very pragmatic, but at the same time an apparently dignified, way of legitimizing what is above, below, and on either side. It is directed towards people and towards God. It is a veil behind which human beings can hide their own 'fallen existence', their trivialization, and their adaptation to the status quo. It is an excuse that everyone can use, from the greengrocer, who conceals his fear of losing his job behind an alleged interest in the unification of the workers of the world, to the highest functionary, whose interest in staying in power can be cloaked in phrases about service to the working class. The primary excusatory function of ideology, therefore, is to provide people, both as victims and pillars of the post-totalitarian system, with the illusion that the system is in harmony with the human order and the order of the universe.

The smaller a dictatorship and the less stratified by modernization the society under it, the more directly the will of the dictator can be exercised. In other words, the dictator can employ more or less naked discipline, avoiding the complex processes of relating to the world and of self-justification which ideology involves. But the more complex the mechanisms of power become, the larger and more stratified the society they embrace, and the longer they have operated historically, the more individuals must be connected to them from outside, and the greater the importance attached to the ideological excuse. It acts as a kind of bridge between the regime and the people, across which the regime approaches the people and the people approach the regime. This explains why ideology plays such an important role in the post-totalitarian system: that complex machinery of units, hierarchies, transmission belts, and indirect instruments of manipulation which insure in countless ways the integrity of the regime, leaving nothing to chance, would be quite simply unthinkable without ideology acting as its all-embracing excuse and as the excuse for each of its parts.

## IV

Between the aims of the post-totalitarian system and the aims of life there is a yawning abyss: while life, in its essence, moves towards plurality, diversity, independent self-constitution and self-organization, in short, towards the fulfilment of its own freedom, the post-totalitarian system demands conformity, uniformity, and discipline. While life ever strives to create new and 'improbable' structures, the post-totalitarian system contrives to force life into its most probable states. The aims of the system reveal its most essential characteristic to be introversion, a movement towards being ever more completely and unreservedly *itself*, which means that the radius of its influence is continually widening as well. This system serves people only to the extent necessary to ensure that people will serve it. Anything beyond this, that is to say, anything which leads people to overstep their predetermined roles is regarded by the system as an attack upon itself. And in this respect it is correct: every instance of such transgression is a genuine denial of the system. It can be said, therefore, that the inner aim of the post-totalitarian system is not mere preservation of power in the hands of a ruling clique, as appears to be the case at first sight. Rather, the social phenomenon of self-preservation is subordinated to something higher, to a kind of blind *automatism* which drives the system. No matter what position individuals hold in the hierarchy of power, they are not considered by the system to be worth anything in themselves, but only as things intended to fuel and serve this automatism. For this reason, an individual's desire for power is admissible only in so far as its direction coincides with the direction of the automatism of the system.

Ideology, in creating a bridge of excuses between the system and the individual, spans the abyss between the aims of the system and the aims of life. It pretends that the requirements of the system derive from the requirements of life. It is a world of appearances trying to pass for reality.

The post-totalitarian system touches people at every step, but it does so with its ideological gloves on. This is why life in the system is so thoroughly permeated with hypocrisy and lies: government by bureaucracy is called popular government; the working class is enslaved in the name of the working class; the complete degradation of the individual is presented as his or her ultimate liberation; depriving people of information is called making it available; the use of power to manipulate is called the public control of power, and the arbitrary abuse of power is called observing the legal code; the repression of culture is called its development; the expansion of imperial influence is presented as support for the oppressed; the lack of free expression becomes the highest form of freedom; farcical elections become the highest form of democracy; banning independent thought becomes the most scientific of world views; military occupation becomes fraternal assistance. Because the regime is captive to its own lies, it must falsify everything. It falsifies the past. It falsifies the present, and it falsifies the future. It falsifies statistics. It pretends not to possess an omnipotent and unprincipled police apparatus. It pretends to respect human rights. It pretends to persecute no one. It pretends to fear nothing. It pretends to pretend nothing.

Individuals need not believe all these mystifications, but they must behave as though they did, or they must at least tolerate them in silence, or get along well with those who work with them. For this reason, however, they must *live within a lie*. They need not accept the lie. It is enough for them to have accepted their life with it and in it. For by this very fact, individuals confirm the system, fulfil the system, make the system, *are* the system.

## V

We have seen that the real meaning of the greengrocer's slogan has nothing to do with what the text of the slogan actually says. Even so, this real meaning is quite clear and generally comprehensible because the code is so familiar: the greengrocer declares his loyalty (and he can do no other if his declaration is to be accepted) in the only way the regime is capable of hearing; that is, by accepting the prescribed *ritual*, by accepting appearances as reality, by accepting the given rules of the game. In doing so, however, he has himself become a player in the game, thus making it possible for the game to go on, for it to exist in the first place.

If ideology was originally a bridge between the system and the individual as an individual, then the moment he or she steps on to this bridge it becomes at the same time a bridge between the system and the individual as a component of the system. That is, if ideology originally facilitated (by acting outwardly) the constitution of power by serving as a psychological excuse, then from the moment that excuse is accepted, it constitutes power inwardly, becoming an active component of that power. It begins to function as the principal instrument of ritual communication *within* the system of power.

The whole power structure (and we have already discussed its physical articulation) could not exist at all if there were not a certain 'metaphysical' order binding all its components together, interconnecting them and subordinating them to a uniform method of accountability, supplying the combined operation of all these components with rules of the game, that is, with certain regulations, limitations, and legalities. This metaphysical order is fundamental to, and standard throughout, the entire power structure; it integrates its communication system and makes possible the internal exchange and transfer of information and instructions. It is rather like a collection of traffic signals and directional signs, giving the process shape and structure. This metaphysical order guarantees the inner coherence of the totalitarian power structure. It is the glue holding it together, its binding principle, the instrument of its discipline. Without this glue the structure as a totalitarian structure would vanish; it would disintegrate into individual atoms chaotically colliding with one another in their unregulated particular interests and inclinations. The entire pyramid of totalitarian power, deprived of the element that binds it together, would collapse in upon itself, as it were, in a kind of material implosion.

As the interpretation of reality by the power structure, ideology is always subordinated ultimately to the interests of the structure. Therefore, it has a natural tendency to disengage itself from reality, to create a world of appearances, to become ritual. In societies where there is public competition for power and therefore public control of that power, there also exists quite naturally public control of the way that power legitimates itself ideologically. Consequently, in such conditions there are always certain correctives that effectively prevent ideology from abandoning reality altogether. Under totalitarianism, however, these correctives disappear, and thus there is nothing to prevent ideology from becoming more and more removed from reality, gradually turning into what it has already become in the post-totalitarian system: a world of appearances, a mere ritual, a formalized language deprived of semantic contact with reality and transformed into a system of ritual signs that replace reality with pseudo-reality.

Yet, as we have seen, ideology becomes at the same time an increasingly important component of power, a pillar providing it with both excusatory legitimacy and an inner coherence. As this aspect grows in importance, and as it gradually loses touch with reality, it acquires a peculiar but very real strength. It becomes reality itself, albeit a reality altogether self-contained, one that on certain levels (chiefly inside the power structure) may have even greater weight than reality as such. Increasingly, the virtuosity of the ritual becomes more important than the reality hidden behind it.

The significance of phenomena no longer derives from the phenomena themselves, but from their locus as concepts in the ideological context. Reality does not shape theory, but rather the reverse. Thus power gradually draws closer to ideology than it does to reality; it draws its strength from theory and becomes entirely dependent on it. This inevitably leads, of course, to a paradoxical result: rather than theory, or rather ideology, serving power, power begins to serve ideology. It is as though ideology had appropriated power from power, as though it had become dictator itself. It then appears that theory itself, ritual itself, ideology itself, makes decisions that affect people, and not the other way around.

If ideology is the principal guarantee of the inner consistency of power, it becomes at the same time an increasingly important guarantee of its *continuity*. Whereas succession to power in classical dictatorships is always a rather complicated affair (the pretenders having nothing to give their claims reasonable legitimacy, thereby forcing them always to resort to confrontations of naked power), in the post-totalitarian system power is passed on from person to person, from clique to clique, and from generation to generation in an essentially more regular fashion. In the selection of pretenders, a new 'king-maker' takes part: it is ritual legitimation, the ability to rely on ritual, to fulfil it and use it, to allow oneself, as it were, to be borne aloft by it. Naturally, power struggles exist in the post-totalitarian system as well, and most of them are far more brutal than in an open society, for the struggle is not open, regulated by democratic rules, and subject to public control, but hidden behind the scenes. (It is difficult to recall a single instance in which the First Secretary of a ruling Communist Party has been replaced without the various military and security forces being placed at least on alert.) This struggle, however, can never (as it can in classical dictatorships) threaten the very essence of the system and its continuity. At most it will shake up the power structure, which will recover quickly, precisely because the binding substance – ideology – remains undisturbed. No matter who is replaced by whom, succession is only possible against the backdrop and within the framework of a common ritual. It can never take place by denying that ritual.

Because of this dictatorship of the ritual, however, power becomes clearly *anonymous*. Individuals are almost dissolved in the ritual. They allow themselves to be swept along by it and frequently it seems as though ritual alone carries people from obscurity into the light of power. Is it not characteristic of the post-totalitarian system that, on all levels of the power hierarchy, individuals are increasingly being pushed aside by faceless people, puppets, those uniformed flunkies of the rituals and routines of power?

The automatic operation of a power structure thus dehumanized and made anonymous is a feature of the fundamental automatism of this system. It would seem that it is precisely the *diktats* of this automatism which select people lacking individual will for the power structure, that it is precisely the *diktat* of the empty phrase which summons to power people who use empty phrases as the best guarantee that the automatism of the post-totalitarian system will continue.

Western Sovietologists often exaggerate the role of individuals in the post-totalitarian system and overlook the fact that the ruling figures, despite the immense power they possess through the centralized structure of power, are often no more than blind executors of the system's own internal laws – laws they themselves never can, and never do, reflect upon. In any case, experience has taught us again and again that this automatism is far more powerful than the will of any individual; and should someone possess a more independent will, he or she must conceal it behind a ritually anonymous mask in order to have an opportunity to enter the power hierarchy at all. And when the individual finally gains a place there and tries to make his or her will felt within it, that automatism, with its enormous inertia, will triumph sooner or later, and either the individual will be ejected by the power structure like a foreign organism, or he or she will be compelled to resign his or her individuality gradually, once again blending with the automatism and becoming its servant, almost indistinguishable from those who preceded him or her and those who will follow. (Let us recall, for instance, the development of Husák or Gomulka.) The necessity of continually hiding behind and relating to ritual means that even the more enlightened members of the power structure are often obsessed with ideology. They are never able to plunge straight to the bottom of naked reality, and they always confuse it, in the final analysis, with ideological pseudo-reality. (In my opinion, one of the reasons the Dubček leadership lost control of the situation in 1968 was precisely because, in extreme situations and in final questions, its members were never capable of extricating themselves completely from the world of appearances.)

It can be said, therefore, that ideology, as that instrument of internal communication which assures the power structure of inner cohesion is, in the post-totalitarian system, something that transcends the physical aspects of power, something that dominates it to a considerable degree and, therefore, tends to assure its continuity as well. It is one of the pillars of the system's external stability. This pillar, however, is built on a very unstable foundation. It is built on lies. It works only as long as people are willing to live within the lie.

## VI

Why in fact did our greengrocer have to put his loyalty on display in the shop window? Had he not already displayed it sufficiently in various internal or semi-public ways? At trade-union meetings, after all, he had always voted as he should. He had always taken part in various competitions. He voted in elections like a good citizen. He had even signed the 'anti-Charter'. Why, on top of all that, should he have to declare his loyalty publicly? After all, the people who walk past his window will certainly not stop to read that, in the greengrocer's opinion, the workers of the world ought to unite. The fact of the matter is, they don't read the slogan at all, and it can be fairly assumed they don't even see it. If you were to ask a woman who had stopped in front of his shop what she saw in the window, she could certainly tell you whether or not they had tomatoes today, but it is highly unlikely that she noticed the slogan at all, let alone what it said.

It seems senseless to require the greengrocer to declare his loyalty publicly. But it makes sense nevertheless. People ignore his slogan, but they do so because such slogans are also found in other shop windows, on lamp posts, bulletin boards, in apartment windows, and on buildings; they are everywhere, in fact. They form part of the panorama of everyday life. Of course, while they ignore the details, people are very aware of that panorama as a whole. And what else is the greengrocer's slogan but a small component in that huge backdrop to daily life?

The greengrocer had to put the slogan in his window, therefore, not in the hope that someone might read it or be persuaded by it, but to contribute, along with thousands of other slogans, to the panorama that everyone is very much aware of. This panorama, of course, has a subliminal meaning as well: it reminds people where they are living and what is expected of them. It tells them what everyone else is doing, and indicates to them what they must do as well, if they don't want to be excluded, to fall into isolation, alienate themselves from society, break the rules of the game, and risk the loss of their peace and tranquillity and security.

The woman who ignored the greengrocer's slogan may well have hung a similar slogan just an hour before in the corridor of the office where she works. She did it more or less without thinking, just as our greengrocer did, and she could do so precisely because she was doing it against the background of the general panorama and with some awareness of it, that is, against the background of the panorama of which the greengrocer's shop window forms a part. When the greengrocer visits her office, he will not notice her slogan either, just as she failed to notice his. Nevertheless their slogans are mutually dependent: both were displayed with some awareness of the general panorama and, we might say, under its *diktat*. Both, however, assist in the creation of that panorama, and therefore they assist in the creation of that *diktat* as well. The greengrocer and the office worker have both adapted to the conditions in which they live, but in doing so, they help to create those conditions. They do what is done, what is to be done, what must be done, but at the same time - by that very token - they confirm that it must be done in fact. They conform to a particular requirement and in so doing they themselves perpetuate that requirement. Metaphorically speaking, without the greengrocer's slogan the office worker's slogan could not exist, and vice versa. Each proposes to the other that something be repeated and each accepts the other's proposal. Their mutual indifference to each other's slogans is only an illusion: in reality, by exhibiting their slogans, each compels the other to accept the rules of the game and to confirm thereby the power that requires the slogans in the first place. Quite simply, each helps the other to be obedient. Both are objects in a system of control, but at the same time they are its subjects as well. They are both victims of the system and its instruments.

If an entire district town is plastered with slogans that no one reads, it is on the one hand a message from the district secretary to the regional secretary, but it is also something more: a small example of the principle of social *auto-totality* at work. Part of the essence of the post-totalitarian system is that it draws everyone into its sphere of power, not so they may realize themselves as human beings, but so they may surrender their human identity in favour of the identity of the system, that is, so they may become agents of the system's general automatism and servants of its self-determined goals, so they may participate in the common responsibility for it, so they may be pulled into and ensnared by it, like Faust with Mephistopheles. More than this: so they may create through their involvement a general norm and, thus, bring pressure to bear on their fellow citizens. And further: so they may learn to be comfortable with their involvement, to identify with it as though it were something natural and inevitable and, ultimately, so they may – with no external urging – come to treat any non-involvement as an abnormality, as arrogance, as an attack on themselves, as a form of dropping out of society. By pulling everyone into its power structure, the post-totalitarian system makes everyone instruments of a mutual totality, the auto-totality of society.

Everyone, however, is in fact involved and enslaved, not only the greengrocers but also the prime ministers. Differing positions in the hierarchy merely establish differing degrees of involvement: the greengrocer is involved only to a minor extent, but he also has very little power. The prime minister, naturally, has greater power, but in return he is far more deeply involved. Both, however, are unfree, each merely in a somewhat different way. The real accomplice in this involvement, therefore, is not another person, but the system itself. Position in the power hierarchy determines the degree of responsibility and guilt, but it gives no one unlimited responsibility and guilt, nor does it completely absolve anyone. Thus the conflict between the aims of life and the aims of the system is not a conflict between two socially defined and separate communities; and only a very generalized view (and even that only approximative) permits us to divide society into the rulers and the ruled. Here, by the way, is one of the most important differences between the post-totalitarian system and classical dictatorships, in which this line of conflict can still be drawn according to social class. In the post-totalitarian system, this line runs *de facto* through each person, for everyone in his or her own way is both a victim and a supporter of the system. What we understand by the system is not, therefore, a social order imposed by one group upon another, but rather something which permeates the entire society and is a factor in shaping it, something which may seem impossible to grasp or define (for it is in the nature of a mere principle), but which is expressed by the entire society as an important feature of its life.

The fact that human beings have created, and daily create, this self-directed system through which they divest themselves of their innermost identity, is not therefore the result of some incomprehensible misunderstanding of history, nor is it history somehow gone off its rails. Neither is it the product of some diabolical higher will which has decided, for reasons unknown, to torment a portion of humanity in this way. It can happen and did happen only because there is obviously in modern humanity a certain tendency towards the creation, or at least the toleration, of such a system. There is obviously something in human beings which responds to this system, something they reflect and accommodate, something within them which paralyses every effort of their better selves to revolt. Human beings are compelled to live within a lie, but they can be compelled to do so only because they are in fact capable of living in this way. Therefore not only does the system alienate humanity, but at the same time alienated humanity supports this system as its own involuntary masterplan, as a degenerate image of its own degeneration, as a record of people's own failure as individuals.

The essential aims of life are present naturally in every person. In everyone there is some longing for humanity's rightful dignity, for moral integrity, for free expression of being and a sense of transcendence over the world of existences. Yet, at the same time, each person is capable, to a greater or lesser degree, of coming to terms with living within the lie. Each person somehow succumbs to a profane trivialization of his or her inherent humanity, and to utilitarianism. In everyone there is some willingness to merge with the anonymous crowd and to flow comfortably along with it down the river of pseudo-life. This is much more than a simple conflict between two identities. It is something far worse: it is a challenge to the very notion of identity itself.

In highly simplified terms, it could be said that the post-totalitarian system has been built on foundations laid by the historical encounter between dictatorship and the consumer society. Is it not true that the far-reaching adaptability to living a lie and the effortless spread of social auto-totality have some connection with the general unwillingness of consumption-oriented people to sacrifice some material certainties for the sake of their own spiritual and moral integrity? With their willingness to surrender higher values when faced with the trivializing temptations of modern civilization? With their vulnerability to the attractions of mass indifference? And in the end, is not the greyness and the emptiness of life in the post-totalitarian system only an inflated caricature of modern life in general? And do we not in fact stand (although in the external measures of civilization, we are far behind) as a kind of warning to the West, revealing to it its own latent tendencies?

## VII

Let us now imagine that one day something in our greengrocer snaps and he stops putting up the slogans merely to ingratiate himself. He stops voting in elections he knows are a farce. He begins to say what he really thinks at political meetings. And he even finds the strength in himself to express solidarity with those whom his conscience commands him to support. In this revolt the greengrocer steps out of living within the lie. He rejects the ritual and breaks the rules of the game. He discovers once more his suppressed identity and dignity. He gives his freedom a concrete significance. His revolt is an attempt to *live within the truth*.

The bill is not long in coming. He will be relieved of his post as manager of the shop and transferred to the warehouse. His pay will be reduced. His hopes for a holiday in Bulgaria will evaporate. His children's access to higher education will be threatened. His superiors will harass him and his fellow workers will wonder about him. Most of those who apply these sanctions, however, will not do so from any authentic inner conviction but simply under pressure from conditions, the same conditions that once pressured the greengrocer to display the official slogans. They will persecute the greengrocer either because it is expected of them, or to demonstrate their loyalty, or simply as part of the general panorama, to which belongs an awareness that this is how situations of this sort are dealt with, that this, in fact, is how things are always done, particularly if one is not to become suspect oneself. The executors, therefore, behave essentially like everyone else, to a greater or lesser degree: as components of the post-totalitarian system, as agents of its automatism, as petty instruments of the social auto-totality.

Thus the power structure, through the agency of those who carry out the sanctions, those anonymous components of the system, will spew the greengrocer from its mouth. The system, through its alienating presence in people, will punish him for his rebellion. It must do so because the logic of its automatism and self-defence dictate it. The greengrocer has not committed a simple, individual offence, isolated in its own uniqueness, but something incomparably more serious. By breaking the rules of the game, he has disrupted the game as such. He has exposed it as a mere game. He has shattered the world of appearances, the fundamental pillar of the system. He has upset the power structure by tearing apart what holds it together. He has demonstrated that living a lie is living a lie. He has broken through the exalted façade of the system and exposed the real, base foundations of power. He has said that the emperor is naked. And because the emperor is in fact naked, something extremely dangerous has happened: by his action, the greengrocer has addressed the world. He has enabled everyone to peer behind the curtain. He has shown everyone that it *is* possible to live within the truth. Living within the lie can constitute the system only if it is universal. The principle must embrace and permeate everything. There are no terms whatsoever on which it can coexist with living within the truth, and therefore everyone who steps out of line *denies it in principle and threatens it in its entirety*.

This is understandable: as long as appearance is not confronted with reality, it does not seem to be appearance. As long as living a lie is not confronted with living the truth, the perspective needed to expose its mendacity is lacking. As soon as the alternative appears, however, it threatens the very existence of appearance and living a lie in terms of what they are, both their essence and their all-inclusiveness. And at the same time, it is utterly unimportant how large a space this alternative occupies: its power does not consist in its physical attributes but in the light it casts on those pillars of the system and on its unstable foundations. After all, the greengrocer was a threat to the system not because of any physical or actual power he had, but because his action went beyond itself, because it illuminated its surroundings and, of course, because of the incalculable consequences of that illumination. In the post-totalitarian system, therefore, living within the truth has more than a mere existential dimension (returning humanity to its inherent nature), or a noetic dimension (revealing reality as it is), or a moral dimension (setting an example for others). It also has an unambiguous *political* dimension. If the main pillar of the system is living a lie, then it is not surprising that the fundamental threat to it is living the truth. This is why it must be suppressed more severely than anything else.

In the post-totalitarian system, truth in the widest sense of the word has a very special import, one unknown in other contexts. In this system, truth plays a far greater (and above all, a far different) role as a factor of power, or as an outright political force. How does the power of truth operate? How does truth as a factor of power work? How can its power – as power – be realized?


## VIII

Individuals can be alienated from themselves only because there is *something* in them to alienate. The terrain of this violation is their authentic existence. Living the truth is thus woven directly into the texture of living a lie. It is the repressed alternative, the authentic aim to which living a lie is an inauthentic response. Only against this background does living a lie make any sense: it exists *because* of that background. In its excusatory, chimerical rootedness in the human order, it is a response to nothing other than the human predisposition to truth. Under the orderly surface of the life of lies, therefore, there slumbers the hidden sphere of life in its real aims, of its hidden openness to truth.

The singular, explosive, incalculable political power of living within the truth resides in the fact that living openly within the truth has an ally, invisible to be sure, but omnipresent: this hidden sphere. It is from this sphere that life lived openly in the truth grows; it is to this sphere that it speaks, and in it that it finds understanding. This is where the potential for communication exists. But this place is hidden and therefore, from the perspective of power, very dangerous. The complex ferment that takes place within it goes on in semi-darkness, and by the time it finally surfaces into the light of day as an assortment of shocking surprises to the system, it is usually too late to cover them up in the usual fashion. Thus they create a situation in which the regime is confounded, invariably causing panic and driving it to react in inappropriate ways.

It seems that the primary breeding ground for what might, in the widest possible sense of the word, be understood as an opposition in the post-totalitarian system is living within the truth. The confrontation between these opposition forces and the powers that be, of course, will obviously take a form essentially different from that typical of an open society or a classical dictatorship. Initially, this confrontation does not take place on the level of real, institutionalized, quantifiable power which relies on the various instruments of power, but on a different level altogether: the level of human consciousness and conscience, the existential level. The effective range of this special power cannot be measured in terms of disciples, voters, or soldiers, because it lies spread out in the fifth column of social consciousness, in the hidden aims of life, in human beings' repressed longing for dignity and fundamental rights, for the realization of their real social and political interests. Its power, therefore, does not reside in the strength of definable political or social groups, but chiefly in the strength of a potential, which is hidden throughout the whole of society, including the official power structures of that society. Therefore this power does not rely on soldiers of its own, but on the soldiers of the enemy as it were – that is to say, on everyone who is living within the lie and who may be struck at any moment (in theory, at least) by the force of truth (or who, out of an instinctive desire to protect their position, may at least adapt to that force). It is a bacteriological weapon, so to speak, utilized when conditions are ripe by a single civilian to disarm an entire division. This power does not participate in any direct struggle for power; rather it makes its influence felt in the obscure arena of being itself. The hidden movements it gives rise to there, however, can issue forth (when, where, under what circumstances, and to what extent are difficult to predict) in something visible: a real political act or event, a social movement, a sudden explosion of civil unrest, a sharp conflict inside an apparently monolithic power structure, or simply an irrepressible transformation in the social and intellectual climate. And since all genuine problems and matters of critical importance are hidden beneath a thick crust of lies, it is never quite clear when the proverbial last straw will fall, or what that straw will be. This, too, is why the regime prosecutes, almost as a reflex action preventively, even the most modest attempts to live within the truth.

Why was Solzhenitsyn driven out of his own country? Certainly not because he represented a unit of real power, that is, not because any of the regime's representatives felt he might unseat them and take their place in government. Solzhenitsyn's expulsion was something else: a desperate attempt to plug up the dreadful wellspring of truth, a truth which might cause incalculable transformations in social consciousness, which in turn might one day produce political debacles unpredictable in their consequences. And so the post-totalitarian system behaved in a characteristic way: it defended the integrity of the world of appearances in order to defend itself. For the crust presented by the life of lies is made of strange stuff. As long as it seals off hermetically the entire society, it appears to be made of stone. But the moment someone breaks through in one place, when one person cries out, 'The emperor is naked!' – when a single person breaks the rules of the game, thus exposing it as a game – everything suddenly appears in another light and the whole crust seems then to be made of a tissue on the point of tearing and disintegrating uncontrollably.

When I speak of living within the truth, I naturally do not have in mind only products of conceptual thought, such as a protest or a letter written by a group of intellectuals. It can be any means by which a person or a group revolts against manipulation: anything from a letter by intellectuals to a workers' strike, from a rock concert to a student demonstration, from refusing to vote in the farcical elections, to making an open speech at some official congress, or even a hunger strike, for instance. If the suppression of the aims of life is a complex process, and if it is based on the multifaceted manipulation of all expressions of life then, by the same token, every free expression of life indirectly threatens the post-totalitarian system politically, including forms of expression to which, in other social systems, no one would attribute any potential political significance, not to mention explosive power.

The Prague Spring is usually understood as a clash between two groups on the level of real power: those who wanted to maintain the system as it was and those who wanted to reform it. It is frequently forgotten, however, that this encounter was merely the final act and the inevitable consequence of a long drama originally played out chiefly in the theatre of the spirit and the conscience of society. And that somewhere at the beginning of this drama, there were individuals who were willing to live within the truth, even when things were at their worst. These people had no access to real power, nor did they aspire to it. The sphere in which they were living the truth was not necessarily even that of political thought. They could equally have been poets, painters, musicians, or simply ordinary citizens who were able to maintain their human dignity. Today it is naturally difficult to pinpoint when and through which hidden, winding channel a certain action or attitude influenced a given milieu, and to trace the virus of truth as it slowly spread through the tissue of the life of lies, gradually causing it to disintegrate. One thing, however, seems clear: the attempt at political reform was not the cause of society's reawakening, but rather the final outcome of that reawakening.

I think the present also can be better understood in the light of this experience. The confrontation between 1000 Chartists and the post-totalitarian system would appear to be politically hopeless. This is true, of course, if we look at it through the traditional lens of the open political system, in which, quite naturally, every political force is measured chiefly in terms of the positions it holds on the level of real power. Given that perspective, a mini-party like the Charter would certainly not stand a chance. If, however, this confrontation is seen against the background of what we know about power in the post-totalitarian system, it appears in a fundamentally different light. For the time being, it is impossible to say with any precision what impact the appearance of Charter 77, its existence, and its work has had in the hidden sphere, and how the Charter's attempt to rekindle civic self-awareness and confidence is regarded there. Whether, when, and how this investment will eventually produce dividends in the form of specific political changes is even less possible to predict. But that, of course, is all part of living within the truth. As an existential solution, it takes individuals back to the solid ground of their own identity; as politics it throws them into a game of chance where the stakes are all or nothing. For this reason it is undertaken only by those for whom the former is worth risking the latter, or who have come to the conclusion that there is no other way to conduct real politics in Czechoslovakia today. Which, by the way, is the same thing: this conclusion can be reached only by someone who is unwilling to sacrifice his or her own human identity to politics, or rather who does not believe in a politics that requires such a sacrifice.

The more thoroughly the post-totalitarian system frustrates any rival alternative on the level of real power, as well as any form of politics independent of the laws of its own automatism, the more definitively the centre of gravity of any potential political threat shifts to the area of the existential and the prepolitical: usually without any conscious effort, living within the truth becomes the one natural point of departure for all activities that work against the automatism of the system. And even if such activities ultimately grow beyond the area of living within the truth (which means they are transformed into various parallel structures, movements, institutions, they begin to be regarded as political activity, they bring real pressure to bear on the official structures and begin in fact to have a certain influence on the level of real power), they always carry with them the specific hallmark of their origins. Therefore it seems to me that not even the so-called dissident movements can be properly understood without constantly bearing in mind this special background from which they emerge.

IX

The profound crisis of human identity brought on by living within a lie, a crisis which in turn makes such a life possible, certainly possesses a moral dimension as well; it appears, among other things, as *a deep moral crisis in society*. A person who has been seduced by the consumer value system, whose identity is dissolved in an amalgam of the accoutrements of mass civilization, and who has no roots in the order of being, no sense of responsibility for anything higher than his or her own personal survival, is a *demoralized* person. The system depends on this demoralization, deepens it, is in fact a projection of it into society.

Living within the truth, as humanity's revolt against an enforced position, is, on the contrary, an attempt to regain control over one's own sense of responsibility. In other words, it is clearly a moral act, not only because one must pay so dearly for it, but principally because it is not self-serving: the risk may bring rewards in the form of a general amelioration in the situation, or it may not. In this regard, as I stated previously, it is an all-or-nothing gamble, and it is difficult to imagine a reasonable person embarking on such a course merely because he or she reckons that sacrifice today will bring rewards tomorrow, be it only in the form of general gratitude. (By the way, the representatives of power invariably come to terms with those who live within the truth by persistently ascribing utilitarian motivations to them – a lust for power or fame or wealth – and thus they try, at least, to implicate them in their own world, the world of general demoralization.)

If living within the truth in the post-totalitarian system becomes the chief breeding ground for independent, alternative political ideas, then all considerations about the nature and future prospects of these ideas must necessarily reflect this moral dimension as a political phenomenon. (And if the revolutionary Marxist belief about morality as a product of the 'superstructure' inhibits any of our friends from realizing the full significance of this dimension and, in one way or another, from including it in their view of the world, it is to their own detriment: an anxious fidelity to the postulates of that world view prevents them from properly understanding the mechanisms of their own political influence, thus paradoxically making them precisely what they, as Marxists, so often suspect others of being – victims of 'false consciousness'.) The very special political significance of morality in the post-totalitarian system is a phenomenon that is at the very least unusual in modern political history, a phenomenon that might well have – as I shall soon attempt to show – far-reaching consequences.


## X

Undeniably, the most important political event in Czechoslovakia after the advent of the Husák leadership in 1969 was the appearance of Charter 77. The spiritual and intellectual climate surrounding its appearance, however, was not the product of any immediate political event. That climate was created by the trial of some young musicians associated with a rock group called 'The Plastic People of the Universe'. Their trial was not a confrontation of two differing political forces or conceptions, but two differing conceptions of life. On the one hand, there was the sterile puritanism of the post-totalitarian establishment and, on the other hand, unknown young people who wanted no more than to be able to live within the truth, to play the music they enjoyed, to sing songs that were relevant to their lives, and to live freely in dignity and partnership. These people had no past history of political activity. They were not highly motivated members of the opposition with political ambitions, nor were they former politicians expelled from the power structures. They had been given every opportunity to adapt to the status quo, to accept the principles of living within a lie and thus to enjoy life undisturbed by the authorities. Yet they decided on a different course. Despite this, or perhaps precisely because of it, their case had a very special impact on everyone who had not yet given up hope. Moreover, when the trial took place, a new mood had begun to surface after the years of waiting, of apathy and of scepticism towards various forms of resistance. People were 'tired of being tired'; they were fed up with the stagnation, the inactivity, barely hanging on in the hope that things might improve after all. In some ways the trial was the final straw. Many groups of differing tendencies which until then had remained isolated from each other, reluctant to co-operate, or which were committed to forms of action that made co-operation difficult, were suddenly struck with the powerful realization that freedom is indivisible. Everyone understood that an attack on the Czech musical underground was an attack on a most elementary and important thing, something that in fact bound everyone together: it was an attack on the very notion of 'living within the truth', on the real aims of life. The freedom to play rock music was understood as a human freedom and thus as essentially the same as the freedom to engage in philosophical and political reflection, the freedom to write, the freedom to express and defend the various social and political interests of society. People were inspired to feel a genuine sense of solidarity with the young musicians and they came to realize that not standing up for the freedom of others, regardless of how remote their means of creativity or their attitude to life, meant surrendering one's own freedom. (There is no freedom without equality before the law, and there is no equality before the law without freedom; Charter 77 has given this ancient notion a new and characteristic dimension, which has immensely important implications for modern Czech history. What Slábeček, the author of the book *Sixty-eight*, in a brilliant analysis, calls the 'principle of exclusion', lies at the root of all our present-day moral and political misery. This principle was born at the end of the Second World War in that strange collusion of democrats and communists and was subsequently developed further and further, right to the 'bitter end'. For the first time in decades this principle has been overcome, by Charter 77: all those united in the Charter have, for the first time, become equal partners. Charter 77 is not merely a coalition of communists and non-communists – that would be nothing historically new and, from the moral and political point of view, nothing revolutionary – but it is a community that is *a priori* open to anyone, and no one in it is *a priori* assigned an inferior position.) This was the climate, then, in which Charter 77 was created. Who could have foreseen that the prosecution of one or two obscure rock groups would have such far-reaching consequences?

I think that the origins of Charter 77 illustrate very well what I have already suggested above: that in the post-totalitarian system, the real background to the movements that gradually assume political significance does not usually consist of overtly political events of confrontations between different forces or concepts that are openly political. These movements for the most part originate elsewhere, in the far broader area of the 'pre-political', where 'living within a lie' confronts 'living within the truth', that is, where the demands of the post-totalitarian system conflict with the real aims of life. These real aims can naturally assume a great many forms. Sometimes they appear as the basic material or social interests of a group or an individual; at other times, they may appear as certain

intellectual and spiritual interests; at still other times, they may be
the most fundamental of existential demands, such as the simple
longing of people to live their own lives in dignity. Such a conflict
acquires a political character, then, not because of the elementary
political nature of the aims demanding to be heard but simply
because, given the complex system of manipulation on which the
post-totalitarian system is founded and on which it is also dependent, every free human act or expression, every attempt to live
within the truth, must necessarily appear as a threat to the system
and, thus, as something which is political *par excellence.* Any eventual political articulation of the movements that grow out of this
'pre-political' hinterland is secondary. It develops and matures as a
result of a subsequent confrontation with the system, and not
because it started off as a political programme, project or impulse.

Once again, the events of 1968 confirm this. The communist
politicians who were trying to reform the system came forward with
their programme not because they had suddenly experienced a
mystical enlightenment, but because they were led to do so by
continued and increasing pressure from areas of life that had
nothing to do with politics in the traditional sense of the word. In
fact they were trying in political ways to solve the social conflicts
(which in fact were confrontations between the aims of the system
and the aims of life) that almost every level of society had been
experiencing daily, and had been thinking about with increasing
openness for years. Backed by this living resonance throughout
society, scholars and artists had defined the problem in a wide
variety of ways and students were demanding solutions.

The genesis of Charter 77 also illustrates the special political
significance of the moral aspect of things that I have mentioned.
Charter 77 would have been unimaginable without that powerful
sense of solidarity among widely differing groups, and without the
sudden realization that it was impossible to go on waiting any
longer, and that the truth had to be spoken loudly and collectively,
regardless of the virtual certainty of sanctions and the uncertainty of
any tangible results in the immediate future. 'There are some things
worth suffering for', Jan Patočka wrote shortly before his
death.* I think that Chartists understand this not only as
Patočka's legacy, but also as the best explanation of why they do

---

* *Editor's note*: a highly influential philosopher and disciple of Edmund Husserl, Jan
Patočka was also one of the three founding spokespersons for Charter 77.  He

what they do.

Seen from the outside, and chiefly from the vantage point of the system and its power structure, Charter 77 came as a surprise, as a bolt out of the blue. It was not a bolt out of the blue, of course, but that impression is understandable, since the ferment that led to it took place in the 'hidden sphere', in that semi-darkness where things are difficult to chart or analyse. The chances of predicting the appearance of the Charter were just as slight as the chances are now of predicting where it will lead. Once again, it was that shock, so typical of moments when something from the hidden sphere suddenly bursts through the moribund surface of 'living within a lie'. The more one is trapped in the world of appearances, the more surprising it is when something like that happens.

## XI

In societies under the post-totalitarian system, all political life in the traditional sense has been eliminated. People have no opportunity to express themselves politically in public, let alone to organize politically. The gap that results is filled by ideological ritual. In such a situation, people's interest in political matters naturally dwindles and independent political thought, in so far as it exists at all, is seen by the majority as unrealistic, far-fetched, a kind of self-indulgent game, hopelessly distant from their everyday concerns; something admirable, perhaps, but quite pointless, because it is on the one hand entirely utopian and on the other hand extraordinarily dangerous, in view of the unusual vigour with which any move in that direction is persecuted by the regime.

Yet even in such societies, individuals and groups of people exist who do not abandon politics as a vocation and who, in one way or another, strive to think independently, to express themselves and in some cases even to organize politically, because that is a part of their attempt to live within the truth.

The fact that these people exist and work is in itself immensely important and worthwhile. Even in the worst of times, they

---

was severely harassed by the police, subjected to lengthy interrogations, and literally hounded by the police to his hospital death bed. The quotation above is taken from his final public statement, translated as 'Political testament', *Telos*, **31** (spring 1977), pp. 151–2.

maintain the continuity of political thought. If some genuine political impulse emerges from this or that 'pre-political' confrontation and is properly articulated early enough, thus increasing its chances of relative success, then this is frequently due to these isolated 'generals without an army' who, because they have maintained the continuity of political thought in the face of enormous difficulties, can at the right moment enrich the new impulse with the fruits of their own political thinking. Once again, there is ample evidence for this process in Czechoslovakia. Almost all those who were political prisoners in the early 1970s, who had apparently been made to suffer in vain because of their quixotic efforts to work politically among an utterly apathetic and demoralized society, belong today – inevitably – among the most active Chartists. In Charter 77, the moral legacy of their earlier sacrifices is valued, and they have enriched this movement with their experience and that element of political thinking.

And yet it seems to me that the thought and activity of those friends who have never given up direct political work and who are always ready to assume direct political responsibility very often suffer from one chronic fault: an insufficient understanding of the historical uniqueness of the post-totalitarian system as a social and political reality. They have little understanding of the specific nature of power that is typical for this system and therefore they over-estimate the importance of direct political work in the traditional sense. Moreover, they fail to appreciate the political significance of those 'pre-political' events and processes that provide the living humus from which genuine political change usually springs. As political actors – or, rather, as people with political ambitions – they frequently try to pick up where natural political life left off. They maintain models of behaviour that may have been appropriate in more normal political circumstances and thus, without really being aware of it, they bring an outmoded way of thinking, old habits, conceptions, categories and notions to bear on circumstances that are quite new and radically different, without first giving adequate thought to the meaning and substance of such things in the new circumstances, to what politics as such means now, to what sort of thing can have political impact and potential, and in what way. Because such people have been excluded from the structures of power and are no longer able to influence those structures directly (and because they remain faithful to traditional notions of politics established in more or less democratic societies or in classical dictatorships) they frequently, in a sense, lose touch with reality. Why make compromises with reality, they say, when none of our proposals will ever be accepted anyway? Thus they find themselves in a world of genuinely utopian thinking.

As I have already tried to indicate, however, genuinely far-reaching political events do not emerge from the same sources and in the same way in the post-totalitarian system as they do in a democracy. And if a large portion of the public is indifferent to, even sceptical of, alternative political models and programmes and the private establishment of opposition political parties, this is not merely because there is a general feeling of apathy towards public affairs and a loss of that sense of 'higher responsibility'; in other words, it is not just a consequence of the general demoralization. There is also a bit of healthy social instinct at work in this attitude. It is as if people sensed intuitively that 'nothing is what it seems any longer', as the saying goes, and that from now on, therefore, things must be done entirely differently as well.

If some of the most important political impulses in Soviet bloc countries in recent years have come initially – that is, before being felt on the level of actual power – from mathematicians, philosophers, physicians, writers, historians, ordinary workers and so on, more frequently than from politicians, and if the driving force behind the various 'dissident movements' comes from so many people in 'non-political' professions, this is not because these people are more clever than those who see themselves primarily as politicians. It is because those who are not politicians are also not so bound by traditional political thinking and political habits and therefore, paradoxically, they are more aware of genuine political reality and more sensitive to what can and should be done under the circumstances.

There is no way around it: no matter how beautiful an alternative political model may be, it can no longer speak to the 'hidden sphere', inspire people and society, call for real political ferment. The real sphere of potential politics in the post-totalitarian system is elsewhere: in the continuing and cruel tension between the complex demands of that system and the aims of life, that is, the elementary need of human beings to live, to a certain extent at least, in harmony with themselves, that is, to live in a bearable way, not to be humiliated by their superiors and officials, not to be continually watched by the police, to be able to express themselves freely, to find an outlet for their creativity, to enjoy legal security, and so on.

Anything that touches this field concretely, anything that relates to this fundamental, omnipresent and living tension, will inevitably speak to people. Abstract projects for an ideal political or economic order do not interest them to anything like the same extent – and rightly so – not only because everyone knows how little chance they have of succeeding, but also because today people feel that the less political policies are derived from a concrete and human 'here and now' and the more they fix their sights on an abstract 'some day', the more easily they can degenerate into new forms of human enslavement. People who live in the post-totalitarian system know only too well that the question of whether one or several political parties are in power, and how these parties define and label themselves, is of far less importance than the question of whether or not it is possible to live like a human being.

To shed the burden of traditional political categories and habits and open oneself up fully to the world of human existence and then to draw political conclusions only after having analysed it: this is not only politically more realistic but at the same time, from the point of view of an 'ideal state of affairs', politically more promising as well. A genuine, profound and lasting change for the better – as I shall attempt to show elsewhere – can no longer result from the victory (were such a victory possible) of any particular traditional political conception, which can ultimately be only external, that is, a structural or systemic conception. More than ever before, such a change will have to derive from human existence, from the fundamental reconstitution of the position of people in the world, their relationships to themselves and to each other, and to the universe. If a better economic and political model is to be created, then perhaps more than ever before it must derive from profound existential and moral changes in society. This is not something that can be designed and introduced like a new car. If it is to be more than just a new variation on the old degeneration, it must above all be an expression of life in the process of transforming itself. A better system will not automatically ensure a better life. In fact the opposite is true: only by creating a better life can a better system be developed.

Once more I repeat that I am not underestimating the importance of political thought and conceptual political work. On the contrary, I think that genuine political thought and genuinely political work is precisely what we continually fail to achieve. If I say 'genuine', however, I have in mind the kind of thought and conceptual work that has freed itself of all the traditional political schemata that have been imported into our circumstances from a world that will never return (and whose return, even were it possible, would provide no permanent solution to the most important problems).

The Second and Fourth Internationals, like many other political powers and organizations, may naturally provide significant political support for various efforts of ours, but neither of them can solve our problems for us. They operate in a different world and are a product of different circumstances. Their theoretical concepts can be interesting and instructive to us but one thing is certain: we cannot solve our problems simply by identifying with these organizations. And the attempt in our country to place what we do in the context of some of the discussions that dominate political life in democratic societies often seems like sheer folly. For example, is it possible to talk seriously about whether we want to change the system or merely reform it? In the circumstances under which we live, this is a pseudo-problem, since for the time being there is simply no way we can accomplish either goal. We are not even clear about where reform ends and change begins. We know from a number of harsh experiences that neither reform nor change is in itself a guarantee of anything. We know that ultimately it is all the same to us whether or not the system in which we live, in the light of a particular doctrine, appears 'changed' or 'reformed'. Our concern is whether we can live with dignity in such a system, whether it serves people rather than people serving it. We are struggling to achieve this with the means available to us, and the means it makes sense to employ. Western journalists, submerged in the political banalities in which they live, may label our approach as overly legalistic, as too risky, revisionist, counter-revolutionary, bourgeois, communist, or as too right-wing or left-wing. But this is the very last thing that interests us.


# XII

One concept that is a constant source of confusion chiefly because it has been imported into our circumstances from circumstances that are entirely different, is the concept of an opposition. What exactly is an opposition in the post-totalitarian system?

In democratic societies with a traditional parliamentary system of government, political opposition is understood as a political force on the level of actual power (most frequently a party or coalition of

parties) which is not a part of the government. It offers an alternative political programme, it has ambitions to govern, and it is
recognized and respected by the government in power as a natural
element in the political life of the country. It seeks to spread its
influence by political means, and competes for power on the basis of
agreed-upon legal regulations.

In addition to this form of opposition, there exists the phenomenon of the 'extra-parliamentary opposition', which again consists
of forces organized more or less on the level of actual power, but
which operate outside the rules created by the system, and which
employ different means than are usual within that framework.

In classical dictatorships, the term opposition is understood to
mean the political forces which have also come out with an alternative political programme. They operate either legally or on the outer
limits of legality, but in any case they cannot compete for power
within the limits of some agreed-upon regulations. Or the term
opposition may be applied to forces preparing for a violent confrontation with the ruling power, or who feel themselves to be in this
state of confrontation already, such as various guerrilla groups or
liberation movements.

An opposition in the post-totalitarian system does not exist in any
of these senses. In what way, then, can the term be used?

1 Occasionally the term 'opposition' is applied, mainly by western
journalists, to persons or groups inside the power structure who find
themselves in a state of *hidden* conflict with the highest authorities.
The reasons for this conflict may be certain differences (not very
sharp differences, naturally) of a conceptual nature, but more
frequently it is quite simply a longing for power or a personal antipathy to others who represent that power.
2 Opposition here can also be understood as everything that does or
can have an indirect political effect in the sense already mentioned,
that is, everything the post-totalitarian system feels threatened by,
which in fact means everything it *is* threatened by. In this sense, the
opposition is every attempt to live within the truth, from the greengrocer's refusal to put the slogan in his window to a freely written
poem; in other words, everything in which the genuine aims of life
go beyond the limits placed on them by the aims of the system.
3 More frequently, however, the opposition is usually understood
(again, largely by western journalists) as groups of people who make
public their non-conformist stances and critical opinions, who make

no secret of their independent thinking and who, to a greater or lesser degree, consider themselves a political force. In this sense, the notion of an 'opposition' more or less overlaps with the notion of 'dissent', although, of course, there are great differences in the degree to which that label is accepted or rejected. It depends not only on the extent to which these people understand their power as a directly political force, and on whether they have ambitions to participate in actual power, but also on how each of them understands the notion of an 'opposition'.

Again, here is an example: in its original declaration, Charter 77 emphasized that it was not an opposition because it had no intention of presenting an alternative political programme. It sees its mission as something quite different, for it has not presented such programmes. In fact, if the presenting of an alternative programme defines the nature of an opposition in post-totalitarian states, then the Charter cannot be considered an opposition.

The Czechoslovak government, however, has considered Charter 77 as an expressly oppositional association from the very beginning, and has treated it accordingly. This means that the government – and this is only natural – understands the term 'opposition' more or less as I defined it in point 2, that is, as everything that manages to avoid total manipulation and which therefore denies the principle that the system has an absolute claim on the individual.

If we accept this definition of opposition, then of course we must, along with the government, consider the Charter a genuine opposition, because it represents a serious challenge to the integrity of post-totalitarian power, founded as it is on the universality of 'living with a lie'.

It is a different matter, however, when we look at the extent to which individual signatories of Charter 77 think of themselves as an opposition. My impression is that most base their understanding of the term opposition on the traditional meaning of the word as it became established in democratic societies (or in classical dictatorships); therefore, they understand 'opposition', even in Czechoslovakia, as a politically defined force which, although it does not operate on the level of actual power, and even less within the framework of certain rules respected by the government, would still not reject the opportunity to participate in actual power because it has, in a sense, an alternative political programme whose proponents are prepared to accept direct political responsibility for it. Given this notion of an opposition, some Chartists – the great majority – do not see themselves in this way. Others – a minority – do, even though they fully respect the fact that there is no room within Charter 77 for 'oppositional' activity in this sense. At the same time, however, perhaps every Chartist is familiar enough with the specific nature of conditions in the post-totalitarian system to realize that it is not only the struggle for human rights that has its own peculiar political power, but incomparably more 'innocent' activities as well, and therefore they can be understood as an aspect of opposition. No Chartist can really object to being considered in 'opposition' in this sense.

There is another circumstance, however, that considerably complicates matters. For many decades, the power ruling society in the Soviet bloc has used the label 'opposition' as the blackest of indictments, as synonymous with the word 'enemy'. To brand someone 'a member of the opposition' is tantamount to saying he or she is trying to overthrow the government and put an end to socialism (naturally in the pay of the imperialists). There have been times when this label led straight to the gallows, and of course this does not encourage people to apply the same label to themselves. Moreover, it is only a word, and what is actually done is more important than how it is labelled.

The final reason why many reject such a term is because there is something negative about the notion of an 'opposition'. People who so define themselves do so in relation to a prior 'position'. In other words, they relate themselves specifically to the power that rules society and through it, define themselves, deriving their own 'position' from the position of the regime. For people who have simply decided to live within the truth, to say aloud what they think, to express their solidarity with their fellow citizens, to create as they want and simply to live in harmony with their better 'self', it is naturally disagreeable to feel required to define their own, original and positive 'position' negatively, in terms of something else, and to think of themselves primarily as people who are against something, not simply as people who *are* what they are.

Obviously, the only way to avoid misunderstanding is to say clearly – before one starts using them – in what sense the terms 'opposition' and 'member of the opposition' are being used and how they are in fact to be understood in our circumstances.

XIII

If the term 'opposition' has been imported from democratic societies into the post-totalitarian system without general agreement on what the word means in conditions that are so different, then the term 'dissident' was, on the contrary, chosen by western journalists and is now generally accepted as the label for a phenomenon peculiar to the post-totalitarian system and almost never occurring – at least not in that form – in democratic societies.

Who are these 'dissidents'?

It seems that the term is applied primarily to citizens of the Soviet bloc who have decided to live within the truth and who, in addition, meet the following criteria:

1 They express their non-conformist positions and critical opinions publicly and systematically, within the very strict limits available to them, and because of this, they are known in the West.

2 Despite being unable to publish at home and despite every possible form of persecution by their governments, they have, by virtue of their attitudes, managed to win a certain esteem, both from the public and from their government, and thus they actually enjoy a very limited and very strange degree of indirect, actual power in their own milieu as well. This either protects them from the worst forms of persecution, or at least it ensures that if they are persecuted, it will mean certain political complications for their governments.

3 The horizon of their critical attention and their commitment reaches beyond the narrow context of their immediate surroundings or special interests to embrace more general causes and, thus, their work becomes political in nature, although the degree to which they think of themselves as a directly political force may vary a great deal.

4 They are people who lean towards intellectual pursuits, that is, they are 'writing' people, people for whom the written word is the primary – and often the only – political medium they command, and that can gain them attention, particularly from abroad. Other ways in which they seek to live within the truth are either lost to the foreign observer in the elusive local milieu or – if they reach beyond this local framework – they appear to be only somewhat less visible complements to what they have written.

5 Regardless of their actual vocations, these people are talked

about in the West more frequently in terms of their activities as committed citizens, or in terms of the critical, political aspects of their work, than in terms of the 'real' work they do in their own fields. From personal experience, I know that there is an invisible line you cross – without even wanting to or becoming aware of it – beyond which they cease to treat you as a writer who happens to be a concerned citizen and begin talking of you as a 'dissident' who almost incidentally (in his or her spare time, perhaps?) happens to write plays as well.

Unquestionably, there are people who meet all of these criteria. What is debatable is whether we should be using a special term for a group defined in such an essentially accidental way, and specifically, whether they should be called 'dissidents'. It does happen, however, and there is clearly nothing we can do about it. Sometimes, to facilitate communication, we even use the label ourselves, although it is done with distaste, rather ironically, and almost always in quotations marks.

Perhaps it is now appropriate to outline some of the reasons why 'dissidents' themselves are not very happy to be referred to in this way. In the first place, the word is problematic from an etymological point of view. A 'dissident', we are told in our press, means something like 'renegade' or 'backslider'. But dissidents do not consider themselves renegades for the simple reason that they are not primarily denying or rejecting anything. On the contrary, they have tried to affirm their own human identity, and if they reject anything at all, then it is merely what was false and alienating in their lives, that aspect of 'living within a lie'.*

But that is not the most important thing. The term 'dissident' frequently implies a special profession, as if, along with the more normal vocations, there was another special one – grumbling about the state of things. In fact, a 'dissident' is simply a physicist, a sociologist, a worker, a poet, individuals who are merely doing what they feel they must and, consequently, who find themselves in open conflict with the regime. This conflict has not come about through any conscious intention on their part, but simply through the inner

---

* *Editor's note*: In this paragraph, Havel is in effect replying to the official Czechoslovak newspapers, in which 'dissident' is sometimes rendered as *odpadlík*, which means literally 'one who has fallen out', hence 'renegade' or 'backslider'.

logic of their thinking, behaviour or work (often confronted with external circumstances more or less beyond their control). They have not, in other words, consciously decided to be professional malcontents, rather as one decides to be a tailor or a blacksmith.

In fact, of course, they do not usually discover they are 'dissidents' until long after they have actually become one. 'Dissent' springs from motivations far different from the desire for titles or fame. In short, they do not decide to become 'dissidents', and even if they were to devote twenty-four hours a day to it, it would still not be a profession, but primarily an existential attitude. Moreover, it is an attitude that is in no way the exclusive property of those who have earned themselves the title of 'dissident' just because they happen to fulfil those accidental external conditions already mentioned. There are thousands of nameless people who try to live within the truth and millions who want to but cannot, perhaps only because to do so in the circumstances in which they live, they would need ten times the courage of those who have already taken the first step. If several dozen are randomly chosen from among all these people and put into a special category, this can utterly distort the general picture. It does so in two different ways. Either it suggests that 'dissidents' are a group of prominent people, a 'protected species' who are permitted to do things others are not and whom the government may even be cultivating as living proof of its generosity; or it lends support to the illusion that since there is no more than a handful of malcontents to whom not very much is really being done, all the rest are therefore content, for were they not so, they would be 'dissidents' too.

But that is not all. This categorization also unintentionally supports the impression that the primary concern of these 'dissidents' is some vested interest that they share as a group, as though their entire argument with the government were no more than a rather abstruse conflict between two opposed groups, a conflict that leaves society out of it altogether. But such an impression profoundly contradicts the real importance of the 'dissident' attitude, which stands or falls on its interest in others, in what ails society as a whole, in other words, on an interest in all those who do not speak up. If 'dissidents' have any kind of authority at all and if they have not been exterminated long ago like exotic insects that have appeared where they have no business being, then this is not because the government holds this exclusive group and their exclusive ideas in such awe, but because it is perfectly aware of the potential political power of 'living within the truth' rooted in the hidden sphere, and well aware too of the kind of world 'dissent' grows out of and the world it addresses: the everyday human world, the world of daily tension between the aims of life and the aims of the system. (Can there be any better evidence of this than the government's action after Charter 77 appeared, when it launched a campaign to compel the entire nation to declare that Charter 77 was wrong? Those millions of signatures proved, among other things, that just the opposite was true.) The political organs and the police do not lavish such enormous attention on 'dissidents' – which may give the impression that the government fears them as they might fear an alternative power clique – because they actually are such a power clique, but because they are ordinary people with ordinary cares, differing from the rest only in that they say aloud what the rest cannot say or are afraid to say. I have already mentioned Solzhenitsyn's political influence: it does not reside in some exclusive political power he possesses as a individual, but in the experience of those millions of Gulag victims which he simply amplified and communicated to millions of other people of good will.

To institutionalize a select category of well-known or prominent 'dissidents' means in fact to deny the most intrinsic moral aspect of their activity. As we have seen, the 'dissident movement' grows out of the principle of equality, founded on the notion that human rights and freedoms are indivisible. After all, did not 'well-known dissidents' unite in *KOR** to defend unknown workers? And was it not precisely for this reason that they became 'well-known dissidents'? And did not the 'well-known dissidents' unite in Charter 77 after they had been brought together in defence of those unknown musicians, and did they not unite in the Charter precisely *with them*, and did they not become 'well-known dissidents' precisely because of that? It is truly a cruel paradox that the more some citizens stand up in defence of other citizens, the more they are labelled with a word that in effect separates them from those 'other citizens'.

This explanation, I hope, will make clear the significance of the

---

* *Editor's note*: The Workers' Defence Commitee, a Polish organization that preceded the birth of Solidarity in August, 1980. It was later renamed *KSS–KOR* (Committee for Social Self-Defence – KOR) to indicate its commitment to defending civil rights as well as its support of all social initiatives against the institutions of the totalitarian state.

quotation marks I have put around the word 'dissident' throughout this essay.


# XIV

At the time when the Czech lands and Slovakia were an integral part of the Austro-Hungarian Empire, and when there existed neither the historical nor the political, psychological or social conditions that would have enabled the Czechs and Slovaks to seek their identity outside the framework of this empire, T. G. Masaryk established a Czechoslovak national programme based on the notion of 'small-scale work' (*drobná práce*). By that he meant honest and responsible work in widely different areas of life but within the existing social order, work that would stimulate national creativity and national self-confidence. Naturally he placed particular emphasis on intelligent and enlightened upbringing and education, and on the moral and humanitarian aspects of life. Masaryk believed that the only possible starting point for a more dignified national destiny was humanity itself. Humanity's first task was to create the conditions for a more human life; and in Masaryk's view, the task of transforming the stature of the nation began with the transformation of human beings.

This notion of 'working for the good of the nation' took root in Czechoslovak society and in many ways it was successful and is still alive today. Along with those who exploit the notion as a sophisticated excuse for collaborating with the regime, there are still many, even today, who genuinely uphold the ideal and, in some areas at least, can point to indisputable achievements. It is hard to say how much worse things would be if there were not many hard working people who simply refused to give up and try constantly to do the best they can, paying an unavoidable minimum to 'living within a lie' so that they might give their utmost to the authentic needs of society. These people assume, correctly, that every piece of good work is an indirect criticism of bad politics, and that there are situations where it is worthwhile going this route, even though it means surrendering one's natural right to make direct criticisms.

Today, however, there are very clear limitations to this attitude, even compared to the situation in the 1960s. More and more frequently, those who attempt to practise the principle of 'small-scale work' come up against the post-totalitarian system and find themselves facing a dilemma: either one retreats from that position, dilutes the honesty, responsibility and consistency on which it is based and simply adapts to circumstances (the approach taken by the majority), or one continues on the way begun and inevitably comes into conflict with the regime (the approach taken by a minority).

If the notion of small-scale work was never intended as an imperative to survive in the existing social and political structure *at any cost* (in which case individuals who allowed themselves to be excluded from that structure would necessarily appear to have given up 'working for the nation') then today it is even less significant. There is no general model of behaviour, that is, no neat, universally valid way of determining the point at which small-scale work ceases to be 'for the good of the nation' and becomes 'detrimental to the nation'. It is more than clear, however, that the danger of such a reversal is becoming more and more acute and that small-scale work, with increasing frequency, is coming up against that limit beyond which avoiding conflict means compromising its very essence.

In 1974, when I was employed in a brewery, my immediate superior was a certain Š., a person well-versed in the art of making beer. He was proud of his profession and he wanted our brewery to brew good beer. He spent almost all his time at work, continually thinking up improvements and he frequently made the rest of us feel uncomfortable because he assumed that we loved brewing as much as he did. In the midst of the slovenly indifference to work that socialism encourages, a more constructive worker would be difficult to imagine.

The brewery itself was managed by people who understood their work less and were less fond of it, but who were politically more influential. They were bringing the brewery to ruin and not only did they fail to react to any of Š.'s suggestions, but they actually became increasingly hostile towards him and tried in every way to thwart his efforts to do a good job. Eventually the situation became so bad that Š. felt compelled to write a lengthy letter to the manager's superior, in which he attempted to analyse the brewery's difficulties. He explained why it was the worst in the district and pointed to those responsible.

His voice might have been heard. The manager, who was politically powerful but otherwise ignorant of beer, a man who loathed workers and was given to intrigue, might have been replaced and conditions in the brewery might have been improved on the basis of

Š.'s suggestions. Had this happened, it would have been a perfect example of small-scale work in action. Unfortunately the precise opposite occurred: the manager of the brewery, who was a member of the Communist Party's district committee, had friends in higher places and he saw to it that the situation was resolved in his favour. Š.'s analysis was described as a 'defamatory document' and Š. himself was labelled a 'political saboteur'. He was thrown out of the brewery and shifted to another one where he was given a job requiring no skill. Here the notion of small-scale work had come up against the wall of the post-totalitarian system. By speaking the truth, Š. had stepped out of line, broken the rules, cast himself out, and he ended up as a sub-citizen, stigmatized as an enemy. He could now say anything he wanted, but he could never, as a matter of principle, expect to be heard. He had become the 'dissident' of the Eastern Bohemian Brewery.

I think this is a model case which, from another point of view, illustrates what I have already said in the preceding section: you do not become a 'dissident' just because you decide one day to take up this most unusual career. You are thrown into it by your personal sense of responsibility, combined with a complex set of external circumstances. You are cast out of the existing structures and placed in a position of conflict with them. It begins as an attempt to do your work well, and ends with being branded an enemy of society. This is why our situation is not comparable to the Austro-Hungarian Empire, when the Czech nation, in the worst period of Bach's absolutism,* had only one real 'dissident', Karel Havlíček, who was imprisoned in Brixen. Today, if we are not to be snobbish about it, we must admit that 'dissidents' can be found on every street-corner.

To rebuke 'dissidents' for having abandoned 'small-scale work' is simply absurd. 'Dissent' is not an alternative to Masaryk's notion, it is frequently its only possible outcome. I say 'frequently' in order to emphasize that this is not always the case. I am far from believing that the only decent and responsible people are those who find

---

* *Editor's note*: Alexander Bach was Minister of the Interior for a decade - 1849–59 - in Vienna. His name has entered the Czech language and is synonymous with police rule. Karel Havlíček Borovský (1821–56) was a poet, literary critic and publicist. He is widely considered as the classical writer in the tradition of Czech political satire, and was involved directly in the Czech movement for nationhood and democracy during the 1840s and 1850s.

themselves at odds with the existing social and political structures. After all, the brewmaster Š. might have won his battle. To condemn those who have kept their positions simply because they have kept them, in other words, for not being 'dissidents', would be just as absurd as to hold them up as an example to the 'dissidents'. In any case, it contradicts the whole 'dissident' attitude – seen as an attempt to live within the truth – if one judges human behaviour not according to what it is and whether it is good or not, but according to the personal circumstances such an attempt has brought one to.

## XV

Our greengrocer's attempt to live within the truth may be confined to not doing certain things. He decides not to put flags in his window when his only motive for putting them there in the first place would have been to avoid being reported by the house warden; he does not vote in elections that he considers false; he does not hide his opinions from his superiors. In other words, he may go no further than 'merely' refusing to comply with certain demands made on him by the system (which of course is not an insignificant step to take). This may, however, grow into something more. The greengrocer may begin to do something concrete, something that goes beyond an immediately personal self-defensive reaction against manipulation, something that will manifest his new-found sense of higher responsibility. He may, for example, organize his fellow greengrocers to act together in defence of their interests. He may write letters to various institutions, drawing their attention to instances of disorder and injustice around him. He may seek out unofficial literature, copy it and lend it to his friends.

If what I have called living within the truth is a basic existential (and of course potentially political) starting point for all those 'independent citizens' initiatives ' and 'dissident' or 'opposition' movements dealt with in the essays to follow, this does not mean that every attempt to live within the truth automatically belongs in this category. On the contrary, in its most original and broadest sense, living within the truth covers a vast territory whose outer limits are vague and difficult to map, a territory full of modest expressions of human volition, the vast majority of which will remain anonymous and whose political impact will probably never be felt or described any more concretely than simply as a part of a social climate or mood. Most of these expressions remain elementary revolts against manipulation: you simple straighten your backbone and live in greater dignity as an individual.

Here and there – thanks to the nature, the assumptions and the professions of some people, but also thanks to a number of accidental circumstances such as the specific nature of the local milieu, friends, and so on – a more coherent and visible initiative may emerge from this wide and anonymous hinterland, an initiative that transcends 'merely' individual revolt and is transformed into more conscious, structured and purposeful work. The point where living within the truth ceases to be a mere negation of living with a lie and becomes articulate in a particular way, is the point at which something is born that might be called 'the independent spiritual, social and political life of society'. This independent life is not separated from the rest of life ('dependent life') by some sharply defined line. Both types frequently coexist in the same people. Nevertheless, its most important focus is marked by a relatively high degree of inner emancipation. It sails upon the vast ocean of the manipulated life like little boats, tossed by the waves but always bobbing back as visible messengers of living within the truth, articulating the supressed aims of life.

What is this independent life of society? The spectrum of its expressions and activities is naturally very wide. It includes everything from self-education and thinking about the world, through free creative activity and its communication to others, to the most varied free, civic attitudes, including instances of independent social self-organization. In short, it is an area in which living within the truth becomes articulate and materializes in a visible way.

Thus what will later be referred to as 'citizens' initiatives', 'dissident movements' or even 'oppositions', emerge, like the proverbial one-tenth of the iceberg visible above the water, from that area, from the independent life of society. In other words, just as the independent life of society develops out of living within the truth in the widest sense of the word, as the distinct, articulated expression of that life, so 'dissent' gradually emerges from the 'independent life of society'. Yet there is a marked difference: if the independent life of society, externally at least, can be understood as a higher form of living within the truth, it is far less certain that 'dissident movements' are necessarily a higher form of the 'independent life of society'. They are simply one manifestation of it and

though they may be the most visible and, at first glance, the most
political (and most clearly articulated) expression of it, they are far
from necessarily being the most mature or even the most important,
not only in the general social sense but even in terms of direct
political influence. After all, 'dissent' has been artificially removed
from its place of birth by having been given a special name. In fact,
however, it is not possible to think of it separated from the whole
background out of which it develops, of which it is an integral part,
and from which it draws all its vital strength. In any case, it follows
from what has already been said about the peculiarities of the post-
totalitarian system that what *appears* to be the most political of
forces in a given moment, and what thinks of itself in such terms,
need not necessarily in fact *be* such a force. The extent to which it is a
real political force is due exclusively to its pre-political context.

What follows from this description? Nothing more and nothing
less than this: it is impossible to talk about what in fact 'dissidents'
do and the effect of their work without first talking about the work
of all those who, in one way or another, take part in the independent
life of society and who are not necessarily 'dissidents' at all. They
may be writers who write as they wish without regard for censorship
or official demands and who issue their work – when official
publishers refuse to print them – as *samizdat*. They may be philosophers, historians, sociologists and all those who practise independent scholarship and, if it is impossible through official or semi-
official channels, who also circulate their work in *samizdat* or who
organize private discussions, lectures and seminars. They may be
teachers who privately teach young people things that are kept from
them in the state schools; clergymen who either in office or, if they
are deprived of their charges, outside it, try to carry on a free religious life; painters, musicians and singers who practise their work
regardless of how it is looked upon by official institutions; everyone
who shares this independent culture and helps to spread it; people
who, using the means available to them, try to express and defend
the actual social interests of workers, to put real meaning back into
trade unions or to form independent ones; people who are not afraid
to call the attention of officials to cases of injustice and who strive to
see that the laws are observed; and the different groups of young
people who try to extricate themselves from manipulation and live in
their own way, in the spirit of their own hierarchy of values. The list
could go on.

Very few would think of calling all these people 'dissidents'. And yet are not the well-known 'dissidents' simply people like them? Are not all these activities in fact what 'dissidents' do as well? Do they not produce scholarly work and publish it in *samizdat*? Do they not write plays and novels and poems? Do they not lecture to students in private 'universities'? Do they not struggle against various forms of injustice and attempt to ascertain and express the genuine social interests of various sectors of the population?

After having tried to indicate the sources, the inner structure and some aspects of the 'dissident' attitude as such, I have clearly shifted my viewpoint from outside, as it were, to an investigation of what these 'dissidents' *actually* do, how their initiatives are manifested and where they lead.

The first conclusion to be drawn, then, is that the original and most important sphere of activity, one that predetermines all the others, is simply an attempt to create and support the 'independent life of society' as an articulated expression of 'living within the truth'. In other words, serving truth consistently, purposefully and articulately, and organizing this service. This is only natural, after all: if living within the truth is an elementary starting point for every attempt made by people to oppose the alienating pressure of the system, if it is the only meaningful basis of any independent act of political import, and if, ultimately, it is also the most intrinsic existential source of the 'dissident' attitude, then it is difficult to imagine that even manifest 'dissent' could have any other basis than the service of truth, the truthful life and the attempt to make room for the genuine aims of life.

## XVI

The post-totalitarian system is mounting a total assault on humans and humans stand against it alone, abandoned and isolated. It is therefore entirely natural that all the 'dissident movements' are explicitly defensive movements: they exist to defend human beings and the genuine aims of life against the aims of the system.

Today the Polish group *KOR* is called the Committee for Social Self-Defence. The word 'defence' appears in the names of other similar groups in Poland, but even the Soviet Helsinki monitoring group and our own Charter 77 are clearly defensive in nature.

In terms of traditional politics, this programme of defence is understandable, even though it may appear minimal, provisional and ultimately negative. It offers no new conception, model or ideology, and therefore it is not 'politics' in the proper sense of the word, since politics always assumes a 'positive' programme and can scarcely limit itself to defending someone against something.

Such a view, I think, reveals the limitations of the traditionally political way of looking at things. The post-totalitarian system, after all, is not the manifestation of a particular political line followed by a particular government. It is something radically different: it is a complex, profound and long-term violation of society, or rather the self-violation of society. To oppose it merely by establishing a different political line and then striving for a change in government would not only be unrealistic, it would be utterly inadequate, for it would never come near to touching the root of the matter. For some time now, the problem has no longer resided in a political line or programme: it is a problem of life itself.

Thus defending the aims of life, defending humanity is not only a more realistic approach, since it can begin right now and is potentially more popular because it concerns people's everyday lives; at the same time (and perhaps precisely because of this) it is also an incomparably more consistent approach because it aims at the very essence of things.

There are times when we must sink to the bottom of our misery to understand truth, just as we must descend to the bottom of a well to see the stars in broad daylight. It seems to me that today, this 'provisional', 'minimal' and 'negative' programme – the 'simple' defence of people – is in a particular sense (and not merely in the circumstances in which we live) an optimal and most positive programme because it forces politics to return to its only proper starting point, proper that is, if all the old mistakes are to be avoided: individual people. In democratic societies, where the violence done to human beings is not nearly so obvious and cruel, this fundamental revolution in politics has yet to happen, and some things will probably have to get worse there before the urgent need for that revolution is reflected in politics. In our world, precisely because of the misery in which we find ourselves, it would seem that politics has already undergone that transformation: the central concern of political thought is no longer abstract visions of a self-redeeming, 'positive' model (and of course the opportunistic political practices that are the reverse of the same coin), but rather the people who have so far merely been enslaved by those models and their practices.

Every society, of course, requires some degree of organization. Yet if that organization is to serve people and not the other way around, then people will have to be liberated and space created so that they may organize themselves in meaningful ways. The depravity of the opposite approach, in which people are first organized in one way or another (by someone who always knows best 'what the people need') so they may then allegedly be liberated, is something we have known on our own skins only too well.

To sum up: most people who are too bound to the traditional political way of thinking see the weaknesses of the 'dissident movements' in their purely defensive character. In contrast, I see that as their greatest strength. I believe that this is precisely where these movements supercede the kind of politics from whose point of view their programme can seem so inadequate.

## XVII

In the 'dissident movements' of the Soviet bloc, the defence of human beings usually takes the form of a defence of human and civil rights as they are entrenched in various official documents such as the Universal Declaration of Human Rights, the International Covenants on Human Rights, the Final Act of the Helsinki Conference and the constitutions of individual states. These movements set out to defend anyone who is being prosecuted for acting in the spirit of those rights, and they in turn act in the same spirit in their work, by insisting over and over again that the regime recognize and respect human and civil rights, and by drawing attention to the areas of life where this is not the case.

Their work, therefore, is based on the principle of legality: they operate publicly and openly, insisting not only that their activity is in line with the law, but that achieving respect for the law is one of their main aims. This principle of legality, which provides both the point of departure and the framework for their activities, is common to all 'dissident' groups in the Soviet bloc, even though individual groups have never worked out any formal agreement on that point. This circumstance raises an important question: Why, in conditions where a widespread and arbitrary abuse of power is the rule, is there such a general and spontaneous acceptance of the principle of legality?

On the primary level, this stress on legality is a natural expression of specific conditions that exist in the post-totalitarian system, and the consequence of an elementary understanding of that specificity. If there are in essence only two ways to struggle for a free society – that is, through legal means and through (armed or unarmed) revolt – then it should be obvious at once how inappropriate the latter alternative is in the post-totalitarian system. Revolt is appropriate when conditions are clearly and openly in motion, during a war for example, or in situations where social or political conflicts are coming to a head. It is appropriate in a classical dictatorship that is either just setting itself up or is in a state of collapse. In other words, it is appropriate where social forces of comparable strength (for example, a government of occupation vs a nation fighting for its freedom) are confronting each other on the level of actual power, or where there is a clear distinction between the usurpers of power and the subjugated population, or when society finds itself in a state of open crisis. Conditions in the post-totalitarian system – except in extremely explosive situations like the one in Hungary in 1956 – are, of course, precisely the opposite. They are static and stable, and social crises, for the most part, exist only latently (though they run much deeper). Society is not sharply polarized on the level of actual political power, but, as we have seen, the fundamental lines of conflict run right through each person. In this situation, no attempt at revolt could ever hope to set up even a minimum of resonance in the rest of society, because that society is 'soporific', submerged in a consumer rat-race and wholly involved in the post-totalitarian system (that is, participating in it and acting as agents of its 'automatism'), and it would simply find anything like revolt unacceptable. It would interpret the revolt as an attack upon itself and, rather than supporting the revolt, it would very probably react by intensifying its bias towards the system, since, in its view, the system can at least guarantee a certain quasi-legality. Add to this the fact that the post-totalitarian system has at its disposal a complex mechanism of direct and indirect surveillance that has no equal in history and it is clear that not only would any attempt to revolt come to a dead end politically, but it would also be almost technically impossible to carry off. Most probably it would be liquidated before it had a chance to translate its intentions into action. Even if revolt were possible, however, it would remain the solitary gesture of a few isolated individuals and they would be opposed not only by a gigantic apparatus of national (and supra-national) power, but also by the very society in whose name they were mounting their revolt in the first place. (This, by the way, is another reason why the regime and its propaganda have been ascribing terroristic aims to the 'dissident movements' and accusing them of illegal and conspiratorial methods.)

All of this, however, is not the main reason why the 'dissident movements' support the principle of legality. That reason lies deeper, in the innermost structure of the 'dissident' attitude. This attitude is and must be fundamentally hostile towards the notion of violent change as such to the system – and every revolt, essentially, aims at violent change – simply because it places its faith in violence. (Generally, the 'dissident' attitude can only accept violence as a necessary evil in extreme situations, when direct violence can only be met by violence and where remaining passive would in effect mean supporting violence: let us recall, for example, that the blindness of European pacifism was one of the factors that prepared the ground for the Second World War.) As I have already mentioned, 'dissidents' tend to be sceptical about political thought based on the faith that profound social changes can only be achieved by bringing about (regardless of the method) changes in the system or in the government, and the belief that such changes – because they are considered 'fundamental' – justify the sacrifice of 'less fundamental' things, in other words, human lives. Respect for a theoretical concept here outweighs respect for human life. Yet this is precisely what threatens to enslave humanity all over again.

'Dissident movements', as I have tried to indicate, share exactly the opposite view. They understand systemic change as something superficial, something secondary, something that in itself can guarantee nothing. Thus an attitude that turns away from abstract political visions of the future towards concrete human beings and ways of defending them effectively in the here and now is quite naturally accompanied by an intensified antipathy to all forms of violence carried out in the name of 'a better future', and by a profound belief that a future secured by violence might actually be worse than what exists now; in other words, the future would be fatally stigmatized by the very means used to secure it. At the same time, this attitude is not to be mistaken for political conservatism or political moderation. The 'dissident movements' do not shy away from the idea of violent political overthrow because the idea seems too radical, but on the contrary, because it does not seem radical enough. For them, the problem lies far too deep to be settled through mere systemic changes, either governmental or technological.

Some people, faithful to the classical Marxist doctrines of the nineteenth century, understand our system as the hegemony of an exploiting class over an exploited class and, operating from the postulate that exploiters never surrender their power voluntarily, they see the only solution in a revolution to sweep away the exploiters. Naturally, they regard such things as the struggle for human rights as something hopelessly legalistic, illusory, opportunistic and ultimately misleading because it makes the doubtful assumption that you can negotiate in good faith with your exploiters on the basis of a false legality. The problem is that they are unable to find anyone determined enough to carry out this revolution, with the result that they become bitter, sceptical, passive and ultimately apathetic – in other words, they end up precisely where the system wants them to be. This is one example of how far one can be misled by mechanically applying, in post-totalitarian circumstances, ideological models from another world and another time.

Of course, one need not be an advocate of violent revolution to ask whether an appeal to legality makes any sense at all when the laws – and particularly the general laws concerning human rights – are no more than a façade, an aspect of the world of appearances, a mere game behind which lies total manipulation. 'They can ratify anything because they will still go ahead and do whatever they want anyway' – this is an opinion we often encounter. Is it not true that to constantly 'take them at their word', to appeal to laws every child knows are binding only as long as the government wishes, is in the end just a kind of hypocrisy, a Švejkian obstructionism and, finally, just another way of playing the game, another form of self-delusion? In other words, is the legalistic approach at all compatible with the principle of 'living within the truth'?

This question can only be answered by first looking at the wider implications of how the legal code functions in the post-totalitarian system.

In a classical dictatorship, to a far greater extent than in the post-totalitarian system, the will of the ruler is carried out directly, in an unregulated fashion. A dictatorship has no reason to hide its foundations, nor to conceal the real workings of power, and therefore it need not encumber itself to any great extent with a legal code. The post-totalitarian system, on the other hand, is utterly obsessed with the need to bind everything in a single order: life in such a state is thoroughly permeated by a dense network of regulations, proclamations, directives, norms, orders and rules. (It is not called a bureaucratic system without good reason.) A large proportion of those norms functions as direct instruments of the complex manipulation of life that is intrinsic to the post-totalitarian system. Individuals are reduced to little more than tiny cogs in an enormous mechanism and their significance is limited to their function in this mechanism. Their job, housing accommodation, movements, social and cultural expressions, everything, in short, must be cossetted together as firmly as possible, predetermined, regulated and controlled. Every aberration from the prescribed course of life is treated as error, licence and anarchy. From the cook in the restaurant who, without hard-to-get permission from the bureaucratic apparatus, cannot cook something special for his customers, to the singer who cannot perform his new song at a concert without bureaucratic approval, everyone, in all aspects of their life, is caught in this regulatory tangle of red tape, the inevitable product of the post-totalitarian system. With ever-increasing consistency, it binds all the expressions and aims of life to the spirit of its own aims: the vested interests of its own smooth, automatic operation.

In a narrower sense the legal code serves the post-totalitarian system in this direct way as well, that is, it too forms a part of the world of regulations and prohibitions. At the same time, however, it performs the same service in another indirect way, one that brings it remarkably closer – depending on which level of the law is involved – to ideology and in some cases making it a direct component of that ideology.

1 Like ideology, the legal code functions as an excuse. It wraps the base exercise of power in the noble apparel of the letter of the law; it creates the pleasing illusion that justice is done, society protected and the exercise of power objectively regulated. All this is done to conceal the real essence of post-totalitarian legal practice: the total manipulation of society. If an outside observer who knew nothing at all about life in Czechoslovakia were to study only its laws, he or she would be utterly incapable of understanding what we were complaining about. The hidden political manipulation of the courts and of public prosecutors, the limitations placed on lawyers' ability to defend their clients, the closed nature, *de facto*, of trials, the arbitrary actions of the security forces, their position of authority over the judiciary, the absurdly broad application of several deliberately vague sections of that code, and of course the state's utter

disregard for the positive sections of that code (the rights of citizens): all of this would remain hidden from our outside observer. The only thing he or she would take away would be the impression that our legal code is not much worse than the legal code of other civilized countries, and not much different either, except perhaps for certain curiosities, such as the entrenchment in the constitution of a single political party's eternal rule and the state's love for a neighbouring superpower. But that is not all: if our observer had the opportunity to study the formal side of policing and judicial procedures and practices, how they look 'on paper', he or she would discover that for the most part the common rules of criminal procedure are observed: charges are laid within the prescribed period following arrest, and it is the same with detention orders. Indictments are properly delivered, the accused has a lawyer, and so on. In other words, everyone has an excuse: *they have all observed the law.* In reality, however, they have cruelly and pointlessly ruined a young person's life, perhaps for no other reason than because he or she made *samizdat* copies of a novel written by a banned writer, or because the police deliberately falsified their testimony (as everyone knows, from the judge on down to the defendant). Yet all of this somehow remains in the background. The falsified testimony is not necessarily obvious from the trial documents and the section of the criminal code dealing with incitement does not formally exclude the application of that charge to the copying of a banned novel. In other words, the legal code - at least in several areas - is not more than a façade, an aspect of the world of appearances. Then why is it there at all? For exactly the same reason as ideology is there: it provides a bridge of excuses between the system and individuals, making it easier for them to enter the power structure and serve the arbitrary demands of power. The excuse lets individuals fool themselves into thinking they are merely upholding the law and protecting society from criminals. (Without this excuse, how much more difficult it would be to recruit new generations of judges, prosecutors and interrogators!) As an aspect of the world of appearances, however, the legal code deceives not only the conscience of prosecutors, it deceives the public, it deceives foreign observers, and it even deceives history itself.

2 Like ideology, the legal code is an essential instrument of ritual communication outside the power structure. It is the legal code that gives the exercise of power a form, a framework, a set of rules. It is the legal code that enables all components of the system to communicate, to put themselves in a good light, to establish their own

legitimacy. It provides their whole game with its 'rules' and engineers with their technology. Can the exercise of post-totalitarian power be imagined at all without this universal ritual making it all possible, serving as a common language to bind the relevant sectors of the power structure together? The more important the position occupied by the repressive apparatus in the power structure, the more important that it functions according to some kind of formal code. How, otherwise, could people be so easily and inconspicuously locked up for copying banned books if there were no judges, prosecutors, interrogators, defence lawyers, court stenographers and thick files, and if all this were not held together by some firm order? And above all, without that innocent-looking Section 100 on incitement? This could all be done, of course, without a legal code and its accessories, but only in some ephemeral dictatorship run by a Ugandan bandit, not in a system that embraces such a huge portion of civilized humankind and represents an integral, stable and respected part of the modern world. That would not only be unthinkable, it would quite simply be technically impossible. Without the legal code functioning as a ritually cohesive force, the post-totalitarian system could not exist.

The entire role of ritual, façades and excuses appears most eloquently, of course, not in the proscriptive section of the legal code, which sets out what a citizen may not do and what the grounds for prosecution are, but in the section declaring what he or she may do and what his or her rights are. Here there is truly nothing but 'words, words, words'. Yet even that part of the code is of immense importance to the system, for it is here that the system establishes its legitimacy as a whole, before its own citizens, before school children, before the international public and before history. The system cannot afford to disregard this because it cannot permit itself to cast doubt upon the fundamental postulates of its ideology, which are so essential to its very existence. (We have already seen how the power structure is enslaved by its own ideology and its ideological prestige.) To do this would be to deny everything it tries to present itself as and, thus, one of the main pillars on which the system rests would be undermined: the integrity of the world of appearances.

If the exercise of power circulates through the whole power structure as blood flows though veins, then the legal code can be understood as something that reinforces the walls of those veins. Without it, the blood of power could not circulate in an organized way and the body of society would haemorrhage at random. Order would collapse.

A persistent and never-ending appeal to the laws – not just to the laws concerning human rights, but to all laws – does not mean at all that those who do so have succumbed to the illusion that in our system the law is anything other than what it is. They are well aware of the role it plays. But precisely because they know how desperately the system depends on it – on the 'noble' version of the law, that is – they also know how enormously significant such appeals are. Because the system cannot do without the law, because it is hopelessly tied down by the necessity of pretending the laws are observed, it is compelled to react in some way to such appeals. Demanding that the laws be upheld is thus an act of living within the truth that threatens the whole mendacious structure at its point of maximum mendacity. Over and over again, such appeals make the purely ritualistic nature of the law clear to society and to those who inhabit its power structures. They draw attention to its real material substance and thus, indirectly, compel all those who take refuge behind the law to affirm and make credible this agency of excuses, this means of communication, this reinforcement of the social arteries outside of which their will could not be made to circulate through society. They are compelled to do so for the sake of their own consciences, for the impression they make on outsiders, to maintain themselves in power (as part of the system's own mechanism of self-preservation and its principles of cohesion), or simply out of fear that they will be reproached for being 'clumsy' in handling the ritual. They have no other choice: because they cannot discard the rules of their own game, they can only attend more carefully to those rules. Not to react to challenges means to undermine their own excuse and lose control of their mutual communications system. To assume that the laws are a mere façade, that they have no validity and that therefore it is pointless to appeal to them would mean to go on reinforcing those aspects of the law that create the façade and the ritual. It would mean confirming the law as an aspect of the world of appearances and enabling those who exploit it to rest easy with the cheapest (and therefore the most mendacious) form of their excuse.

I have frequently witnessed policemen, prosecutors or judges – if they were dealing with an experienced Chartist or a courageous lawyer, and if they were exposed to public attention (as individuals with a name, no longer protected by the anonymity of the apparatus)

- suddenly and anxiously begin to take particular care that no cracks appear in the ritual. This does not alter the fact that a despotic power is hiding behind that ritual, but the very existence of the officials' anxiety necessarily regulates, limits and slows down the operation of that despotism.

This, of course, is not enough. But an essential part of the 'dissident' attitude is that it comes out of the reality of the human 'here and now'. It places more importance on oft-repeated and consistent concrete action – even though it may be inadequate and though it may ease only insignificantly the suffering of a single insignificant citizen – than it does in some abstract 'fundamental solution' in an uncertain future. In any case, is not this in fact just another form of 'small-scale work' in the Masarykian sense, with which the 'dissident' attitude seemed at first to be in such sharp contradiction?

This section would be incomplete without stressing certain internal limitations to the policy of 'taking them at their own word'. The point is this: even in the most ideal of cases, the law is only one of several imperfect and more or less external ways of defending what is better in life against what is worse. By itself, the law can never create anything better. Its purpose is to render a service and its meaning does not lie in the law itself. Establishing respect for the law does not automatically ensure a better life for that, after all, is a job for people and not for laws and institutions. It is possible to imagine a society with good laws that are fully respected but in which it is impossible to live. Conversely, one can imagine life being quite bearable even where the laws are imperfect and imperfectly applied. The most important thing is always the quality of that life and whether or not the laws enhance life or repress it, not merely whether they are upheld or not. (Often strict observance of the law could have a disastrous impact on human dignity.) The key to a humane, dignified, rich and happy life does not lie either in the constitution or in the criminal code. These merely establish what may or may not be done and, thus, they can make life easier or more difficult. They limit or permit, they punish, tolerate or defend, but they can never give life substance or meaning. The struggle for what is called 'legality' must constantly keep this legality in perspective against the background of life as it really is. Without keeping one's eyes open to the real dimensions of life's beauty and misery, and without a moral relationship to life, this struggle will sooner or later come to grief on the rocks of some self-justifying system of scholastics. Without really wanting to, one would thus become more and more like the observer who comes to conclusions about our system only on the basis of trial documents and is satisfied if all the appropriate regulations have been observed.

## XVIII

If the basic job of the 'dissident movements' is to serve truth, that is, to serve the real aims of life, and if that necessarily develops into a defence of the individual and his or her right to a free and truthful life (that is, a defence of human rights and a struggle to see the laws respected) then another stage of this approach, perhaps the most mature stage so far, is what Václav Benda has called the development of parallel structures.

When those who have decided to live within the truth have been denied any direct influence on the existing social structures, not to mention the opportunity to participate in them, and when these people begin to create what I have called the independent life of society, this independent life begins, of itself, to become structured in a certain way. Sometimes there are only very embryonic indications of this process of structuring; at other times, the structures are already quite well-developed. Their genesis and evolution are inseparable from the phenomenon of 'dissent', even though they reach far beyond the arbitrarily defined area of activity usually indicated by that term.

What are these structures? Ivan Jirous was the first in Czechoslovakia to formulate and apply in practice the concept of a 'second culture'. Although at first he was thinking chiefly of non-conformist rock music and only certain literary, artistic or performance events close to the sensibilities of those non-conformist musical groups, the term 'second culture' very rapidly came to be used for the whole area of independent and repressed culture, that is, not only for art and its various currents but also for the humanities, the social sciences and philosophical thought. This 'second culture', quite naturally, has created elementary organizational forms: *samizdat* editions of books and magazines, private performances and concerts, seminars, exhibitions and so on. (In Poland all of this is vastly more developed: there are independent publishing houses and many more periodicals, even political periodicals; they have means of proliferation other than carbon copies, and so on. In the Soviet Union, *samizdat* has a longer tradition and clearly its forms are quite different.) Culture, therefore, is a sphere in which the 'parallel structures' can be observed in their most highly developed form. Benda, of course, gives thought to potential or embryonic forms of such structures in other spheres as well: from a parallel information network to parallel forms of education (private universities), parallel trade unions, parallel foreign contacts, to a kind of hypothesis on a parallel economy. On the basis of these parallel structures, he then develops the notion of a 'parallel *polis*' or state or, rather, he sees the rudiments of such a *polis* in these structures.

At a certain stage in its development, the independent life of society and the 'dissident movements' cannot avoid a certain amount of organization and institutionalization. This is a natural development and unless this independent life of society is somehow radically suppressed and eliminated, the tendency will grow. Along with it, a parallel political life will also necessarily evolve, and to a certain extent it exists already in Czechoslovakia. Various groupings of a more or less political nature will continue to define themslves politically, to act and confront each other.

These parallel structures, it may be said, represent the most articulated expressions so far of 'living within the truth'. One of the most important tasks the 'dissident movements' have set themselves is to support and develop them. Once again, it confirms the fact that all attempts by society to resist the pressure of the system have their essential beginnings in the pre-political area. For what else are parallel structures than an area where a different life can be lived, a life that is in harmony with its own aims and which in turn structures itself in harmony with those aims? What else are those initial attempts at social self-organization than the efforts of a certain part of society to live – as a society – within the truth, to rid itself of the self-sustaining aspects of totalitarianism and, thus, to extricate itself radically from its involvement in the post-totalitarian system? What else is it but a non-violent attempt by people to negate the system within themselves and to establish their lives on a new basis, that of their own proper identity? And does this tendency not confirm once more the principle of returning the focus to actual individuals? After all, the parallel structures do not grow *a priori* out of a theoretical vision of systemic changes (there are no political sects involved), but from the aims of life and the authentic needs of real people. In fact, all eventual changes in the system, changes we may observe here in their rudimentary forms, have come about as it were *de facto*, from 'below', because life compelled them to, not because they came before life, somehow directing it or forcing some change on it.

Historical experience teaches us that any genuinely meaningful point of departure in an individual's life usually has an element of universality about it. In other words, it is not something partial, accessible only to a restricted community, and not transferable to any other. On the contrary, it must be potentially accessible to everyone; it must foreshadow a general solution and, thus, it is not just the expression of an introverted, self-contained responsibility that individuals have to and for themselves alone, but responsibility to and for the *world*. Thus it would be quite wrong to understand the parallel structures and the parallel *polis* as a retreat into a ghetto and as an act of isolation, addressing itself only to the welfare of those who had decided on such a course, and who are indifferent to the rest. It would be wrong, in short, to consider it an essentially group solution that has nothing to do with the general situation. Such a concept would, from the start, alienate the notion of living within the truth from its proper point of departure, which is concern for others, transforming it ultimately into just another more sophisticated version of 'living within a lie'. In doing so, of course, it would cease to be a genuine point of departure for individuals and groups and would recall the false notion of 'dissidents' as an exclusive group with exclusive interests, carrying on their own exclusive dialogue with the powers that be. In any case, even the most highly developed forms of life in the parallel structures, even that most mature form of the parallel *polis* can only exist – at least in post-totalitarian circumstances – when the individual is at the same time lodged in the 'first', official structure by a thousand different relationships, even though it may only be the fact that one buys what one needs in their stores, uses their money and obeys their laws. Certainly one can imagine life in its 'baser' aspects flourishing in the parallel *polis*, but would not such a life, lived deliberately that way, as a programme, be merely another version of the schizophrenic life 'within a lie' which everyone else must live in one way or another? Would it not just be further evidence that a point of departure that is not a 'model' solution, that is not applicable to others, cannot be meaningful for an individual either? Patočka used to say that the most interesting thing about responsibility is that we carry it with us everywhere. That means that responsibility is ours, that we must accept it and grasp it *here, now*, in this place in time and space where the Lord has set us down, and that we cannot lie our way out of it by moving somewhere else, whether it be to an Indian ashram or to a parallel *polis*. If western young people so often discover that retreat to an Indian monastery fails them as an individual or group solution, then this is obviously because, and only because, it lacks that element of universality, since not everyone can retire to an ashram. Christianity is an example of an opposite way out: it is a point of departure for me here and now – but only because anyone, anywhere, at any time, may avail themselves of it.

In other words, the parallel *polis* points beyond itself and only makes sense as an act of deepening one's responsibility to and for the whole, as a way of discovering the most appropriate locus for this responsibility, not as an escape from it.


## XIX

I have already talked about the political potential of living within the truth and of the limitations upon predicting whether, how and when a given expression of that life within the truth can lead to actual changes. I have also mentioned how irrelevant trying to calculate the risks in this regard are, for an esential feature of independent initiatives is that they are always, initially at least, an all or nothing gamble.

Nevertheless this outline of some of the work done by 'dissident movements' would be incomplete without considering, if only very generally, some of the different ways this work might actually affect society; in other words, about the ways that responsibility to and for the whole *might* (without necessarily meaning that it must) be realized in practice.

In the first place, it has to be emphasized that the whole sphere comprising the independent life of society and even more so the 'dissident movement' as such, is naturally far from being the only potential factor that might influence the history of countries living under the post-totalitarian system. The latent social crisis in such societies can at any time, independently of these movements, provoke a wide variety of political changes. It may unsettle the power structure and induce or accelerate various hidden confrontations, resulting in personnel, conceptual or at least 'climactic' changes. It may significantly influence the general atmosphere of life, evoke unexpected and unforeseen social unrest and explosions of discontent. Power shifts at the centre of the bloc can influence conditions in the different countries in various ways. Economic factors naturally have an important influence, as do broader trends of global civilization. An extremely important area, which could be a source of radical changes and political upsets, is represented by international politics, the policies adopted by the other superpower and all the other countries, the changing structure of international interests and the positions taken by our bloc. Even the people who end up in the highest positions are not without significance, although as I have already said, one ought not overestimate the importance of leading personalities in the post-totalitarian system. There are many such influences and combinations of influence, and the eventual political impact of the 'dissident movement' is thinkable only against this general background and in the context that background provides. That impact is only one of the many factors (and far from the most important one) that affect political developments, and it differs from the other factors perhaps only in that its essential focus is reflecting upon that political development from the point of view of a defence of people and seeking an immediate application of that reflection.

The primary purpose of the outward direction of these movements is always, as we have seen, to have an impact on society, not to affect the power structure, at least not directly and immediately. Independent initiatives address the hidden sphere; they demonstrate that living within the truth is a human and social alternative and they struggle to expand the space available for that life; they help – even though it is, of course, indirect help – to raise the confidence of citizens; they shatter the world of 'appearances' and unmask the real nature of power. They do not assume a messianic role; they are not a social 'avant-garde' or 'élite' that alone knows best, and whose task it is to 'raise the consciousness' of the 'unconscious' masses (that arrogant self-projection is, once again, intrinsic to an essentially different way of thinking, the kind that feels it has a patent on some 'ideal project' and therefore that it has the right to impose it on society). Nor do they want to lead anyone. They leave it up to each individual to decide what he or she will or will not take from their experience and work. (If official Czechoslovak propaganda described the Chartists as 'self-appointees', it was not in order to emphasize any real 'avant-garde' ambitions on their part, but rather a natural expression of how the regime thinks, its tendency to judge others according to itself, since behind any expression of criticism it automatically sees the desire to cast the mighty from their seats and rule in their places 'in the name of the people', the same pretext the regime itself has used for years.)

These movements, therefore, always affect the power structure as such indirectly, as a part of society as a whole, for they are primarily addressing the hidden spheres of society, since it is not a matter of confronting the regime on the level of actual power.

I have already indicated one of the ways this can work: an awareness of the laws and the responsibility for seeing that they are upheld is indirectly strengthened. That, of course, is only a specific instance of a far broader influence, the indirect pressure felt from living within the truth: the pressure created by free thought, alternative values and 'alternative behaviour', and by independent social self-realization. The power structure, whether it wants to or not, must always react to this pressure to a certain extent. Its response, however, is always limited to two dimensions: repression and adaptation. Sometimes one dominates, sometimes the other. For example, the Polish 'Flying University' came under increased persecution and the 'flying teachers' were detained by the police. At the same time, however, professors in existing official universities tried to enrich their own curricula with several subjects hitherto considered taboo and this was a result of indirect pressure exerted by the 'Flying University'. The motives for this adaptation may vary from the 'ideal' (the hidden sphere has received the message and conscience and the will to truth are awakened) to the purely utilitarian: the regime's instinct for survival compels it to notice the changing ideas and the changing mental and social climate and react flexibly to them. Which of these motives happens to predominate in a given moment is not essential in terms of the final affect.

Adaptation is the positive dimension of the regime's response, and it can, and usually does, have a wide spectrum of forms and phases. Some circles may try to integrate values or people from the 'parallel world' into the official structures, to appropriate them, to become a little like them while trying to make them a little like themselves, and thus to adjust an obvious and untenable imbalance. In the 1960s, progressive communists began to 'discover' certain unacknowledged cultural values and phenomena. This was a positive step, although not without its dangers, since the 'integrated' or 'appropriated' values lost something of their independence and originality, and having been given a cloak of officiality and conformity, their credibility was somewhat weakened. In a further phase, this adaptation can lead to various attempts on the part of the official structures to reform, both in terms of their ultimate goals and structurally. Such reforms are usually half-way measures; they are attempts to combine and realistically co-ordinate serving life and serving the post-totalitarian 'automatism'. But they cannot be otherwise. They muddy what was originally a clear demarcation line between living within the truth and living with a lie. They cast a smoke-screen over the situation, mystify society and make it difficult for people to keep their bearings. This, of course, does not alter the fact that it is always essentially good when it happens because it opens out new spaces. But it does make it more difficult to distinguish between 'admissible' and 'inadmissible' compromises.

Another – and higher – phase of adaptation is a process of internal differentiation that takes place in the official structures. These structures open themselves to more or less institutionalized forms of plurality because the real aims of life demand it. (One example: without changing the centralized and institutional basis of cultural life, new publishing houses, group periodicals, artists' groups, parallel research institutes and work places and so on, may appear under pressure from 'below'. Or another example: the single, monolithic youth organization run by the state as a typical post-totalitarian 'transmission belt' disintegrates under the pressure of real needs into a number of more or less independent organizations such as the Union of University Students, the Union of Secondary School Students, the Organization of Working Youth, and so on.) There is a direct relationship between this kind of differentiation, which allows initiatives from below to be felt, and the appearance and constitution of new structures which are already parallel, or rather independent, but which at the same time are respected, or at least tolerated in varying degrees, by official institutions. These new institutions are more than just liberalized official structures adapted to the authentic needs of life; they are a direct expression of those needs, demanding a position in the context of what is already here. In other words, they are genuine expressions of the tendency of society to organize itself. (In Czechoslovakia in 1968 the best known organizations of this type were *KAN*, The Club of Committed Non-Communists, and *K231*, an organization of former political prisoners.)

The ultimate phase of this process is the situation in which the official structures – as agencies of the post-totalitarian system, existing only to serve its automatism and constructed in the spirit of that role – simply begin withering away and dying off, to be replaced by new structures that have evolved from 'below' and are put together in a fundamentally different way.

Certainly many other ways may be imagined in which the aims of life can bring about political transformations in the general organization of things and weaken on all levels the hold that techniques of manipulation have on society. Here I have mentioned only the way in which the general organization of things was in fact changed as we experienced it ourselves in Czechoslovakia around 1968. It must be added that all these concrete instances were part of a specific historical process which ought not be thought of as the only alternative, nor as necessarily repeatable (particularly not in our country), a fact which, of course, takes nothing away from the inportance of the general lessons which are still sought and found in it to this day.

While on the subject of 1968 in Czechoslovakia, it may be appropriate to point to some of the characteristic aspects of developments at that time. All the transformations, first in the general 'mood', then conceptually and finally structurally, did not occur under pressure from the kind of parallel structures that are taking shape today. Such structures – which are sharply defined antitheses of the official structures – quite simply did not exist at the time, nor were there any 'dissidents' in the present sense of the word. The changes that took place were simply a consequence of pressures of the most varied sort, some thorough-going, some partial. There were spontaneous attempts at freer forms of thinking, independent creation and political articulation. There were long-term, spontaneous and inconspicuous efforts to bring about the interpenetration of the independent life of society with the existing structures, usually beginning with the quiet institutionalization of this life on and around the periphery of the official structures. In other words, it was a gradual process of social awakening, a kind of 'creeping' process in which the hidden spheres gradually opened out. (There is some truth in the official propaganda which talks about a 'creeping counter-revolution' in Czechoslovakia, referring to how the aims of life proceed.) The motive force behind this awakening did not have to come exclusively from the independent life of society, considered as a definable social milieu (although of course it did come from there, a fact that has yet to be fully appreciated). It could also have simply come from the fact that people in the official structures who more or less identified with the official ideology came up against reality as it really was and as it gradually became clear to them through latent social crises and their own bitter experiences with the true nature and operations of power. (I am thinking here mainly of the many 'anti-dogmatic' reform communists who grew to become, over the years, a force inside the official structures.) Neither the proper conditions nor the *raison d'être* existed for those limited, 'self-structuring' independent initiatives familiar from the present era of 'dissident movements' that stand so sharply outside the official structures and are unrecognized by them *en bloc*. At that time, the post-totalitarian system in Czechoslovakia had not yet petrified into the static, sterile and stable forms that exist today, forms that compel people to fall back on their own organizing capabilities. For many historical and social reasons, the regime in 1968 was more open. The power structure, exhausted by Stalinist despotism and helplessly groping about for painless reform, was inevitably rotting from within, quite incapable of offering any intelligent opposition to changes in the mood, to the way its younger members regarded things and to the thousands of authentic expressions of life on the 'pre-political' level that sprang up in that vast political terrain between the official and the unofficial.

From the more general point of view, yet another typical circumstance appears to be important: the social ferment that came to a head in 1968 never – in terms of actual structural changes – went any further than the reform, the differentiation or the replacement of structures that were really only of secondary importance. It did not affect the very essence of the power structure in the post-totalitarian system, which is to say its political model, the fundamental principles of social organization, not even the economic model in which all economic power is subordinated to political power. Nor were any essential structural changes made in the direct instruments of power (the army, the police, the judiciary, etc.). On that level, the issue was never more than a change in the mood, the personnel, the political line and, above all, changes in how that power was exercised. Everything else remained at the stage of discussion and planning. The two officially accepted programmes that went furthest in this regard were the April, 1968 Action Programme of the Communist Party of Czechoslovakia and the proposal for economic reforms. The Action Programme – it could not have been otherwise – was full of contradictions and half-way measures that left the physical aspects of power untouched. And the economic proposals, while they went a long way to accommodate the aims of life in the economic sphere (they accepted such notions as a plurality of interests and intiatives, dynamic incentives, restrictions upon the economic command system), left untouched the basic pillar of economic power, that is, the principle of state, rather than genuine *social* ownership of the means of production. So there is a gap here which no social movement in the post-totalitarian system has ever been able to bridge, with the possible exception of those few days during the Hungarian uprising.

What other developmental alternative might emerge in the future? Replying to that question would mean entering the realm of pure speculation. For the time being, it can be said that the latent social crisis in the system has always (and there is no reason to believe it will not continue to do so) resulted in a variety of political and social disturbances (Germany in 1953, Hungary, the USSR and Poland in 1956, Czechoslovakia and Poland in 1968, and Poland in 1970 and 1976), all of them very different in their backgrounds, the course of their evolution and their final consequences. If we look at the enormous complex of different factors that led to such distur- bances, and at the impossibility of predicting what accidental accumulation of events will cause that fermentation in the hidden sphere to break through to the light of day (the problem 'of the final straw'); and if we consider how impossible it is to guess what the future holds, given such opposing trends as, on the one hand, the increasingly profound integration of the 'bloc' and the expansion of power within it, and on the other hand the prospects of the USSR disintegrating under pressure from awakening national conscious- ness in the non-Russian areas (in this regard the Soviet Union cannot expect to remain forever free of the world-wide struggle for national liberation), then we must see the hoplessness of trying to make long-range predictions.

In any case, I do not believe that this type of speculation has any immediate significance for the 'dissident movements' since these movements, after all, do not develop from speculative thinking, and so to establish themselves on that basis would mean alienating them- selves from the very source of their identity.

As far as prospects for the 'dissident movements' as such go, there seems to be very little likelihood that future developments will lead to a lasting coexistence of two isolated, mutually non-interacting and mutually indifferent bodies – the main *polis* and the parallel *polis.* As long as it remains what it is, the practice of living within the truth cannot fail to be a threat to the system. It is quite impossible to imagine it continuing to coexist with the practice of living within a lie without dramatic tension. The relationship of the post-totalitarian system – as long as it remains what it is – and the independent life of society – as long as it remains the locus of a renewed responsibility for the whole and to the whole – will always be one of either latent or open conflict.

In this situation there are only two possibilities: either the post-totalitarian system will go on developing (that is, will be *able* to go on developing), thus inevitably coming closer to some dreadful Orwellian vision of a world of absolute manipulation, while all the more articulate expressions of living within the truth are definitively snuffed out; or the independent life of society (the parallel *polis*), including the 'dissident movements', will slowly but surely become a social phenomenon of growing importance, taking a real part in the life of society with increasing clarity and influencing the general situation. Of course this will always be only one of many factors influencing the situation and it will operate rather in the background, in concert with the other factors and in a way appropriate to the background.

Whether it ought to focus on reforming the official structures or on encouraging differentiation, or on replacing them with new structures, whether the intent is to 'ameliorate' the system or, on the contrary, to tear it down: these and similar questions, in so far as they are not pseudo-problems, can be posed by the 'dissident movement' only within the context of a particular situation, when the movement is faced with a concrete task. In other words, it must pose questions, as it were, *ad hoc*, out of a concrete consideration of the authentic needs of life. To reply to such questions abstractly and to formulate a political programme in terms of some hypothetical future would mean, I believe, a return to the spirit and methods of traditional politics, and this would limit and alienate the work of 'dissent' where it is most instrinsically itself and has the most genuine prospects for the future. I have already emphasized several times that these 'dissident movements' do not have their point of departure in the invention of systemic changes but in a real, everyday struggle for a better life 'here and now'. The political and structural systems that life discovers for itself will clearly always be – for some time to come, at least – limited, half-way, unsatisfying and polluted by debilitating tactics. It cannot be otherwise, and we must expect this and not be demoralized by it. It is of great importance that the main thing – the everyday, thankless and never-ending struggle of human beings to live more freely, truthfully and in quiet dignity – never imposes any limits on itself, never be half-hearted, inconsistent, never trap itself in political tactics, speculating on the outcome of its actions or entertaining fantasies about the future. The purity of this struggle is the best guarantee of optimum results when it comes to actual interaction with the post-totalitarian structures.

## XX

The specific nature of post-totalitarian conditions – with their absence of a normal political life and the fact that any far-reaching political change is utterly unforeseeable – has one positive aspect: it compels us to examine our situation in terms of its deeper coherences and to consider our future in the context of global, long-range prospects of the world of which we are a part. The fact that the most intrinsic and fundamental confrontation between human beings and the system takes place at a level incomparably more profound than that of traditional politics would seem, at the same time, to determine as well the direction such considerations will take.

Our attention, therefore, inevitably turns to the most essential matter: the crisis of contemporary technological society as a whole, the crisis that Heidegger describes as the ineptitude of humanity face to face with the planetary power of technology. Technology – that child of modern science, which in turn is a child of modern metaphysics – is out of humanity's control, has ceased to serve us, has enslaved us and compelled us to participate in the preparation of our own destruction. And humanity can find no way out: we have no idea and no faith, and even less do we have a political conception to help us bring things back under human control. We look on helplessly as that coldly functioning machine we have created inevitably engulfs us, tearing us away from our natural affiliations (for instance from our habitat in the widest sense of that word, including our habitat in the biosphere) just as it removes us from the experience of 'being' and casts us into the world of 'existences'. This situation has already been described from many different angles and many individuals and social groups have sought, often painfully, to find ways out of it (for instance through oriental thought or by forming communes). The only social, or rather political, attempt to do something about it that contains the necessary element of universality (responsibility to and for the whole) is the desperate and, given the turmoil the world is in, fading voice of the ecological movement, and even there the attempt is limited to a particular notion of how to use technology to oppose the dictatorship of technology.

'Only a God can save us now', Heidegger says, and he emphasizes the necessity of 'a different way of thinking', that is, of a departure from what philosophy has been for centuries, and a radical change in the way in which humanity understands itself, the world and its position in it. He knows no way out and all he can recommend is 'preparing expectations'.

Various thinkers and movements feel that this as yet unknown way out might be most generally characterized as a broad 'existential revolution'. I share this view, and I also share the opinion that a solution cannot be sought in some technological sleight of hand, that is, in some external proposal for change, or in a revolution that is merely philosophical, merely social, merely technological or even merely political. These are all areas where the consequences of an 'existential revolution' can and must be felt; but their most intrinsic locus can only be human existence in the profoundest sense of the word. It is only from that basis that it can become a generally ethical – and, of course, ultimately a political – reconstitution of society.

What we call the consumer and industrial (or post-industrial) society, and Ortega y Gasset once understood as 'the revolt of the masses', as well as the intellectual, moral, political and social misery in the world today: all of this is perhaps merely an aspect of the deep crisis in which humanity, dragged helplessly along by the automatism of global technological civilization, finds itself.

The post-totalitarian system is only one aspect – a particularly drastic aspect and thus all the more revealing of its real origins – of this general inability of modern humanity to be the master of its own situation. The automatism of the post-totalitarian system is merely an extreme version of the global automatism of technological civilization. The human failure that it mirrors is only one variant of the general failure of modern humanity.

This planetary challenge to the position of human beings in the world is, of course, also taking place in the western world, the only difference being the social and political forms it takes. Heidegger refers expressly to a crisis of democracy. There is no real evidence that western democracy, that is, democracy of the traditional parliamentary type, can offer solutions that are any more profound. It may even be said that the more room there is in the western democracies (compared to our world) for the genuine aims of life, the better the crisis is hidden from people and the more deeply do they become immersed in it.

It would appear that the traditional parliamentary democracies can offer no fundamental opposition to the automatism of technological civilization and the industrial-consumer society, for they, too, are being dragged helplessly along by it. People are manipulated in ways that are infinitely more subtle and refined than the brutal methods used in the post-totalitarian societies. But this static complex of rigid, conceptually sloppy and politically pragmatic mass political parties run by professional apparatuses and releasing the citizen from all forms of concrete and personal responsibility; and those complex foci of capital accumulation engaged in secret manipulations and expansion; the omnipresent dictatorship of consumption, production, advertising, commerce, consumer culture, and all that flood of information: all of it, so often analysed and described, can only with great difficulty be imagined as the source of humanity's rediscovery of itself. In his June 1978 Harvard lecture,* Solzhenitsyn describes the illusory nature of freedoms not based on personal responsibility and the chronic inability of the traditional democracies, as a result, to oppose violence and totalitarianism. In a democracy, human beings may enjoy many personal freedoms and securities that are unknown to us, but in the end they do them no good, for they too are ultimately victims of the same automatism, and are incapable of defending their concerns about their own identity or preventing their superficialization or transcending concerns about their own personal survival to become proud and responsible members of the *polis*, making a genuine contribution to the creation of its destiny.

Because all our prospects for a significant change for the better are very long range indeed, we are obliged to take note of this deep crisis of traditional democracy. Certainly, if conditions were to be created for democracy in some countries in the Soviet bloc (although this is becoming increasingly improbable), it might be an appropriate transitional solution that would help to restore the devastated

---

* *Editor's note*: This lecture is published as *Alexander Solzhenitsyn Speaks to the West* (London 1978).

sense of civic awareness, to renew democratic discussion, to allow for the crystallization of an elementary political plurality, an essential expression of the aims of life. But to cling to the notion of traditional parliamentary democracy as one's political ideal and to succumb to the illusion that only this 'tried and true' form is capable of guaranteeing human beings enduring dignity and an independent role in society would, in my opinion, be at the very least short-sighted.

I see a renewed focus of politics on real people as something far more profound than merely returning to the everyday mechanisms of western (or if you like bourgeois) democracy. In 1968 I felt that our problem could be solved by forming an opposition party that would compete publicly for power with the Communist Party. I have long since come to realize, however, that it is just not that simple and that no opposition party in and of itself, just as no new electoral laws in and of themselves, could make society proof against some new form of violence. No 'dry' organizational measures in themselves can provide that guarantee, and we would be hard pressed to find in them that God who alone can save us.

## XXI

And now I may properly be asked the question: What is to be done, then?

My scepticism towards alternative political models and the ability of systemic reforms or changes to redeem us does not, of course, mean that I am sceptical of political thought altogether. Nor does my emphasis on the importance of focusing concern on real human beings disqualify me from considering the possible structural consequences flowing from it. On the contrary, if A was said, then B should be said as well. Nevertheless, I will offer only a few very general remarks.

Above all, any existential revolution should provide hope of a moral reconstitution of society, which means a radical renewal of the relationship of human beings to what I have called the 'human order', which no political order can replace. A new experience of being, a renewed rootedness in the universe, a newly grasped sense of 'higher responsibility', a new-found inner relationship to other people and to the human community – these factors clearly indicate the direction in which we must go.

And the political consequences? Most probably they could be reflected in the constitution of structures that will derive from this 'new spirit', from human factors rather than from a particular formalization of political relationships and guarantees. In other words, the issue is the rehabilitation of values like trust, openness, responsibility, solidarity, love. I believe in structures that are not aimed at the 'technical' aspect of the execution of power, but at the significance of that execution in structures held together more by a commonly shared feeling of the importance of certain communities than by commonly shared expansionist ambitions directed 'outward'. There can and must be structures that are open, dynamic and small; beyond a certain point, human ties like personal trust and personal responsibility cannot work. There must be structures that in principle place no limits on the genesis of different structures. Any accumulation of power whatsoever (one of the characteristics of automatism) should be profoundly alien to it. They would be structures not in the sense of organizations or institutions, but like a community. Their authority certainly cannot be based on long-empty traditions, like the tradition of mass political parties, but rather on how, in concrete terms, they enter into a given situation. Rather than a strategic agglomeration of formalized organizations, it is better to have organizations springing up *ad hoc*, infused with enthusiasm for a particular purpose and disappearing when that purpose has been achieved. The leaders' authority ought to derive from their personalities and be personally tested in their particular surroundings, and not from their position in any *nomenklatura*. They should enjoy great personal confidence and even great law-making powers based on that confidence. This would appear to be the only way out of the classic impotence of traditional democratic organizations, which frequently seem founded more on mistrust than mutual confidence, and more on collective irresponsibility than on responsibility. It is only with the full existential backing of every member of the community that a permanent bulwark against 'creeping totalitarianism' can be established. These structures should naturally arise from *below* as a consequence of authentic social 'self-organization'; they should derive vital energy from a living dialogue with the genuine needs from which they arise, and when these needs are gone, the structures should also disappear. The principles of their internal organization should be very diverse, with a minimum of external regulation. The decisive criterion of this 'self-constitution' should be the structure's actual significance, and not just a mere abstract norm.

Both political and economic life ought to be founded on the varied and versatile co-operation of such dynamically appearing and disappearing organizations. As far as the economic life of society goes, I believe in the principle of self-management, which is probably the only way of achieving what all the theorists of socialism have dreamed about, that is, the genuine (i.e. informal) participation of workers in economic decision-making, leading to a feeling of genuine responsibility for their collective work. The principles of control and discipline ought to be abandoned in favour of self-control and self-discipline.

As is perhaps clear from even so general an outline, the systemic consequences of an 'existential revolution' of this type goes significantly beyond the framework of classical parliamentary democracy. Having introduced the term 'post-totalitarian' for the purposes of this discussion, perhaps I should refer to the notion I have just outlined – purely for the moment – as the prospects for a 'post-democratic' system.

Undoubtedly this notion could be developed further, but I think it would be a foolish undertaking, to say the least, because slowly but surely the whole idea would become alienated, separated from itself. After all, the essence of such a 'post-democracy' is also that it can only develop *via facti*, as a process deriving directly *from life*, from a new atmosphere and a new 'spirit' (political thought, of course, would play a role here, though not as a director, merely as a guide). It would be presumptuous, however, to try to foresee the structural expressions of this 'new spirit' without that spirit actually being present and without knowing its concrete physiognomy.

## XXII

I would probably have omitted the entire preceding section as a more suitable subject for private meditation were it not for a certain recurring sensation. It may seem rather presumptuous, and therefore I will present it as a question: Does not this vision of 'post-democratic' structures in some ways remind one of the 'dissident' groups or some of the independent citizens' initiatives as we already know them from our own surroundings? Do not these small communities, bound together by thousands of shared tribulations, give rise to some of those special 'humanly meaningful' political relationships and ties that we have been talking about? Are not these communities (and they *are* communities more than organizations) – motivated mainly by a common belief in the profound significance of what they are doing since they have no chance of direct, external success – joined together by precisely the kind of atmosphere in which the formalized and ritualized ties common in the official structures are supplanted by a living sense of solidarity and fraternity? Do not these 'post-democratic' relationships of immediate personal trust and the informal rights of individuals based on them come out of the background of all those commonly shared difficulties? Do not these groups emerge, live and disappear under pressure from concrete and authentic needs, unburdened by the ballast of hollow traditions? Is not their attempt to create an articulate form of 'living within the truth' and to renew the feeling of higher responsibility in an apathetic society really a sign of some kind of rudimentary moral reconstitution?

In other words, are not these informal, non-bureaucratic, dynamic and open communities that comprise the 'parallel *polis*' a kind of rudimentary prefiguration, a symbolic model of those more meaningful 'post-democratic' political structures that might become the foundation of a better society?

I know from thousands of personal experiences how the mere circumstance of having signed Charter 77 has immediately created a deeper and more open relationship and evoked sudden and powerful feelings of genuine community among people who were all but strangers before. This kind of thing happens only rarely, if at all, even among people who have worked together for long periods in some apathetic official structure. It is as though the mere awareness and acceptance of a common task and a shared experience were enough to transform people and the climate of their lives, as though it gave their public work a more human dimension that is seldom found elsewhere.

. Perhaps all this is only the consequence of a common threat. Perhaps the moment the threat ends or eases, the mood it helped create will begin to dissipate as well. (The aim of those who threaten us, however, is precisely the opposite. Again and again, one is shocked by the energy they devote to contaminating, in various despicable ways, all the human relationships inside the threatened community.)

Yet even if that were so, it would change nothing in the question I have posed.

We do not know the way out of the marasmus of the world, and it would be an expression of unforgivable pride were we to see the little we do as a fundamental solution, or were we to present ourselves, our community and our solutions to vital problems as the only thing worth doing.

Even so, I think that given all these preceding thoughts on post-totalitarian conditions, and given the circumstances and the inner constitution of the developing efforts to defend human beings and their identity in such conditions, the questions I have posed are appropriate. If nothing else, they are an invitation to reflect concretely on our own experience and to give some thought to whether certain elements of that experience do not – without our really being aware of it – point somewhere further, beyond their apparent limits, and whether right here, in our everyday lives, certain challenges are not already encoded, quietly waiting for the moment when they will be read and grasped.

For the real question is whether the 'brighter future' is really always so distant. What if, on the contrary, it has been here for a long time already, and only our own blindness and weakness has prevented us from seeing it around us and within us, and kept us from developing it?

# 2   Spiritual values, independent initiatives and politics*

## Rudolf Battěk

The context of my subject is the 'eternal' conflict between the lives of people ranked vertically above and below each other by political power, and the effort of people to live side by side without any of the priorities established by power. The historical longing for equality is the ideal form of the notion of social justice. Yet every individual who longs for equality is subjected to the reality of the social status quo. So far, historical humanity is proof that permanent equality, stability and full satisfaction are unattainable. As a biotype, human beings cannot expect, in the course of their lives, to attain a 'state' which allows them to stop, relax, and enjoy lasting repose. Individuals usually experience personal satisfaction as a chronologically limited phase of anticipated success, as the achievement of a goal. Permanent self-satisfaction is a threat to life, and presents an extreme danger to humanity as humanity.

## Two moral alternatives
'Not the spirit of revenge, but the will to truth'   *Jan Patočka*

How much scope does an individual have in living his or her life? What choices does he or she have? When and how can he or she decide how far his or her own decisions, actions, and efforts to determine direction and meaning will reach, and what effect they will have?

In principle, there are two alternatives. The first is *spiritual*, which includes ethical postulates, sensitive creation, analytical and synthetic processes of learning and self-discovery in openness and progress, and the relevant concepts are: feeling, knowing, giving, learning, loving, believing. Second, by contrast, the *consumer*

---

* Translated by Paul Wilson.

values (those having to do with consuming and maintaining one's physical existence) include a preference for comfort, surplus, material wealth, and the relevant concepts are: having, getting, receiving and using.

To build and direct one's life exclusively in terms of consumer values leads to 'microcosmic tragedy', to 'a loss of humanity'. Spiritual orientation is the only possible goal that satisfies the meaning of humanity in ways that are accessible to human beings. The defining forms of spiritual self-realization can be perceived in philosophy, culture or religion. Their basic presupposition is an immanent welling forth of truthfulness, ethical clarity, a widely conceived *humanitas* (the postulate of a genuine humanity) and, above all, a *predisposition to truth* and *resistance to evil and lies*. The combination of both (active and passive) leads to *freedom*. These categories are multi-significant, multi-dimensional and temporally imperfect. In other words, they are processes.

No one individual is determined in a single way. Not even the most spiritual type can ignore the need to maintain his or her bodily existence. This fundamental condition of all activity introduces into life certain elements of inevitability and the consequent necessity of fulfilling certain social functions. Social constraint on individuals is an example of such an inevitable element. The multiple significance of social ties is the most outstanding factor both in the search for individual orientation and the group orientation of communities and societies.

It is astonishing how many people find it impossible to grasp the necessity of *balance* when stressing various aspects of their own behaviour, creations, activities, influences and so on. Here the point is not to demand balance as an absolute condition, but merely to point out that rectification in matters of public concern cannot be achieved by emphasizing only one aspect of the struggle, such as a change in one's personal morality, the creation of independent communities, the 'life in truth', passive resistance to a craven regime or the creation of new political institutions, general political commitment and engagement, honestly done work, the writing of critical texts for the 'desk drawer', and so on and so forth. As long as this individual stance springs from inner motivation and is not influenced by deliberate strategic considerations of an external nature (which are not always possible to determine reliably), it is both possible and necessary to think, talk and polemicize about things. One-sided approaches, however, can be disqualified both in theory and in practice, since there evidently exists a rich plurality of opinions on the question: 'What can we do to set things in motion?'

This diversity of opinion grows out of a different understanding of the relationship between the external and the internal, the material and the spiritual, the social and the individual, the political and the private. Such differences, of course, are as deep in the area of political thinking as they are in notions about spiritual values. I could simplify the two extreme options (the spiritual and the consumer–existential) by placing them in a relationship of indirect proportionality: the more one inclines to self-examination, to immanence, to the deity, the less one is concerned with one's external social position and material wealth. But that is not generally valid, even though such a relationship has its own logic and one comes across it quite commonly in practice.

An individual does not make his or her decisions as a 'free' subject. He or she is dependent in many ways, particularly under an authoritarian system of government; he or she must consider a myriad of factors, treat many things with respect and of course his or her character and behavioural disposition are most important as well. Nor is there always perfect accord between what a person theoretically recognizes, respects and values, what he or she would like to achieve in practice and how that person in fact behaves. The decisive factor in determining what position we adopt is *the degree of our moral strength* (that is, the moral condition of the personality). Moreover, an individual does not make up his or her mind once and for all, in so far as he or she makes decisions consciously at all. I would not like to hazard a guess as to what percentage of the population accepts their way of life unthinkingly and adapts passively their opinions and actions to the current customs. But even confident, self-aware individuals can change. However, such changes in opinions, values and attitudes are always difficult and are usually accompanied by inner conflicts, confusions and uncertainties. It takes more effort and courage to change than to cling to one's former ideas.

The way in which an individual decides to engage in activity and display initiative in a totalitarian society is to a large extent determined by the values that dominate his or her personal life – that is, by the *moral alternatives* the individual feels to be important. This is a question of *the power to offer moral resistance* rather than a moralistic rigidity. At the same time, it is irrelevant whether the individual agrees with the ruling power or opposes it. In the former case, it is more difficult to offer moral resistance because agreement entails a wider range of material choice and therefore the temptation to 'abandon' and 'forget' the postulate of moral determination. I consider it especially important that the non-conforming individual in a totalitarian society have more positive social and personal relationships than negative and oppositional ones. If it is the other way round, this can lead to weakness and confusion about oneself and also to false conclusions about one's attitude towards the usurping power.

Those who are 'growing up' or who are morally unstable must have an open environment in which their opinions may mature. They should also realize that the moral qualities of humanity are indispensable, no matter what one's social position or degree of social commitment is. Once one has discovered the proper moral orientation (moral maturity) one then has a basis both for daily personal decisions and for public work. The progress of spiritual orientation, however, guarantees neither political 'success', nor the success of one's efforts in society. In the long run, however, political actors who fail morally always heap shame upon themselves 'for eternity', whereas moral consistency at key historical moments has always meant genuine victory, which has in turn become a model of behaviour for the future. This reflects a Confucian idea that a morally flawed action will sooner or later prove politically ineffective and perhaps quite destructive, even when motivated by the clear hope of practical and political gain.

This principle ought to be immanent in our *human* and *civic* activities, in our efforts to have human rights recognized and respected in present-day European civilization.

**Two social positions**
'Whoever calls for a cultural democracy under the banner of European humanity does so with the intention of transforming the demand for a better, more valuable world into fact.' *Herman Glaser*

Evaluating these two types of moral decision-making is not, of course, a narrowly ethical question. Ethics has an important role to play in it, but it is clearly a problem of coming up with a generally valid conception of the life of individuals in society. The problem is that the same set of circumstances can be viewed in different ways. These differences may be expressed as a tension between two attitudes within the same individual – between his or her attitude as a person (the individual's humanity) and as a citizen (the individual's position in civil society). Essentially, it is tension and conflict between the private and the public, the individual and the collective, the non-political and the political, the personal and the social, between intellectual awareness and public behaviour.

Fellowship between people as individuals creates various communities that are based on relationships of internally motivated *sympathy*. One enters such a community freely and leaves it freely. As a citizen, however, the individual is situated legally and socially in a society organized as a state. He or she behaves as a functional unit, as an employee, as a political or social functionary, as a member of an organization.

These two categories (of being human, and acting as a citizen) are neither exclusive nor separable. The individual cannot split into two different beings, although in authoritarian states citizens seldom become persons until they are in private, with their families, among friends, at their cottages. As citizens, they are more apt to stylize an appropriate role for themselves, maintaining certain rules of behaviour that become habitual. There is always tension between natural, spontaneous behaviour and 'official' behaviour. This can also be demonstrated in the difference between natural and formal authority. In the organization of society, the formalization of behaviour is necessary only to a certain extent. The more social activity is subordinated to a hierarchy (voluntary associations, organizations run by cultural administrators), the greater the emphasis on formalized behaviour (observing not only regulations but also customs). The crisis of modern humanity, and therefore of modern society and of modern politics is, among other things, a result of this self-stylization in individuals who belong to socially 'higher' functional categories.

The higher the functional position one occupies in a society organized as a *state* system, the less time one has for the process of self-awareness. A totalitarian state, in particular, has vast mechanisms for surveillance and monitoring, and this is directed not only at non-conformist elements but, with equal necessity, at the leading cadres, the buttresses of the system. The *public* man who has no time for himself or his family is a living example of this imbalance. The crisis of society is also a crisis of imbalance between the individual's human essence and his or her organizational persona.

But is there, or has there ever been, a person or society that is not in a state of crisis? This is a cardinal question in understanding contemporary Czechoslovakian society. Advancing civilization and culturalization, embracing all the continents in an ever-tighter continuity, has brought with it a degree of inter-societal and inter-human devastation unknown to earlier history.

It would seem that people are beginning to realize the limitations of their technological civilization. They are beginning to express their fears, to study the evidence, and to seek ways to resist the irresponsible power which, to consolidate itself, needs to have the largest arsenal of the most advanced weapons, the biggest energy sources and the most 'human material', regardless of the cost.

Whether one defends the technological civilization or criticizes it from an ecological standpoint depends to a large extent on social position, but also on the extent to which one has thought through the meaning and future of life, and how one views the prospects of the future generation. The mentality of contemporary humanity is determined by new discoveries and technological advances, the ability to produce more and consume it on a massive scale. This, in turn, provides the incentive for more rapid innovation, thus creating new needs and even higher consumption. Add to this the natural desire of deprived sectors of the population to achieve the same standard of living as the higher strata, and it would seem that the citizen of industrial societies has become 'stabilized' in this regard, at least. The heightened private needs of the regular workers converge with the defensive requirements of the ruling bureaucrats. The citizen who wants more consumer goods and works for them is a safe guarantee of conformity, acquiescence and manipulability.

The feeling that human existence is threatened has never been so acute as it is right now. The apocalyptic fears of the past were religious visions that had no rational basis. The possibility that humankind might perish in a natural catastrophe existed only in the overheated imaginations of religious fanatics. In the past, people never dreamed that humanity itself would one day become the divine agent threatening the destruction of the world, as if the crisis of today had sprung from humanity's own indifference towards itself. So far, there is little evidence that this indifference has been sufficiently shaken. Addiction, it would seem, is not something limited to drug users; the entire society is drugged by the need for feverish, ceaseless experience. There is a great deal we might miss, and it is as if we want to know everything, experience everything, get something from everything. Haste goes hand in hand with indifference and they combine to make the entire concept of life, like everything else, superficial. Those in power bombard a dulled and appeased society with a rigid ideological justification for all the manifestations of that power, beginning with a critique of the ruling strata in the 'other' social systems and ending with panoptic conjectures on the 'normative' supply of destructive weapons and materials ready to be used to liquidate those directly involved in wartime military action (armies) or those uninvolved (working people on both sides). Perceptive individuals revolt against such 'guarantees' of peace (which of course mean peace for the developed civilization of industrial societies), in which, with cold premeditation and an eye on business, the Third World is shamelessly used as a testing ground for new weapons and war tactics.

Critical attitudes (or opposition) to the ruling power exist in all systems. Such attitudes sometimes reflect a fundamental disagreement with the system, but often they point to the existence of a wide variety of different opinions on particular questions or even a critical attitude to personalities. Under totalitarian systems of government, opposition assumes dramatic forms, because any open criticism of the system, both as a whole and in part, is forbidden, prosecuted and punished. Simple opposition becomes dissidence.

In those western European political systems traditionally referred to as parliamentary democracies, the kinds of non-political activity (in associations, clubs, tribunes and committees) that are independent of the government and yet within the framework of the legal code must, in the eastern European sphere of Soviet influence, necessarily become like a political opposition because any and every attempt to be 'independent', regardless of whether it conforms to the existing legal code, is considered anti-social and anti-socialist and therefore *politically* harmful and dangerous.

Even the phrase 'independent citizens' initiative' is a provocative anomaly in totalitarian systems of the Soviet type. The most important fact is that since the Soviet occupation of Czechoslovakia in 1968, this kind of activity has spread throughout the communist bloc, and the authorities are incapable of suppressing and eliminationg it, although they do try

1 to keep it under constant surveillance;
2 to limit and contain its radius of action and the intensity and extent of its influence on general social awareness;

3 to prosecute extreme expressions of activity other than the 'respected' ones;
4 to undertake various forms of harassment, i.e. to make the life of activists miserable through illegal tactics; and
5 to exploit differences of opinion so as to spread dissention inside the opposition movement. Of course even tougher, more direct measures cannot be ruled out.

What must become fundamental for us is *initiation*, not *dissidence*. That is, we should consider ourselves first and foremost as *initiators* of future possibilities and not as subversives, drop-outs or rebels who are anti-a, anti-b, or anti-c. We should leave resistance and repression to the ruling powers and transform our *opposition* into an increasingly clear *position*! Charter 77 represents the position of an independent citizens' initiative that understands human rights as something given not *de lege* but *de facto*. And in that sense the initiators of a new position must be able not only to formulate, but also to bring to life the notion of a harmonious relationship between individuals and society.

**Two political tendencies**
'Politics is not only the art of the possible, but as well the *search for*, and even the *creation* of the possible. We cannot passively wait for opportunities to arise, we must actively prepare and create them.'

This is not an abstract essay on individuals living in any society whatsoever, but about human beings and their prospects in a system circumscribed by power, ideology, and social and cultural manipulation. In a totalitarian political structure, just about every facet of human existence is politicized. The hierarchically organized ruling class has at its disposal a highly centralized form of decision-making power. Its totality is best revealed in the dispersive way it controls and influences all the components of society, whose subordinate decision-making power is derived from direct or indirect signals, resolutions, directives and orders, all emanating from the top of the ruling hierarchy.

Discussions about what comprises politics remain vague as long as they do not take into consideration the politicization of 'non-political' spheres and 'non-political' behaviour. In a totalitarian system, every kind of behaviour is 'political' because the ruling power judges every attitude, every accomplishment according to how it serves and supports its own position. Nothing in that changes the evolution and transformation of total power. Today, the regime no longer demands inner belief and active, conformist commitment to the system, as it did in the 1950s and 1960s when such qualities were essential to attaining and maintaining an important position in society. Today, the regime is satisfied with formal expressions of agreement and affirmation, and even with mere silence, non-protest. In other words, one may think what one likes, but if one's thoughts are critical and non-conformist, they must not be expressed.

The problem of *conformity and non-conformity*, position and opposition, consent and dissent, exists solely because there are socio-political differences in society and differences in power, which in turn have differing degrees of privilege attached to them. As I understand it, privilege, which in some instances overlaps with power, means the ability to act and attain certain goals. Privilege can correspond with the political establishment, in which case it is a conforming privilege. To be the son of a government official and thus be guaranteed the right to a university education is to enjoy conformist privilege, one that is positive in that one attains a good position in society but negative in that one forfeits true individual-ity. Non-conformist privilege is associated with membership in the underground or political opposition. Measured by general stand-ards, this brings a low level of social prestige but a large degree of social individuality, independence and authenticity. Everyone is free to choose which category of privilege they consider sufficient for their lives. Individuals who have decided to lead lives consistent with their own moral sense will, in the deprived totalitarian society, lean unequivocally towards non-conformist privilege. In doing so, they will be exposed to many difficulties and stumbling blocks in practical life, but their approach will be characterized by openness, seeking, self-confidence, conviction, a free critical sense, self-criticism and even a smiling self-irony, all factors not to be taken lightly in the preservation of one's sanity under the constant barrage of threats from the authorities.

The situations in which individuals and groups find themselves are widely varied, and this complicates our choice. Present day Czechoslovak society must be characterized as a type of totalitarian state; using the term 'post-totalitarian society' to describe the socio-political system leads to some inappropriate conclusions. There is certainly a difference between a system whose ruling group imposes its will with brute force, and a system in which an equally derivative ruling élite 'totally' controls what happens in society, the only difference being that it 'takes into consideration' the factor of domestic and foreign politics, and instead of instruments of direct liquidation (which are today considered somewhat 'substandard', 'uncultured' and 'inhuman'), uses instruments of indirect, gradual liquidation, such as systematic repression, harassment, deprivation of livelihood, and imprisonment.

But let us be cautious in drawing conclusions – even a well-defined non-conformity is not entirely devoid of social approval, subordination and respect. Moreover, even the most abject supporter of the regime may have occasion to express criticism and disagreement. The problem is not that we are in opposition, for in the given situation we cannot be otherwise. It is that we must find within the context of official repression a way of transforming that opposition gradually and tirelessly into a position – that is, into an actively created way of life. It is a difficult, but by no means impossible, task. Let us realize that we have already been living like this for a long time (more than ten years and some of us more than thirty). Many who exhausted themselves soon after the coups of 1948 and 1968 became quiescent and, to a certain extent, reconciled to the situation, having found a place in society that satisfied their longing for a 'normal' life. But this cannot hide a deepening rift that has existed from the beginning, but which, in the euphoric period after social change, was not as obvious and emphatic.

Any political opposition, that is, any new political position, must be able to offer an alternative conception; in a totalitarian system, this alternative cannot be mere hot air. Those who have no alternative, or who have one but are afraid to express it and stand behind it, are swept by the logic of the situation (social ties and threats) into an acceptable non-conformity. And if this 'polite' or 'proper' opposition is ever declared to be a programme, it will quickly become no more than a fanciful and unrealistic version of what the silent majority of citizens already 'enjoy'; the only difference being that such criticism as there is will be directed not at the authorities but at the 'brothers in suffering' who, thank God, are still capable of actively seeking ways to oppose and resist, both in life and in politics.

The totalitarian system can only be eliminated by eliminating all the elements of political dictatorship that are essential to that system. That is the basic practical and political task of all advanced

European societies. Only fools, however, believe that this will definitively (yet again) solve the problem of tormented, careworn, contemporary human beings, enabling them to live a free and satisfying life. No mere political transformations can achieve that. Efforts to democratize any totalitarian system only make sense when the ground is laid in society and room is created for a free choice between options, so that people may act in a way that is consistent with their character and their notion of social responsibility.

The variety of unofficial civic activity, and its capacity not only to criticize the state of society but also to act in positive and creative ways, must be appreciated and respected. It is also proper that all expressions, attitudes, and activities be subject to criticism and evaluation and be encouraged to argue back. Such dialogue within the opposition can only be welcomed. Moreover, incipient discontent with shortcomings in the system can, with understanding, become transformed into discontent with the general state of society, into an awareness that a non-conformist stance is possible. That, in turn, can grow to become active opposition. Such recognition and understanding is not always accessible or acceptable to everyone, perhaps not even to the majority. An individual's critical attitude towards a given social system depends on many circumstances. Having once accepted the principle of acting in conformity with perceived truth, however, one cannot avoid drawing appropriate conclusions in one's own behaviour and practical life. This evolution of social self-awareness takes place in several stages and each stage has a different scale of values, a different intensity and level of active committment. Finally, it must be realized that even individuals who are openly in opposition have differences of opinion.

Objections are constantly being made, for instance, to commitments of an expressly political nature, as though opposition only stood a chance of succeeding if it eliminated all political commitment. But politics cannot be banished either from one's thoughts or from practical activity merely by declaring them to have no future. Likewise, it is impossible to banish from our active non-conformity any initiative to which people are willing to lend their efforts. In today's system of 'real socialism', political opposition has a fundamental significance that cannot be denied, nor can any other activity take its place. We must think about forms, aims and methods, and about ways of effecting a transition to new, non-traditional ways of working politically. Social structures can be democratized by expanding the elements of self-management, limiting institutional growth, making allowances for ideas as a motivating factor, and strengthening direct democracy by eliminating priorities and privileges. On the other hand, however, we must avoid political leaps into the dark and shun those fascinating social utopias with their visions of the elimination of power, government and the state, visions in which power will be held by all or, better still, by none, and no one will rule over anyone else. Given the complexity of modern social structures, power cannot be eliminated, just as the state form of social organization cannot be done away with. But political power, the highest form of decision-making power, must be prevented, both through law and through 'power', from becoming totally concentrated in a single place. One constant task, therefore, will be to control, limit and criticize power, to make it practically impossible for power to grow to suffocating proportions.

There are many ways to accomplish this. Modern democracies have already shown us many of them. The future democratic, self-managing socialist society, however, will be more consistent in this regard, because it will have more technical means at its disposal and a greater real and general consensus. If the world of today is faced with the task of eliminating unjustified, unwarranted and therefore unjust class and group privileges, it is also faced with the task of breaking down the barriers protecting the political power that totally controls everything that goes on in society, including the behaviour of individuals.

There is not now, nor is there likely to be in the near future, any socio-cultural system or state that can be held up to citizens as an example, including the systems we may ourselves propose. Every proposed organization of society, even one with a maximum of self-management, will need to be balanced by extra-governmental, extra-managerial, extra-organizational activity on the part of voluntary associations established for the widest possible variety of both short-term and long-term needs and purposes.

Hope for those who would liberate themselves, therefore, lies in a symbiosis of the moral and the social, of humanity and democracy, in the realization of a social order in which the formalized and functionalized structure of society will be regulated and controlled by this 'newly discovered' spontaneous civic activity, which will be a permanent and essential source of social self-awareness, while the bureaucracies ruling society shrink to assume merely compliant executive roles.

I am convinced that the human rights movements that have arisen in the authoritarian regimes of eastern Europe are not merely a temporary phenomenon, but that they will play a complex and many-sided role in the social life of the communities of a united Europe.

# 3   Catholicism and politics*

## Václav Benda

Following a none-too-praiseworthy custom, I shall begin by stating what this essay is not. First and foremost, it is not an historical study, and to the extent that I make use of historical facts, I do so quite outside my field of competence and with no pretensions to scholarship. Moreover, such facts are not intended to prove my points but merely to illustrate them, to make them more comprehensible to readers unfamiliar with the conditions under which we live.

This essay is really a reaction to a challenge implied in numerous discussions with Czech and occasionally Slovak and Polish friends – discussions that were, for the most part, rudimentary and rather groping. This points to a second limitation: very craftily, I relinquish in advance any claim to conclusiveness, either in the scope of my subject or the depth of my grasp. The impressions I shall try to express are *my own* and they are deliberately as limited and as partisan as I can make them. My purpose is to provoke discussion, not to summarize and draw conclusions.

Finally, I will be talking exclusively about *Czech* Catholicism, simply because I know regrettably little about conditions in Slovakia. On the whole, my impression is that Slovak Catholicism is far closer to Polish Catholicism than to Czech: it has a relatively massive base of support in the population, its coherence with the national tradition has never been questioned, it has an uninterrupted historical continuity and therefore displays a marked conservatism, and so on. Perhaps the only difference is that *political* Catholicism in Slovakia was linked historically with the quasi-fascist Slovak state during the Second World War and, to this day, not only is this fact abundantly and indiscriminately employed as a political whip, but it also represents a deep trauma with which political Catholicism in Slovakia is still struggling. In this I perceive

* Translated by Paul Wilson.

an important reason – though not the only one – why, despite the many analogies between the Slovak and the Polish Catholic churches, their political influence and activities are utterly incomparable. I apologize in advance to my Slovak and Polish friends for the short-sighted view I have taken of their respective situations, to which I shall occasionally refer in this and other instances.

I would like to add a positive note to these opening qualifications: I am firmly convinced that the churches in eastern Europe are now in a position to lead the world church out of its present state of tension and irresolution. This, however, is not the subject of my essay and I can do no more here than affirm what is at once a joyful hope and an overwhelming responsibility. But the general crisis and deterioration of politics has to be considered here as well. In this connection considerable importance is usually ascribed to the Third World, and many even invest great hopes in it. I agree, in the sense that any solution that ignores the existence and problems of the Third World is doomed to failure, particularly if it is undertaken at the Third World's expense. But I hold out no hope whatsoever for some new political guidance or universal answer coming from the Third World, for what we see in the political picture there (and it contains almost everything, from the best to the worst) are expressions not of crisis, but of chaos. Moreover, this chaos provides little in the way of formative influences, since most of the energy of this greater part of humanity, for a long time to come, will very likely be spent in the immediate struggle for survival. And yet neither the countries of the eastern bloc nor the traditional democracies of the West display much evidence of a healthy, dynamic political life: the signs of crisis are too obvious. But there the similarity (between East and West) ceases, for the symptoms of disease on each side belong to an utterly different order. They cannot be compared on *any* rational, theoretical or practical grounds. The best analogy I can think of is the difference between a diseased organ and a malignant tumor. The western Left, in the widest sense, may be right a hundred times over in their critical assessment of politics in their own countries, but as long as they fail to understand the vast differences between totalitarianism and democracy (and the Left does *not* understand them, and clearly, for very basic reasons, does not even want to), I have no confidence either in what they do nor in the solutions they propose. That is one of many reasons – and I shall refer to others later on – why I believe that at this point the countries of the eastern bloc are the most competent to formulate the basis of a radically new political order, and suggest a way out of the worldwide crisis of politics.

I am convinced that we are, *hic et nunc*, faced with a single problem, one that can be just as easily formulated, theoretically, as the need for a new theology, for a new substance of faith, a new philosophy and science, or for a new *polis*. In practical terms, the political aspect has a certain priority in eastern Europe – which is somewhat unusual in the history of Christianity – if only because here, every expression of faith is automatically considered a political act (and unfortunately, in my country, this usually means the police think so too).

When the independent Czechoslovak Republic was created in 1918, the vast majority of its population – formally, at least – was Catholic, whereas the official idea of the country's statehood derived, to a considerable extent, from an anti-Catholic, reforming tradition (which, although historically absurd, was none the less an appropriate punishment for the spiritual, cultural and political sterility of the Catholic Church in the country at that time). This initial paradox produced a different set of consequences in the two parts of the Republic. Slovak Catholicism – with a wider congregation, more vitally and authentically national – was able to maintain its decisive political influence, though at the cost of denying not only Czechoslovak statehood but, unfortunately, democratic traditions as well. Czech Catholicism, by contrast, essentially withdrew from politics and, in fact, from all other forms of active involvement in creating the general social climate; it limited itself to an irresolute and rather unsuccessful defence of its traditional positions. The only important exception to this was in the field of Catholic-oriented arts and letters, particularly in literature, but of course official church circles either rejected such trends or, at best, regarded them with suspicion.

The communists were able to exploit the historical handicap of Slovak Catholicism and between 1945 and 1948, through an adroit combination of political and police methods, they swept it from the political scene: neither an overwhelming electoral victory, nor reluctant support from the other democratic forces in the republic, nor even the left-wing 'sweet talk' of some Catholic politicians was of any avail.

On the other hand, at the time of the communist takeover in 1948 the Catholic Church in the Czech lands represented the only influential and organized force that was uncompromised and uncorrupted by previous political concessions to the communists or by defensive co-operation with them. At the same time, however, it was politically inexperienced and unprepared for political struggle. Its reaction was what one would have expected in that situation: it made no active effort to influence the course of events, yet it emphatically refused to sanction the coup, to regard the new political conditions 'realistically' and to accede to the inital wooing by the communists. Thanks to this somewhat quixotic stand, the Catholic Church became the first exemplary object of systematic repression. First of all, its organizational and intellectual potential was destroyed. All the bishops were interned or imprisoned. In 1949 the Church orders were *de facto* broken up and 8000 of the 12,000 monks were either imprisoned or interned for an average of five years (the superiors of certain orders were not released until the spring of 1968). A considerable number of secular priests were either imprisoned or not allowed to continue in their calling. Moreover, tens of thousands of Catholic lay people spent long years in prison, and there were very few leading Catholic intellectuals, especially writers, who managed to escape imprisonment. Another 10,000 Catholics in all the above categories avoided a similar fate only by emigrating. *Everyone* who dared to continue professing their faith was subjected to tough discrimination and administrative sanctions.

All things are clear before God and this whole body of suffering will not remain forgotten and, in time, will yield its benefits. But my task here is to evaluate the consequences of the church's attitude from a limited human, and a narrowly political, perspective. For the twenty years between 1948 and 1968 the reply seems clear: the crushing repression, the falling away of the 'luke-warm' majority, the limiting of church life to a minimum of ritual expressions – all of this, to my mind, is more than balanced by the high moral credit the Catholic Church gained in the eyes of society. Protestant churches, in those years, made compromises with the communist regime, and this allowed them some room – albeit a limited amount – for the life of the church and relatively preserved them from systematic repression. Nevertheless, this period confirms the priority of truth over pragmatism: the revitalization – often politically motivated in the beginning – of religious awareness, particularly among young people and the intelligentsia, overwhelmingly focused on the devastated and repressed Catholic Church.

Developments since 1968, however, have considerably complicated this simple assessment. In the Protestant milieu, thanks to its less drastic treatment by the state (although this was purchased with not insignificant offerings at a strange assortment of altars), a situation was created in which the leadership of those churches now react to pressure from the regime with reluctance, at least. Some simple believers and clergymen have, in one way or another, taken an active and courageous part in social matters. The Catholic Church, on the other hand, is now paying a heavy price for its previous heroic period and, apparently suffering from a kind of 'hangover', is now squandering its accumulated stock of suffering and the moral credit that flows from it. Those who survived long periods of imprisonment are now old and, with a few honourable exceptions, tired and sceptical, although those who are clearly 'broken' are very few and far between. The top church hierarchy is composed partly of such people, and partly of those who either voluntarily or under pressure have become puppets or direct agents of the security forces, and naturally, are utterly servile towards the regime. The policy of granting or withdrawing official state permission to function as clergymen (in some periods more than 50 per cent of the priests were thus denied the possibility of serving in parishes) which has been going on for decades, the systematic relocation of the more active priests from parish to parish, the deliberate elimination of the better students and teachers from theological seminaries, even employing psychological and sociological techniques – these and other policies have taken their toll among the clergy. The degree of political and cultural isolation among them is high, and a considerable number of the lower clergy (even though the situation here is incomparably better than in the hierarchy) are to some extent 'involved' with official state power. Worst of all, there is a complete lack of effective solidarity between the community of believers and their pastors, while Protestant congregations, thanks to just such solidarity, have recently been able to resist repression, in some cases successfully. Timid official post-Consilium attempts at involving more laypeople in the life of the church were suppressed after 1968. At the same time, any unofficial extra-liturgical contacts, whether among believers or between priests and laypeople, are subject to administrative sanctions and in some cases to judicial sanctions as well, according to the existing Czechoslovak legal code. I cannot resist mentioning a concrete case, not the most flagrant by far, but interesting in the context of Czechoslovakia and Poland. At an Esperanto camp held in August 1977 in Herbortice, a Polish and a Czech priest (Fr

Zielonek and Fr Srna) apparently held mass in a tent just before reveille, with the knowledge of the camp director J. Šváček, and in the presence of several campers. Shortly afterwards, Fr Srna had his state permission taken from him. Both he and J. Šváček faced criminal charges of 'interfering with the supervision of church and religious communities' and they were sentenced to twelve and fifteen months, respectively, both sentences being suspended for three years.

What I have outlined is the result of a general and thorough 'decimation of cadres' (though the word 'decimation' is a euphemism here); in one way or another, it was inevitable. What is most serious and politically most dangerous, however, is a certain psychological effect of long decades of terror. An overwhelming majority of Czech Catholics are convinced (and unfortunately their own experience has largely confirmed it) that merely by attending church and privately professing their faith, they are expressing so much courage and willingness to suffer for Christ that no one has the right to expect of them any further expressions of civic courage and commitment. Naturally there is an element of backsliding in this attitude; they are exchanging the 'Kingdom of God' for a certain form of habitation in this world – albeit as second-class citizens and victims of discrimination. It also contains an element of justified mistrust of their former persecutors who now, having been denied their rights, make loud appeals for general solidarity, frequently without giving sufficient guarantees that when they speak of rights, they are not really talking about their lost privileges. Nevertheless, whether we condemn it or apologize for it, this attitude remains a political fact and it will have to be taken into account in the future as well. Moreover, there is the danger that even those who daily encounter the absurdities and injustices of social life, and are thus aware of the moral insupportability of such an attitude (and this happens occasionally to every honest believer who has eyes to see and ears to hear), will still limit their reaction, pressured by an already automatic self-censorship, to some form of 'minimal gesture'. To illustrate what I mean by this, let me mention the kind and well-educated Catholic woman who recently refused to sign a petition of protest drawn up by a group of believers because she felt it was a foolish provocation of the powers that be, pointing out that even in the 1950s things could be accomplished quietly. She herself, for example, would occasionally send parcels of muffins to priests who were interned or in prison. I would not want you to underestimate the persistent and courageous dedication of this woman and treat 'muffin Catholicism' on the same level as 'goulash socialism'; for just such good works, many in this country were sent, and are still being sent, to prison for many years. In terms of an individual's efforts to approach the Truth (I mean the truth about salvation), and also because it sets an example to those close by, I consider such good works indispensible and worthy of the highest praise. The problem is that we are in a situation when the very foundations of the universal church, and the *polis* in the widest sense of the word, are in grave danger and everyone, like it or not, is faced with a challenge: which would you rather save, your own life or the life of this community, this brutally tortured body of Christ? Confronted with such a challenge, the kind of behaviour described above is not in itself enough, and may even be dangerously deceptive as an example to others. Just as the overwhelming majority has retreated from civic life into the close circle of family and friends, this too represents a retreat, perhaps more honourable, but a retreat none the less, into a ghetto; it is a voluntary resignation of openness and universal sharing of responsibility.

If I have expressed the challenge now facing Czech Catholics (and probably their Slovak, Polish and other brothers and sisters in the faith as well) in a deliberately callous way, I wanted to emphasize the callous and uncompromising conditions in which their hopes of becoming 'the salt of the earth' must be realized.

By shifting the meaning of Christ's statement from the spiritual level – from that of a personal approach to the Kingdom of God – to the political level and even, I am bold to say, to the level of a struggle for political power, I have opened a way to that fundamental source of all hope, including hope on this earth. For most Czech Christians, communism was and is identical with Satan and the Anti-Christ – and I readily agree. Yet communism had two historical forms: in the 1950s it was more like Lucifer ('the bearer of light'), the most sublime of the Lord's angels, the spirit of deception and deceit and eternal fickleness. It was essentially a Manichean struggle between the principles of Good and Evil in which mendacity took the place of truth by being louder, appearance took the place of reality by seeming more logical, and the way to the Fall took the place of historical salvation because it was easier. At a time like this, when mulititudes fell by the wayside and many were destroyed as a warning to others, those who looked to their own souls and remained in Truth could be said to have acquitted themselves well.

But since 1968, communism has become more like that Nietzschean 'spirit of gravity', callous, gloomy and all-consuming: against truth stands power, against reality, non-entity or nothingness, against history, the motionless cycle 'from anniversary to anniversary'. To acquit oneself in this period, which is more burdensome than cruel, it is therefore not enough merely to look out for one's own soul and believe that Truth – the Truth which in a particular place and time took on human form and walked among people and assumed their suffering – is no more than a *position* which has to be *maintained*.

For as long as evil was aggressive and polemical (and always had an arsenal of physical violence for use in cases where it lacked arguments), it was possible to 'hedge' against it and, from the position thus assumed, to oppose it, either in active polemics or through passive suffering. If, however, the chief form of the present political evil is a restrictive heaviness that all citizens carry on their shoulders and at the same time bear *within* them, then the only possibility is to shake that evil off, escape its power and to seek truth. Under such circumstances, every genuine struggle for one's own soul becomes an openly political act, and a creative political act at that, because it is no longer merely 'defining oneself' against something else (there is nothing to define oneself against), but rather a jettisoning of ballast and opening oneself up to what is new and unknown. And thus, in a society whose typical features are a mass exodus into private life and utter indifference to the stage scenery of official pseudo-politics, it is paradoxically possible to observe a latent politicization, the growth of a political potential. Christians can and should become one of the means by which this potential is released and made manifest. My earlier pessimism about the present state of things is based on the fact that it would seem to be almost humanly impossible to grasp this opportunity, accept it without reservation, and be willing to gamble everything on it. The historical perspectives are hopelessly blocked, the regime is more cohesive and powerful than ever before, the government of fear even more widespread. But my optimism springs from the fact that all this is true only *at the moment* and that the slightest social groundswell (which may mean only a few people displaying the courage to take a chance, despite everything, on the opportunity I have mentioned) may call into life processes whose tempo and consequences no one can foresee.

The point is that fear is largely a fiction maintained by nothing more than inertia. A system that has deliberately rejected its fanatical adherents and relies on a mass of pliant, passive opportunists may have guaranteed itself *easy* obedience, but not *blind* obedience, because any form of personal responsibility presents too great a risk for its machinery and so, in the end, even the regime's terroristic purposes are worn down and degenerate in a complicated jungle of bureaucracy. Even its cohesiveness and power are deceptive because they are not the functions of a living organism, but the mechanical operations of a worn-out machine that can be brought to a halt when the least important of its parts seizes up. Christians, in particular, should be clear about the hopelessness of the present historical perspectives and the stability of earthly 'thousand-year' empires. Here, then, is where I see the basic source of hope, especially hope for the future role of political Catholicism. Add to this the fact that the election of Pope John Paul II has lent new dimensions to the traditional Catholic respect for authority which has had such an unhappy influence here, particularly after the installation of a collaborationist hierarchy, then despite everything, this hope seems realistic and its realization only a matter of time.

If it is possible to outline what might be achieved in politics and Catholicism in our lands, it should also be possible to articulate what we might do to help resolve the crisis of the contemporary world, and in particular the crisis of its politics. I should say, however, that I cannot do this, nor is it possible, because such an articulation would be a political programme and the transformation I have in mind is essentially above political programmes or, rather, it bypasses them altogether and deals directly with life. This is to some an emotional claim, but emotional feeling is one factor to which that 'treasury of suffering' built up over the past decades has given back a positive meaning. Nevertheless, a partial answer can perhaps be provided: we may point out what that change ought *not* to be and sketch in a few of the levels of reality with which it must *necessarily* come to terms.

To begin with, an extremely simplified scheme of political stratification in Czechoslovakia today: the vast majority of the population is 'loyal' to the system; at the same time, the regime sees loyalty not as consensus, but as 'collective guilt', decently rewarded. The degrees of collective guilt and its rewards are graduated, but everyone has a share in it, from the most insignificant worker right up to the prime minister. Tactically, the system is almost flawless: practically everyone has a vested interest in maintaining the status quo and practically everyone has a share in carrying out the repressive functions of the regime. Strategically, however, the system is catastrophic. In the first place, no one believes (perhaps not even the First Secretary of the Communist Party) that there is any future in it and so everyone tries to evade the obligations of his or her position, while squeezing the maximum personal advantage from it as rapidly as possible. The slogan here is 'after us, the flood'. In the second place, the system of constant humiliation and compulsory participation in shameful actions and events creates a sensation of powerlessness and guilt in the manipulated majority. One consequence of this is an intensified hatred of the regime. In recent years I have been in a wide variety of social situations and the degree of this hatred has often horrified me. If this 'loyal' mass of citizens ever does awaken (or is aroused) from its torpor, then its vision will probably be directed towards the past. Among these citizens, there is a nebulous, half-conscious longing to restore the past and a savage desire to exact revenge for their squandered lives and at the same time to wash away their guilt in a bloodbath. If the regime is terrified by these suppressed passions, and although it may be only dimly aware of them, then the opposition also sees them more as a threat to some future opportunity for rectification than as something that strengthens its own position.

The tiny minority that is consciously and *openly* politically disloyal can be roughly divided into two categories. The first consists of the 'liberals', who focus on the present and attempt to manifest and legitimize their stance exclusively in the here and now. Characteristically, they emphasize the moral and existential aspects of being, the reform of contemporary humanity and, in some cases, 'small-scale work' leading to a change for the better. Along with this, they are sceptical of changes in political forms and of radicalism that attempts any more than setting a 'moral example'. The second category includes the whole range of 'socialist' tendencies – from socialists of an uncertain stamp, through social democrats and Euro-communists to Trotskyites. What they all share is a clear orientation towards the future, connected in one way or another to a transformation (revolutionary or reformist) of the present state of things. The positive aspects of this orientation – it is precise and comprehensible and therefore attractive – are also a source of its negative qualities: it overlooks the present and interprets the past voluntaristically, thus creating the constant danger that the ideals it proclaims will remain mere theories at the cost of exacting cruelly real sacrifices.

Nevertheless, because the political situation is so utterly elementary and 'naked', and because there is no political life (or political opposition) in Czechoslovakia as it is commonly understood in Europe, and because any freely conceived initiative automatically becomes a political act *par excellence* with all the consequences for the initiators, a kind of bridge is starting to form across the gap between the differences I have schematically described.

So far, the fullest and most typical expression of this is the free citizens' initiative, Charter 77. The community of Charter 77 signatories and the far wider circle of those who sympathize with them and in one way or another actively support them, not only includes almost all currents in the 'conscious' political opposition, but also those who, out of a need to express themselves as free human beings, have refused to become 'established' at the cost of sharing the guilt and have tried to escape from political life altogether. Most of the cultural underground, which forms one of the largest identifiable constituencies inside the Charter, belongs to the latter category. These are people who learned their ABCs of civic virtues – that is to say, political virtues in the proper sense of the word – within the context of Charter 77, while at the same time giving the 'political' members of Charter 77 a proper lesson in what human freedom and living within the Truth mean. This unity among people of disparate opinion and background is a great forum of learning, and is something new from which many lessons might be learned. Unfortunately, external observers appear to find it puzzling. The regime explains this unity by mutual antagonism, which is largely nonsense, of course, although there is a grain of truth in it. On the other side, western observers try to determine, to the point of stupefaction, which political grouping and which tactical point of view this unity serves. I can assure them that even the most precise answer to this question will not bring them a single step closer to understanding what it is really all about.

Yet the very source of this unity is also its greatest handicap: it is a defensive unity, a unity born of necessity which in its present form is incapable of achieving anything more concrete than it has already. Those who share that unity have given up on politics – that is, on politics as a *techné* – in the name of a struggle against everything that makes human life unfree and undignified. To the extent that the *techné* of politics is identified with authority and manipulation, such a resignation is justified and stimulating. The problem is that freedom and human dignity are not absolute givens, but are rather gifts that humanity and society must learn to accept in their history, and for which they must also learn to struggle. Therefore in my opinion, politics as *techné* (i.e. as the art of waging a struggle over the fate of the *polis*) will be justified in the future as well – even though, clearly, it will constantly oscillate between that sense of futility and the necessity of Jacob's struggle with the angel. And in this sense the unity enjoyed so far in Charter 77 seems provisional and inadequate.

In concluding I shall try, from what I take to be the Catholic point of view, to indicate the possibilities open to a new politics and a 'more essential' unity. Despite elements of a potential synthesis, this is not a proposal for reconciliation or historical compromise, but an appeal to those who, in the given conditions and despite all their fundamental disagreements, are willing to work together to move the conflagration to a new, less well mapped and therefore more interesting field.

Before I so this, however, I must backtrack somewhat. The political stratification mentioned above has a parallel in the Christian context. Protestants – thanks, among other things, to a certain puritanism – are relatively immune to the combination of loyalty to the regime, a sense of shared guilt for its existence and a hatred of it. On the other hand, they frequently exhibit an unconditionally moralistic (or, in my terminology, 'liberal') attitude or, conversely, they may support the idea of creating a radically new and just society according to a formula laid down in advance. In other words, they support what is in essence a socialist idea. Both the liberal and the socialist positions derive from the same moralistic conception of politics: they differ only in whether they emphasize the 'private' or the 'public' nature of morality.

Among Catholics, on the contrary, the relative distribution of the three basic positions – 'loyalist', 'liberal' and 'socialist' – is apparently about the same as it is in the rest of the population. Still, there is an important shift here: regardless of which political orientation Catholics favour, they almost always keep their distance from them and at the same time are almost always willing to give fundamental credit to the contributions of other orientations. They are 'more sinful', or at least more tolerant of sin, than Protestants, and understand better the positive significance of sin in the history of redemption (*viz.*, the reference to *felix culpa* or fortunate sin in the Easter liturgy). For this reason, they are both able to tolerate and to appreciate human failings, while nurturing a healthy scepticism towards the liberal or socialist faith in radical individual or social reform. At the same time, however, they see the problem of redemption chiefly in its social and historical dimensions, and they therefore pose the question of co-responsibility and collective guilt even more acutely than the most puritan of puritans. They are even willing to admit that a desire for revenge has its place, modified to a form of penance and the righting of wrongs in historical time. Catholicism, after all, has given dogmatic form to the redemptive role of individual 'moral' example in the worship of the saints. And finally, the arrival of the Kingdom of Christ is, more clearly than ever before, seen as being conditional on our concrete efforts to prepare the ground for it in historical time and to build its foundations. (The decision of the Vatican II Concilium, which replaces the liturgical prayer for the conversion of the apostate Jews with a prayer that they remain faithful to their own God and their mission to be the visible prefiguration of the history of Redemption, serves to illustrate this.)

Catholics, therefore, are more 'involved' and more guilty, not just because of their momentary human weaknesses, but also by virtue of the fact that communist regimes have found tried and true models for their worst practices in the history of the institutional church. At the same time, however, this awareness of guilt means that Catholics have a tougher, less compromising attitude, a clearer notion of the difference between 'good and evil'. Catholics are also open to the positive aspects of particular solutions, while maintaining a certain immunity towards them. Finally, they are extremely sceptical of politics in general, while being aware that only 'something like politics' can save us at the present time.

When, in my excursions into the past, I spoke of 'political Catholicism', I was deeply aware of the dubiousness and the inner contradictions of such a phrase, although it is commonly used. I did not try to avoid it, simply because I believed that it would acquire a positive sense in the context of how I perceived the future form of politics, as something light years away from politics in the present sense of a struggle for power and, at the same time, as something even 'more political' if we understand by that a commitment to a playful and sacred concern for the affairs of the *polis*.

The starting point for this new politics is allied closely with the attitudes mentioned above, which I indicated were typical for the political awakening (or re-awakening) of Catholic citizens; it is also linked with the special character which these atttitudes, thanks to historical circumstances, are acquiring. If we accept, or allow ourselves to be forced into accepting, the current definition of politics, there will in fact be nothing we can do. But there is another choice: we can also proceed, starting right now, with an entirely new kind of politics. The word 'new' is in fact misleading, for it suggests an inevitable and automatically positive idea of 'progress'. Nothing could be further from what I really think. I believe that the 'only thing that can save us' is a 'return to the sources' of life and politics – the sources being considered not nineteenth-century practices, with their arbitrary division between 'right' and 'wrong' at an arbitrarily chosen point in history (which usually meant the devaluation and misinterpretation of both notions), but rather as a genuine quest in which everything 'good and evil' in the development of politics will be re-examined, thought through and reinterpreted, in which the past will be given new significance that will help us clarify our present-day problems. The election of Pope John Paul II demonstrates that such a view of the 'new' is not just a personal folly of mine, and that it can become realistic on a worldwide scale (and especially for 'Catholics', from one point of view, and for the 'eastern bloc countries' from another). On the theological level, at least, his election suddenly called into question the generally accepted polarization of conservatives and progressives in the church, and raised the possibility that such a division may no longer make any sense. It is a mere possibility. Nevertheless, I believe it will come, and that it will have a beneficial influence on other areas of human culture.

In the same way, I believe that the 'new politics' I have mentioned is possible, that it is the only alternative to the apocalypse, and that our nations in general, and their Catholic inhabitants in particular, have a unique chance to articulate its initial stages. It should be a notion of politics that is deadly serious, involving people up to their necks, yet it should be unbloody and (necessarily) playful. It should demand an obligation (to set an example, I have taken this obligation upon myself, although political activity was the last thing I wanted to get involved in). Yet it should not tie one down: a state or any other type of social organization, for instance, may be perceived as a useful factor in limiting evil, but it must never become an instrument for creating a 'heaven on earth'. It should be a politics in which human rights and the rules of parliamentary democracy and even, for instance, the privileges and freedoms of the 'feudal' world and the demands of social justice, are all a matter of course, because they have already, in one way or another, been realized and at the same time, been found wanting. Because it occasionally becomes necessary, for technical reasons, to use current buzz-words, I will – to the considerable disgust of my left-thinking friends – call this political concept of mine radical conservatism. I am very curious as to whether, after reading this essay, they will consider our political disagreements a consequence of verbal misunderstanding or of genuine antagonism. Still, on the basis of many indications, I am convinced that there are only two paths open to Catholics in the Czech lands at the present time: the path leading to political and therefore to Christian failure, or the path – toilsome and thorny – of looking for a new, conservatively radical politics.

# 4  On the question of Chartism*

## Václav Černý

Charter 77 regarded and proclaimed itself as an independent citizens' campaign. At the outset, it deliberately refuted the allegation that it sought to be a political party. It was blindingly clear that it had none of the means to become one. There is nothing illegal or anti-state in the idea of a voluntary movement of citizens to defend human rights and civil liberties. On the contrary, the creation of the Charter, just like its declared aims, was fully in accord with the letter of the State Constitution and the freedoms which, on paper, our state guaranteed our citizens when it endorsed the Human Rights Conventions and the Helsinki Agreement, and committed itself internationally to ensuring their implementation in respect of its own citizens. If you read the first text of the Charter, i.e., its proclamation, you will find that, apart from its detailing of proven instances of actual wrongs done to citizens *in contravention* of the undertakings and guarantees of existing legislation, it is composed in its entirety of quotations of passages from the State Constitution and references to the principles embodied both therein and in the international agreements endorsed by the state. Therefore, it was a political mistake of the first order for the powers that be to have rejected from the outset the dialogue proposed by the Charter. Their mistake was even graver because that dialogue was chiefly in their own interest. After all, not only would it have been possible, but it would have been a wise and circumspect move to have accepted the Charter as an expression of discontent at the violation of the state's *own* laws, and to have entered into a debate with it regarding the ways and means of guaranteeing these laws.

The powers that be further compounded their error by blindly declaring the Charter to be *a priori* a political intrigue, and by abdicating their responsibility by placing the matter in the hands

---

* Translated by A. G. Brain.

of the police and penal authorities. Each and every one of their measures was an irrational act of political blindness and a moral abomination. But of course, it was no more than one further act in a long history of well-entrenched brutal despotism which relies on vicious repression and threats when argument fails it. The usual pattern is for this to be followed by misrepresentation and abuse, but it cannot deny itself the final pleasure for long, and fists soon take the place of arguments. There is nothing new in this. We have all had direct experience of it. It went on for years: the sort of persuasion that started with a punch in the mouth and sometimes ended with a noose around the neck. Needless to say, such tactics do not work in this country any more. Today's policeman, if they have not yet squeezed all morals out of him, even has his reservations about such methods. And even when they have, his power of reasoning has usually remained intact, and he can even prove quite bright. His experience, which in many cases goes back years, is no longer solely experience of 'third-degree' tactics or professional extermination techniques. I am quite willing to admit without reservations that this has been true of my numerous secret police interrogators of the past two years, from the lieutenant up to the colonel.

The fundamental, and very first mistake that the political establishment made with respect to Charter 77 – its refusal to hold a dialogue about the duty to respect the Constitution – had immediate repercussions. This error could not help but lead to further error, and falsehood to breed still more falsehood until, in the end, the established power bloc was bringing down a torrent of misfortune on its own head and endlessly making a fool of itself. In the media the Charter was described as a project conceived by 'turncoats and double-dealers', and elsewhere as 'has-beens'. The miserable bungling oaf who thought those expressions up deserved a good kick in the pants from his political masters. The Chartists were indeed 'has-beens' in the sense that they lacked any sort of political power. But the same can be said of 90 per cent of the Czechoslovak population. What else is a double-dealing turncoat but someone who hands his country over to a foreign power for personal gain, like those who collaborated with the Germans, for example? It is fairly obvious that it is quite inappropriate to call traitors those who demand strict observance of the constitution. This allegation is in fact a boomerang which rebounds on those it suits best: those who ordered the notorious media articles in the first place.

They organized the notorious anti-Charter 'protest' among the wider public of so-called 'cultural workers'. But those present at the meetings were not read the text of the Charter, so they did not know precisely what it was they were protesting against. By this time they were the laughing stock of the entire nation and the campaign disappeared into thin air with a wave of the hand, in an act of sheer absurdity. The upshot of it was that the members of the country's cultural community were henceforth divided, by name, into those who had signed the Charter and those who, in the field of Czech 'culture' (!), were prepared, in response to a call from above for extra-special obedience, to condemn something without giving it a hearing. Each of those who condemned the Charter will no doubt find, individually and collectively, suitable ways of describing themselves and their actions. They include those who immediately sought some excuse or other. After all, the Czechs are past masters of the art of finding excuses. Judged merely in general terms, one can say that Czech national culture and its sense of morality had never before suffered the sort of outrage they did from the organizers of the 'protest' against the Charter and what was intended as a mass disavowal of it. The fact that the establishment gave the task of defending its positions to the usual political and journalistic hacks was probably a case of Hobson's choice in an emergency, but it gained it nothing and was just one further error, since those gentlemen's standards are notorious. As could be expected, they immediately brought into play against the Charter a whole set of slanders, distortions, abuse, half-truths and absolute falsehoods which all represent the dismal range of their capacity. I speak from experience as one who has been a favourite target for their sort of behaviour for the past thirty years, and who could well lay claim to the laurels of seniority and worthy service. Though the powers that be may not know it, or rather, would sooner not know it, nay, *cannot afford to know it* (for where else would they find more obedient, unscrupulous and servile creatures), the media are the principal, albeit unintentional, creators and encouragers of opposition, since they are totally suspect and nobody believes them. People almost automatically take for gospel the opposite of what the papers say. Once all-powerful, the media were capable of pointing the finger that condemned people to death. As they lost all credibility they also lost some of their power, and at the very least were obliged to change their methods, if not their ends. Nowadays, they do not directly fix the noose around people's necks, but they do endeavour to destroy their honour and slay them with a hail of repeated slanders and lies, even if they no longer stoop so low as to employ such provocative expressions as 'hanging from lamp-posts'. As in the past, the intention remains that of eliminating troublesome elements. The king is dead, long live the king! Stalin is no longer acceptable, long live neo-Stalinism!

But to return to the Charter: the authorities nicknamed it dissidence. I see no reason why the Charter should accept being branded in this way. It is an expression that was thought up as a means of discrediting the Charter and knocking it on the head with a single word. In today's political jargon, dissidence equals subversion. It suits the media's paymasters for the Charter to be dressed up in wolf's clothing as a means of putting the wind up the faint-hearted and creating a pretext for its persecution. The only others who might be happy to employ the term are propagandists abroad, who are only too pleased to find further evidence of national discord in our country. The Charter, however, is under no obligation to accept names given to it by either side. It chose its own name: it is the *Charter* and its signatories are *Chartists* and they need no other title. I use it myself and am proud to do so.

I am not out to write the history of the Charter and Chartism here. Its history may not be long, but it has one, and someone will write it one day, without a doubt. And there is also no doubt that when it is written it will contain quite a few surprises, even for many Chartists, because, like all human history, it will include not only the merits, but also the demerits, not only the achievements but also certain over-blown and over-trumpeted ambitions: not so much a history of personal errors as of errors in personalities. But that is by the by. The main issue is the fundamental purpose of the Charter and its mission in the nation's life. The purpose of the Charter, from the outset, was a critical and moral one, and still is. The Charter decided that its aim was freely and openly to demand genuine implementation of the promises and undertakings embodied in the state constitution and the international conventions endorsed by our country. It does not aspire to power. It is solely an appeal to people's consciences and a call for words to mean what they say. What it does aspire to is to create a general awareness of the need for justice for all, and to encourage citizens to voice this demand. It sees no other way forward to a hopeful and promising future for our nation, the state authorities and the government. Its aim is to shake consciences, not the constitution. Its strength is derived solely from the morality of its cause in the face of lies, subterfuge, manipulation of people and the hegemony of police power.

The Charter is not a resistance movement, it is a pressure group. The constitution guarantees citizens complete freedom of expression and religious worship, but time and again this freedom is systematically flouted in all its aspects. The law speaks of an equal and universal right to education, yet countless numbers of promising Czech children, despite their acknowledged gifts and talents, are denied higher education just because of their social background or their parents' views. The constitution, the law and the international conventions endorsed by our state all unequivocally guarantee freedom of speech and literary expression, yet 150 of our most distinguished writers have, for the past ten years or more, been silenced by the Party for political reasons. Meanwhile, to the shock and horror of the entire world, our national literature has been forcibly transformed into a wasteland of inconsequentiality and servile ideological conformity, hiding grotesquely behind a smokescreen of official statistics about the numbers of books printed and a bizarre and unending stream of vainglorious nominations of 'national laureates', chosen for their servility and submissiveness.

The importance of Chartism is that it pricks these empty bladders, tears down the sham façades and takes the law at its word, and forces that word to mean what it says and to speak the truth. If we accept that throughout the ages there has been a tradition in Czech culture of ethical struggle for truthfulness and freedom of conscience, then there is no doubt that Chartism is the direct descendent in a long and noble line. The most recent of its ancestors is Havlíček, and I would recommend that his 1851 essay, 'A few words about legal resistance',* be given the widest possible publicity as Chartism's basic text. In accordance with the principle of *legal* criticism, all actions and activities of the Charter are open, direct, never anonymous, and, so to speak, bear a *signature*. They rule out deceit, trickery and intrigue. And since they are carried out in full view of the nation, any suspicion or charge of underhandedness, treachery, subversion or terrorism can have no grounds. Instead, such accusations merely rebound on those who naïvely and maliciously try to pin them on the Charter. The Charter was refused a

---

* *Editor's note*: Unavailable in English translation, this nineteenth-century essay argues that the rule of law is a basic condition of freedom, and that legal resistance (of the type practised by the Irish against British oppression) is the most appropriate means of defending the freedom of citizens against the abuses and excesses of political power.

dialogue with the top echelons of state power. Instead it had to be content with one-sided 'dialogues' with the police and the security organs of state power.

Even at that level, whatever happens, the Charter will keep to its rule of courtesy, openness and forthrightness. This follows logically from its moral stand and its principle of a common citizenry. Even though not every interrogator will be capable of responding in kind, he will not be considered at fault unless he infringes the basic rules of civil behaviour. This approach, which is one I have always adopted myself, is the only guarantee of the Charter's success, whether in the long or the short term. It has always been a principle with the Charter never to point the finger of guilt at the wrong persons, even when they unwittingly share that guilt. It has always made a point of addressing its remarks to those in power. And the fact that the supreme authorities refuse to speak to the Charter, itself represents an obvious victory for the Charter. Victories are victories, even when they are concealed. Because of what it has said and done, the Charter will always remain a watershed in the nation's cultural evolution and a milestone in its spiritual life, a moment when the Czech people sought to renew their moral fibre, revive their sense of rights and justice, their human dignity and their striving for the truth. The Charter was a warning and sign to the political lords and masters – all of them, wherever they may be, from one end of the Earth to the other. After all, it has always been the renown of the Czech ethos at its greatest to speak with the voice of universal humanity and to reject evil, wrong-doing and falsehood unconditionally.

It is folly to rely on totalitarian power. It only arouses fear, not respect and esteem. You have power, but no authority. You vaunt your pretended total authority and unanimous support, but this is only the product of fear: the people's and your own. The people fear your arms and your prisons, and fear for their livelihoods. As for your own fear, which is what unites you, it is fear for your skins. It is fear bred from your awareness of your own crimes and their consequences, because you realize you are wrong. And there is no way you can be right, because you do not know, nor do you even want to know, what human dignity is; because you do not realize that the authority which inspires trust, the authority which is absolute, albeit invisible, is the authority which derives from personal integrity and from an independence of spirit which broaches no compromise with servility. You are incapable of the least respect for this type of authority. You are not prepared to budge an inch in the face of demands for human rights or the slightest measure of democratization. You have degraded and debased yourselves to such an extent that everything you now do is but a further indictment of yourselves, and proves the bankruptcy of your policies. You live in a *de facto* state of permanent crisis. By crisis I mean the inability to act according to your own reason and conscience and to give independent consideration to the matter of human rights, justice and the welfare of the nation. I mean the inability to take critical stock of what you do, because if you did, you might just have the courage to ease off, change course, make rectifications and reparations, pursue reforms, and so on. By crisis, I mean the state of total abdication of personal responsibility, whereby you are incapable of planning and implementing anything but suicidal policies. As time goes on, the chances dwindle for you to mend your ways and introduce the rectifications that would save you. By crisis I mean the level to which you have sunk of describing every attempt at improving the status quo and restoring the health of national life as a conspiracy or as organized subversion, or of trying to find 'networks' or links abroad, seeking to prove that everything originates in a foreign conspiracy.

Such practices are common when arguments fail. Should the slightest speck of common sense still remain in those parts of your brains which are reputedly the seat of self-criticism, tell your paid hacks, who have surely done all the damage they are capable of doing you, to stop blindly throwing 'socialism with a human face' into their attacks on the Charter! Since when was socialism anything other than the fulfilment of human aspirations? Socialism cannot help but possess human features. The concept of humanity is built into the very concept of socialism. Logically, and experience bears this out, the only alternative is 'socialism with a brazen face' which presents violence as freedom; or socialism pulling a terrifying face when it seeks to frighten people into submission rather than consider the justice of the people's grievances. It is time to stop your hamfisted scribblers before they point the finger directly at you through their figurative or factual allusions.

I should now like to turn to the question of scepticism about the Charter. People ask what it has in fact achieved and, in general, what it is capable of achieving. What did you expect it to do? Did you think that, at a stroke, it would do away with the lies? Such questions and scepticism I consider to be misplaced and to betray a failure to understand the significance of the Charter. In my view, the Charter has achieved a moral victory, and in the given circumstances this means a complete and total victory. It has spoken the truth about the ways things are and placed them in a correct perspective. Has that been such a mean achievement? Renewal cannot commence nor even be envisaged until the truth is first stated. But since you undoubtedly require specific material proof, you shall have it. Here are at least three pieces of evidence.

First, the Charter shook the nation's conscience. It provided a shock to a torpid and dispirited public opinion. However invisible the multitude of shock-waves have been, however much its effect has been denied or news of it forcibly blacked out, nobody, not even those who refute it, harbours any private doubts about the effectiveness and wider significance of that shock. The mass of public opinion became aware of the Charter, albeit often only in a fragmented form, and the overwhelming majority agreed with it, either tacitly or explicitly. Is it a mean achievement to have provoked throughout the nation a wave of criticism and scarcely concealed distrust of the slogans and of the official news and commentaries of the 'information' media? You would have had to have slept through the whole of last year not to know about it, and anyone in that predicament is probably best left to their comforting, albeit unhealthy, slumber. The Charter put to the authorities a series of demands of a legal and moral character. Since the authorities responded with repression, accusations and victimization, the Charter has chosen to defend itself by fully documenting and investigating the cases of repression and openly publishing and filing this information. This I consider to be its second fundamental achievement, i.e., that no manifestation of repression or violence is anonymous any more. Its authors and mechanism are named and identified.

The most violent case of spiritual oppression in our nation's history, and one without precedent of its kind in the history of world culture, was the obliteration of Czech literature at the height of its spiritual evolution, along with the values and emancipatory ethos it espoused. The fact that that literature, with the help of certain writers and voluntary helpers, was able to evolve the self-help system of *samizdat* I regard as the third definite positive achievement of Chartism, even though *samizdat* is rather more a parallel phenomenon of Chartist inspiration than a direct consequence of the Charter itself. This *samizdat* publishing is now world-renowned.

It already numbers some 200 titles. All the nation's literature worthy of the name and of its great past has been published in this form over recent years. Through their failure to have displayed the slightest degree of courage or solidarity with the oppressed, or to have offered assistance, the representatives of printed, officially-condoned and rewarded literature have, because of the existence of *samizdat*, placed themselves at an abject moral level that has not even an approximate precedent in the history of Czech culture.

In view of the achievements it has already scored, the Charter ought to continue and will do so. It is frivolous and immaterial to give thought to the possibility of its voluntary dissolution. After all, apart from the objective fact of the Charter, there is the moral reality of Chartism, and this will not just dissipate either as a result of the Charter's voluntary liquidation or its suppression and dispersal by means of outside violence. If the Charter is destroyed, it will re-emerge under the same or another name. And subsequent attempts to destroy it would continue to have the same result, perhaps indefinitely. The only way to end the movement for renewal is to eliminate or correct the social causes which give rise to it. Otherwise, there can be no end to Charters and Chartism.

Quite another matter are the considerations about how it is to be run and what forms this will take. These may change. They could dwindle or grow. It all depends on considerations of need, suitability and effectiveness. It also depends on how the Charter is treated. There is the whole question of solidarity and relations with other independent constitutional citizens' campaigns in other countries of the socialist bloc, such as Poland, and to that question there can be just one possible response: yes, a thousand times, yes.

# 5 The human rights movement and social progress*

## Jiří Hájek

Now that society is coming to maturity in those countries whose official propaganda in recent years has dubbed them 'really existing socialism' – a clearly imprecise term, since their 'socialism' is no more real than the socialism of Yugoslavia or China or, for that matter, of Algeria and other African states which have proclaimed socialism of their own variety – the need emerges within them for genuine democratization in order to make them consistent with the fundamentally democratic nature of socialism. This need is also growing in the consciousness of their populations, whose basic social security is assured by the socialist organization of society and whose material needs are being satisfied in terms of consumer values (for which this social system has yet to find an alternative). What also highlights the need for freedom is the contrast between, on the one hand, the people's material and educational level and, on the other, the obstacles they face in this society in their efforts to lead full lives.

Even the authorities pay lip-service to this need, recognizing it in general terms in such phrases as 'the deepening of socialist democracy'. Indeed, the new Soviet constitution pays greater attention to the rights of its citizens than did the 1936 constitution, and much more than the constitutions of those states which were, to all intents and purposes, modelled on the Soviet system. In this respect, some of the clauses recall the wording of the International Conventions or, in general terms, are consistent with the ideas of the 'Eurocommunists'.

However, the Stalinist-style power structures have the effect of limiting these recognized rights or even suppressing them. Universally-proclaimed freedoms are strictly circumscribed (in no less universal a fashion) in the 'interests of society', the latter being

---

* Translated by A.G. Brain.

defined in practice as the interests of the leading force of that society: the Communist Party. As a rule, specific criticism is permitted only from the top downwards; only generalized criticism is countenanced from below. So long as they accept and tolerate the opinions, directives and actions of their regimes, and, when required, take part in ritual displays of 'commitment' to them, citizens have the right to untramelled enjoyment of social, economic and, to a certain extent, cultural rights. At the same time, they have the opportunity to satisfy their personal needs and wants in a consumerist sense. Meanwhile, because of the present state of the economy, particularly in the service or tertiary sector, enjoyment of these opportunities requires much time and effort on the part of the individual citizen. The Stalinist style of rule and its corresponding practices limit the citizens' choice to one of two alternatives: either to accept it (whether sincerely or not is immaterial) or reject it, and thereby place themselves outside the uniform social consensus, adopting a negative, ostentatiously different, or even hostile attitude to this concept which is identified officially with socialism, patriotism and internationalism. The second option has the effect of calling down on themselves the wrath of the regime, the consequences of which are unpleasant to say the least (albeit not as cruel as in the 1950s and, in contrast to those days, calculable in terms of the regime's particular interpretation of democracy). For people with socialist ideas and feelings, the stigma of 'anti-socialism' or 'anti-communism' and relegation to the enemy camp is conceivably the most powerful deterrent, and they therefore think twice before countering this interpretation and this practice of democracy, rights and freedom with a concept and an interpretation branded by the regime and its propaganda as 'non-class-conscious', 'bourgeois' or even 'hostile'. It is possible that this is more powerful and decisive a deterrent than any fear about the problems, harassment and discrimination waiting ready to afflict them and their families.

This inhibition diminishes and finally disappears, however, the moment that a regime which imposes on society and its citizens its narrow and restrictive, even repressive, interpretation of democracy, rights and freedoms, proclaims or indicates elsewhere, and in other circumstances, its readiness to accept, or at least tolerate, other interpretations. Even in 1948, at the height of the Cold War, when what was to be condemned in 1956 as the 'personality cult' was still in full swing, the USSR and its allies expressed reservations about the Universal Declaration of Human Rights; this document was seen to specify an interpretation of democrary and human rights at odds with what was practised in those countries, and therefore was to be ignored within those states, even though they had taken part at the UN in the work of transforming it into international covenants and supported its use in the anti-colonial struggle. The situation has been different since the adoption of the International Covenants in 1966, when the socialist states also voted in favour of them, and even ratified them and incorporated them into their national legislation. In so doing, they endorsed positions at variance with their previous official interpretation of human rights and civil liberties. The fact that these Covenants are not interpretations infiltrated cunningly by bourgeois diplomacy and propaganda is confirmed, were any such confirmation necessary, by the Berlin Conference of European Communist and Workers' Parties, which fully upheld the view that respect for human rights is one of the fundamental principles of the policy of peaceful coexistence, and went on to call for the ratification and consistent implementation of the International Covenants on Human Rights by all European states, particularly, and above all, by those where communist parties have a decisive, or exclusive say in policy-making.

These are significant factors which banish the doubts of the active socialist-motivated citizens of the Warsaw Pact countries, and dispel any fear they might have had that the implementation of just such an interpretation of democracy as that set out in those documents might be viewed as falling outside the scope and framework of socialist society, or even regarded as hostile to it. Corresponding to this realization, the participants in Charter 77 represent a wide spectrum of ideological standpoints. Their common denominator is an endeavour to induce the authorities of the socialist state to observe fully socialist principles in their relations with all citizens, in accordance with what the state leadership proclaims and what it pledged to observe as part of its active involvement in the process of détente and the strengthening of peaceful coexistence in Europe.

The reaction of the political authorities to this initiative has been absurd: bringing or summoning people *en masse* to interrogations for allegedly criminal, subversive acts; dismissals from employment for signing the Charter; a campaign of slander, accusations, and tirades, as well as false, unsubstantiated claims throughout the mass media for weeks and even months, without the victims having any means of defence; the organization of stage-managed meetings or rallies at workplaces, where workers express their 'indignation' and, for fear of losing their jobs, sign or adopt declarations drawn up by bureaucrats 'spontaneously' condemning the Charter which they have neither read nor been permitted to read; the warning, issued by the Public Prosecutor to the Charter spokespeople and their supporters, describing their action as criminal, for which no legal justification was given, just a virtual paraphrase of the media nonsense.

The point is that this was taking place in the 1970s, after the 'hour of truth' of 1968, which no 'normalization' will erase from the memory of the socialist society of the Czechoslovak Socialist Republic, and at a time when no responsible person in Europe could have gained anything from a return to the atmosphere of former times (neither Stalinism nor McCarthyism). This is why the Czechoslovak public has refused to accept the pretended legality of the anti-Charter actions and rejected the lies and slanders which were used to justify it. Despite the smokescreen of invective, slander, stage-managed 'protests', repression, discrimination and pressure of every variety, the original 240 signatures were joined by hundreds more until the number of public suppporters of the Charter swelled to 1000, although many times more expressed sympathy and support while not considering, for one reason or another, that it was appropriate and useful to expose themselves to the above-mentioned pressures.

Thus, by the beginning of 1978, the citizens' campaign had become a recognized factor in the life of the country. It is a reminder to all who hear, read or learn of its call, that it is not essential (or makes them seriously consider if it *is* essential) to limit one's options to the alternatives of obedient conformity (real or feigned) and negation (expressed or real). It offers another, third way: the path of constructive criticism and legal debate. It warns and shows that in a society that has been atomized by the regime and geared to the values of consumerism (which, contrary to official propaganda, is officially tolerated and encouraged), it is possible freely and voluntarily to opt for moral values which are closer to the essence of socialism than those for which the majority toil, and which they pretend to believe in so as to keep the authorities at bay. I have to admit, however, that since August 1968, unhappily, fewer and fewer people here are concerned about something being nearer to, or further from, the essence of socialism.

The Charter remains a challenge awaiting a response from those to whom it was addressed. Possibly, it will have to try anew in a different form or from another quarter. It is not to its authors that a reply should be directed, nor does it even have to be a reply in the literal sense. It might well take the form of a conscious and courageous stand on civil rights issues by those who genuinely care about the future of our society, its national identity, its socialist character and its humane nature. All the more effective will an eventual reply be if it comes from those whose work and qualifications are recognized as vitally important even by the present leadership. The Charter will also have to gain the sympathy and support of those in the ranks of power and in the supreme decision-making circles who have not yet been (apparently) overwhelmed by the tide of dogmatism, bureaucracy and plain and simple careerism and double-dealing associated with the post-August 1968 'normalization' process. It will have to be accepted by those who have retained a speck of Marxist thinking, not to mention normal human thinking and the ability to behave responsibly in a decent human fashion. And the sooner this happens, the better it will be for this society, and for this nation and its people.

The structure of this society, with its unprecedented concentration of power over people in the hands of a bureaucratic machine, precludes the possibility of sudden upheavals which might replace the bureaucratic machine with a democratic socialist power structure, in line both with what Marx and Engels had envisaged and with the experience of the Paris Commune (with the differences deriving from the degree of scientific and technological development, and the level of people's maturity attained in the course of the century since then). In view of the fact that, at least among the developed industrialized countries, the recognition of the status quo (in territorial and political terms) is viewed by all sides as a factor of stability for the coexistence of different economic and social systems and power blocs, there can be no hope of the sort of coincidence of internal and external factors capable of provoking instant radical changes in the systems either side of the dividing line in Europe. This is as true for the efforts of the revolutionary socialist and communist forces in western Europe, as it is for attempts to overcome the rigidity and stagnation of the bureaucratic regime of 'existing socialism' in eastern Europe.

The power structure will continue to fight tooth and nail to resist change. Nonetheless, the need for such change continues to grow in the social consciousness, and this need is lent still greater urgency by the weight of contradictions and problems in the economy, in intrasocial relations, and in culture, science and the arts. The reality of these contradictions and problems is more than a match for the existing ideological and organizational hold of the political system over a system already buckling under their pressure. Not only is society unable to withstand the strain but, in addition, the ideological and organizational structures are now devoid of any of the genuine content and usefulness they might once have had; they are also losing all their effectiveness, so that they are maintained solely by the brute force of the regime. This state of affairs is coming home at least to that part of the ruling élite that is involved directly in these pressing issues. It throws into disarray their routine ideological schemas and stereotypes rooted in their group interests. Because of the nature of their experience hitherto, the atmosphere they live in, and the need to safeguard their immediate interests, these groups will continue to seek a solution to these crucial problems chiefly through organizational and technological measures; at best, they can be expected to replace bureaucratic methods with technocratic ones. None the less, the attempt to move in that direction provides a space for the initiatives of the democratic forces and currents within society. In such situations, citizens' initiatives, emphasizing the rights of individuals, citizens and society in general, could help bring about democratic modifications to technologically-geared solutions, and act as a corrective to the general direction being taken by the society as a whole.

Such a change of direction, long and slow though it may be, can be assisted also by international developments. In the present approximate state of balance of military forces, in which both superpowers have the capacity to wipe out not only their enemies but also their allies and themselves (a situation which can be expected to remain for a long time into the future in relations between the USSR and the USA and their respective alliances), other considerations are creeping into their political jousting. These are by no means only economic considerations. In the real ideological struggle being waged, it is not censorship or other barriers to information or opinions inimical to the ruling élite that is proving decisive, but rather the extent to which people in a given social system enjoy personal freedom. While it is true that people cannot be really free unless they enjoy the right to work, education and social security, it is equally true, and experience in the socialist countries has proved it, that these eminent social, economic and cultural rights are not worth the paper they are printed on for many people if there is a failure to guarantee and implement those 'classic' civil and political rights and freedoms, and if restrictions are placed on what people may think and say.

Socialist society is far better equipped than any other society to realize this unity and sustain it. It is clearly unpleasant for anyone convinced of socialism's advantages when its opponents raise the matter of this unity in international discussions, and when their arguments are given credence by the conditions and shortcomings of the countries of eastern Europe. But if socialism does not fear economic competition with capitalism and if it is even prepared to accept unpleasant criticism from the other side when it is to its own advantage, how can it avoid conflict in the sphere of human rights and freedoms? The fact that the regime reacts to criticism of its failure to implement laws and international pledges by persecuting or discriminating against its domestic critics, and that it refuses to discuss the implementation of these pledges with its co-signatories, proves that it does not have a clear conscience. When this is done by a regime describing itself as socialist it is a disservice, to say the least, to the cause of socialism, its democratic and humanizing mission and, thus, to social progress itself.

# 6 Prospects for democracy and socialism in eastern Europe*

## Ladislav Hejdánek

Since the end of the Second World War, democratic strivings have surfaced again and again in the socialist bloc countries of eastern Europe within the Soviet Union's sphere of influence. These efforts have always been blocked or suppressed, only to reappear somewhere else at a later moment. Such attempts to win greater democracy have varied in their character and form according to the social structures and political traditions of the country concerned. However, in the course of time, the differences have become less marked and specific factors have ceased to play such an important role, with the result that we are now seeing a convergence of emphasis on political democratization, which is viewed increasingly as a *sine qua non* of a developed socialist society. The latest development to confirm this by now undeniable trend is the establishment of distinctly analogous groups and even movements in a number of socialist countries. All of these groups and movements call for the restoration of democratic practices or, where applicable, their institution and gradual assertion within the framework of the given social order, and emphasize the need to implement and respect inalienable human and civil rights. These groups and movements have already been successful in establishing a degree of continuity which shows hopeful signs of being able to survive periods of increased political rigidity in individual countries or even on a bloc-wide scale. Although it is far too early to speak of this trend assuming really international proportions, there is, none the less, a widening acceptance of the vital need for co-operation and a common platform, at least within the bloc.

The intervention of a victorious Soviet Union at the end of the Second World War, during which it had been transformed into a world power, effectively checked and halted the evolution of democracy in central and eastern Europe; this region now found itself part of a widened Soviet sphere of influence as a result of the

---

* Translated by A.G. Brain.

new political settlement in Europe. Czechoslovakia was arguably the worst hit, after having remained a firm bastion of democracy in central Europe throughout both the inter-war decades. During the last quarter of a century, however, the political, cultural, social and even economic situations in the European countries of the Soviet bloc have grown to resemble each other to such a degree that, for the foreseeable future, the trend towards convergence seems likely to prevail over tendencies to assert national peculiarities. This represents a significant change. Until now, all attempts to counteract the compulsory Soviet archetype and assert a degree of autonomy have based themselves on the specific conditions of the individual national societies. Henceforth, they will be in a position to refer to generalized conditions when confronting directives rooted in the remnants of the political and social anomaly of Russian autocracy. It is high time to jettison, once and for all, the idea that the democratic forces in the individual Soviet bloc countries should concentrate on asserting some sort of independent path, some kind of 'private' emancipation from the Kremlin's economic and political control and governance. It is necessary to examine the issue in terms of political power, and to concentrate on co-operation between the democratic forces of all the countries concerned. It must be absolutely plain that it is not the goal of the democratic forces to destroy the bloc (or socialism, for that matter) but, rather, to achieve democratic transformations in the social, economic and political life of all countries of so-called 'existing socialism'. And in support of this goal, it is essential to unite the democratic forces in the individual countries on a genuinely democratic footing and, if possible, by democratic means. These days, this means establishing and maintaining direct personal and working contacts between them, quite separate from official contacts and irrespective of them. In recent years, this has actually started to happen, as I indicated at the beginning of this chapter.

    Meanwhile, it is vital to maintain contacts and engage in talks with the western European democratic forces, even though one has the impression that in western Europe they have no clear notion of what the coming, i.e., post-capitalist society will look like. However, these days there are substantially fewer people, among the socialist-minded inhabitants of western Europe, who regard the states of so-called 'existing socialism' as examples worth emulating. The difficulties which their own political efforts encounter in those countries are quite different from those encountered in eastern

Europe by the democratic supporters of human rights and freedom. It is therefore all the more important that we should achieve the maximum possible degree of mutual understanding and knowledge of each other's problems. There can be no doubt that, in the long term, the future of Europe in the broadest sense depends on the preparedness of the democratic movements in both currently separate parts to lay the foundations of a new, more open, just and humane society. Only then will Europe be able to share effectively in building a new world and assist substantially in finding solutions to global problems, instead of constituting an obstacle as it does at present.

There are many reasons for the partisans of democracy (and socialism) to concentrate on long-term tasks and the broadest of objectives. Attempts to form a political opposition in the countries of central and eastern Europe which fall within the Soviet sphere of military, political and economic control are, at this particular moment, not only premature and ill-prepared, but actually misguided, and they are proving an obstacle by delaying the settlement of the really burning problems confronting us. Besides, the whole issue of opposition is far from clear. By its very nature, political opposition implies having something in common with the regime it opposes. And this is more than just the common framework of the same social structure. It also requires a space, a common level at which differences can be thrashed out, not to mention a whole set of basic principles which the opposition shares with the regime. Furthermore, any opposition is deeply influenced by the form and quality of the political 'position' which it rejects and confronts. On the other hand, an opposition can only play its role if the regime 'recognizes' it in some way, i.e., takes it into account and acknowledges it. All this clearly demonstrates that the establishment of opposition political groups would do nothing to solve the most important and crucial problems facing the societies of so-called 'existing socialism', particularly in central and eastern Europe. Besides, not only are the structures and machinery of the regime not ready for the integration of an opposition into the life of the country; they are also unsuited for the task. Unhappily, the only prospect for reforming the regime is a gradual change of personnel involving an increasing liberalization, or, rather, a softening of the repressive methods, so as to permit a certain limited influx of 'rational' measures in a technocratic sense. The only possible alternative is an upheaval which is inconceivable in a single country in view of the above-mentioned framework of bloc-wide control, while a shake-up of the entire bloc is unthinkable without catastrophic consequences, both immediate and long term; and only the blind can harbour any illusions on that score. If our countries are to count on a future better than their past and their present, thought must be given to more than mere methods of political conflict. The greatest failure of socialist programmes to date, and particularly of the Bolshevik revolution, was that they did not tackle the question of what the new society was to look like and, above all, what sort of person was going to feel at home in it (nor, for that matter, did they do anything to ensure that anyone could feel at home in it).

This is all linked to the need to re-evaluate the roots of the socialist movement and to seek the reasons for its numerous failures and cases of outright deviation. By now, it must be obvious to all thinking people that socialism is the offspring of liberal-democratic traditions and is far from capable of prefiguring, or of even presenting itself as, a new historical epoch or, as Marx and his supporters thought, a new socio-economic system. Socialism's historical justification is its extrapolation of democratic principles into social and economic realms and its practical implementation of them. Socialism is democracy taken to all its conclusions in every field. Whenever the settlement of social demands has been violently divorced from its democratic roots, and whenever democratic structures have been abolished in the name of social progress, or deprived of any real meaning, socialism has entered a historical blind alley and become a negative example to all who might seek to follow in its footsteps. In order to conceal the true facts about such deviant socialism, the socialist programme was transformed into an ideology capable of acting as a cover even for expansionism, using socialism and socialist feelings as a strategic weapon, i.e., as an instrument. At the same time, the social realities of so-called 'existing socialism' had to be hidden as far as possible from view, so as to minimize control and inspection. This was the principal motivation behind drawing the so-called iron curtain (which was not at all a defence against subversion or espionage). And even after so many appalling revelations, the fear that the veil might be lifted on the internal social and political situation in extensive areas of the Soviet Union constitutes the chief obstacle to extending economic and cultural ties beyond a strictly official and narrowly selective minimum.

It will therefore be necessary to subject socialist ideology to the severest and most open criticism from within in order to expose its fraudulent and mendacious pretentions and, instead, rehabilitate its genuine roots and the true core of socialism as the social implementation of democracy's political principles. There must be a radical effort to take the ideology out of socialism. And, of course, this must not fail to tackle the democratic programme and its fundamental principles, for democracy as well as socialism has failed on many occasions.

In today's Europe (and today's world in general) Christianity is the only current or movement capable of ensuring that democratic programmes are re-instituted on a firm moral and spiritual footing. But, at the same time, one must acknowledge how many times in the past Christians and the Christian church failed disastrously to live up to expectations in the political sphere. Hence, it is far from easy to predict whether they will rise to this task or whether they will even be capable of undertaking it properly. For this reason, we should especially welcome the course chosen by groups and movements calling for the recognition, and implementation of human rights. They do not consider themselves a political opposition, nor have they any intention of constituting the first rung on the ladder for some alternative power bloc. The political role of such groups and movements is obvious: they hold a mirror up to the face of the regime which claims to be democratic and humane, but rejects any criticism of its undemocratic and inhumane nature as a slander (when voiced from within the society) or as inadmissible interference (when it comes from outside). By playing this role, they might indeed begin to represent an opposition-in-formation in a situation where the regime would refuse to broach any opposition at all. In the long term, however, the principle of keeping at arm's length any pretensions to power and, likewise, any political power conflict, opens up a new dimension of political, or should we say 'apolitical', public activity. The goal of an opposition political movement is to expose the regime, in which the act of drawing attention to individual acts of injustice, illegality or cruelty becomes an instrument of political struggle. As soon as the opposition wins power, its criticism of injustice, illegality, etc., ceases to be functional since, no longer an instrument of opposition, it is instead influenced by whether, after its victory, this former opposition has put matters right, or is in fact committing the same excesses. On the other hand, a human rights movement maintaining its detachment from all political power conflicts and not striving to share power, will continue to pursue its vital work whatever the regime or social system, and in every political situation. It can afford to support minorities even when this does not generate any political (i.e. power-political) capital. The sole reason for its activity is to ensure that there should be no flouting of basic human rights and freedoms. It is then immaterial who is responsible for violation or from whence come threats to them.

The creation of a living organism of 'alternative culture' is of fundamental importance in overcoming the decline of social life and reviving it at every level. Of special importance for the future will be educational and discussion circles and even workshops where gifted young people will be able to receive instruction in subjects that today's universities are unable or forbidden to teach from older specialists who have been deprived of their jobs. The political significance of these 'non-political' activities is extensive, not only within the individual national societies, but also in so far as it holds out a prospect of achieving broader international understanding, above all within the bloc. Without the background of a vigorous and lively 'alternative' cultural front independent of official structures, the activity of the defenders of human rights and freedoms would inevitably atrophy and decline. Human rights and freedoms are particularly important for those citizens who have committed themselves most deeply and accepted greater responsibility than others; and that applies chiefly to genuinely creative people. Freedom does not consist in alleviating people's lives, but rather in giving them the opportunity to accept the most difficult and important tasks which, for that reason, are the most pressing. Only then do the principles of democratic respect for the basic freedoms and inalienable rights of every human being become bulwarks against the victimization and exploitation of the weak, and this only as a result of the vigorous efforts of those who assume the major tasks.

This 'alternative culture' is already a fact of life in the countries of the Soviet bloc. Whole *samizdat* editions of banned and suppressed authors, as well as translations and minor literary productions, newsletters, popular studies and essays, not to mention highly specialised learned commentaries and literary and specialist reviews, are all published in typewritten form. Then there are musical groups, private theatrical publications, study circles and seminars, and so on. In many cases, these are of a much higher standard than the official culture. In fact, it is fair to say that it constitutes a 'position' in relation to which the officially sanctioned productions of state publishing houses are no more than an opposition, and frequently a feeble one at that. Despite all this, one hears complaints from time to time that the human rights groups are linked too closely with the life of the unofficial culture, and that they do too little to publicize their own specific positions among the population at large. I fear, though, that despite the slight element of truth in these complaints, their weakness lies in their failure to free themselves from power-political evaluations, such that they regard 'the masses' in the first analysis as their allies and the basis of their political (or at least social) support. None the less, we should be clear in our minds that not even a cultural front dissociated from the regime and official policies is capable of keeping up its essential independent stance without a wider social back-up. This is not a question of having a large number of sympathizers but, rather, of the nature and quality of that sympathy, and the degree to which social support is firmly anchored. In brief, what is chiefly required is 'moral' support rather than political support, however numerically strong it might be.

Human rights defenders will always have difficulty in finding the terms in which to address the majority of the population who have adapted themselves and discovered a *modus vivendi* in a situation of pressure from all sides. And it is in this task that the former need the extensive and long-term (or, rather, permanent) support of those working in the field of culture who will find the words to explain the situation to the public at large, kindle people's awareness and help promote the establishment in ordinary people of a moral sense and strength of character. Without such eminently important mediation, human rights groups will remain relatively isolated and on the fringe of events most of the time. Furthermore, at moments of tension and conflict, they will be powerless in the face of pragmatic and utilitarian misuses of the principles they espouse. Such mediation makes sense, however, only on two conditions. One is that the creative people involved should display moral integrity in their own lives and work – something which cannot be taken for granted in today's conditions of generalized moral decay. The second condition, which clearly relates to the first, is that the cultural front should speak to the public at large in a non-ideological fashion. The main tasks facing us now are long term: raising the people's political understanding to a much higher level, kindling and encouraging the moral integrity and independence of mind of ordinary citizens, and promoting a profound spiritual renewal grounded firmly in the lives of the widest sections of society. Without this, our efforts to achieve respect for inalienable human rights and the extension of human and civil liberties will soon founder.

The countries of the Soviet bloc are entering what might be described as a latter-day national renaissance, in which the intelligentsia could play a decisive role, so long as it does not renege on its essential mission and, instead, contents itself with acting as mere technical specialists. The way forward must consist chiefly in providing practical and tangible proof that the state and political power are not the supreme expression of the life of societies, but are merely one function – a function that is by no means the most essential and, indeed, that will have to play an increasingly minor role. Society must gradually overcome its enthralment by a state which seeks, with the help of its bureaucratic machinery and powers of coercion, to achieve total domination of the life of society as a whole and of every individual down to the last detail. This tendency is worldwide, which is why it will take a worldwide programme to halt and suppress it. It is obvious that such a grandiose project can be sure of success only if it will be undertaken in all countries and not just in one part of the world. International understanding of a non-governmental and extra-governmental character is becoming absolutely vital in this connection. What is more, we are talking about a considerably long-term operation. None the less, the first steps allow no delay. We can never be sure when, as a result of all sorts of disorder, breakdown or catastrophe on the existing international scene, these systems will become less rigid and tense, and susceptible to the introduction of new elements and principles. We must certainly count on such an eventuality by the end of the century at least. It would be unforgivable if we were caught unawares, inadequately prepared for a new situation.

In the countries of so-called 'existing socialism' (and not only there), the state has taken over the entire economic life of the nation and, in so doing, has forced every individual and the whole of society into a state of dependence and subjection. The purpose of human rights campaigns was, at the outset, to establish the bounds beyond which all state and government intervention ceases to be legitimate and legal: in short, to prevent the political enslavement of the citizen. It has turned out that the defence of civil and human rights must be looked at in a much wider sense: the citizen is also in need of economic liberation. So-called 'existing socialism' may well have freed citizens from want, but it did so by increasing their economic and, therefore, their general social dependence. The root cause of this failure and deviation of socialism was the linking of the machinery of state and its political structures with a country's economic structures. In accordance with the trend towards total control over society at every level, the state also gained ascendancy in other major fields, such as culture, scientific and technical research, the media, education, such that it now increasingly penetrates the private lives of citizens through every channel. There is only one way to right this: by emancipating civil society from domination by the state and its machinery. And this can only be achieved by completely emancipating every main area of civil society, starting with the workplace. As a complement to the old and, in general, well-tested separation of powers and the decentralization of the state machine, it is necessary to separate culture, information and communication media, education, etc., from the state, on the same lines as the church/state separation. A consequence of this will be that the economic organization of a country will assume greater importance, since it is a task which is impossible without a certain degree of central control; the dangers inherent in this can only be avoided by means of thorough-going democratization, i.e., the establishment of self-managing bodies at every level, and the systematic separation of all economic structures from the field of government control.

There can be no doubt that these aims cannot be attained by piecemeal or marginal reforms of the existing societies. It is also clear that a similar solution is called for in other parts of the world. The route described is, as far as we can see, the only one which would assist, instead of impede, the reconciliation of different countries and societies, and one which, with the inevitable unification of the continents and, eventually, the entire world, will contain defence mechanisms against the hegemony of the powerful and the monopoly of the entrenched. One thing is, nevertheless, indisputable: the establishment of a political opposition does not accord with the course I have indicated, and nor does it answer its needs. Power struggles inevitably enhance the importance of political power, whether they occur within states or between them. The evolution we seek can be brought closer and assisted only if there is a winding down of tension both internationally and between the blocs, as well as within the blocs and in individual countries. The right way to tackle this will be by slow but steady pressure, avoiding confrontation and wide-scale conflict. Social upheavals and catastrophes cannot be ruled out, of course, but in no event can they be regarded as a solution or even as a means of accelerating developments. Concentrated, and at the same time widely exerted pressure, avoiding all excesses, may (and should) achieve concessions on the part of those in power, and also constitute important experience for human rights activists. The goal must not be to share power, however, but to force the powers-that-be into legal and legitimate paths.

Democracy and socialism both have their roots in Europe, and not only in its political, but above all in its spiritual and moral traditions. There are hopeful signs that as a result of the progressive decline of these traditions (a phenomenon which can be explained partly as a temporary outcome of social and historical upheavals and shifts), Europe will be the first to realize the need to move into a new phase of the centuries-old struggle for basic human freedom and inalienable human rights. And since it is immediately obvious that in the course of this continuing fight the existing states will look on the defenders of these rights and freedoms as a threat to their power, there will be a vital need to make every effort to achieve understanding between groups and movements of this type across state frontiers and, above all, beyond the blocs. If the trend towards international *détente* can be maintained, and progress can be made in talks about European security and co-operation, and if, in other parts of the world, the forces of peace succeed in isolating and extinguishing the hot-beds of tension and conflict, perhaps we can look forward with hope to the day when, in Europe itself, we witness the liberation of society from total state domination and the emergence of a situation precluding the centralization of the means of production, which have for so long been kept out of people's hands and removed from human ends by governments. Perhaps then we would see the end of the division of Europe. This could in turn set an example to other parts of the world of how to construct a society in which peace will not only be preserved superficially but also inwardly, on the basis of the thorough-going democratization of all aspects of life, not only in political terms, but also in the broadest economic and social sense. This will be inconceivable without the emancipation of the overwhelming majority of the lives of societies and individuals from the clutches of *dirigisme* and control by the machinery of state. Furthermore, this will not be achieved without the patient struggle of creative people and defenders of fundamental human values, a process that can only be jeopardized by political agitation, organization, coercion and violence. These human values, and these values alone, justify the battle for human freedoms and rights. Democratic political, social and economic structures have as their highest purpose the creation of a space in which to bring these values to life and introduce and assert them in the lives of individuals and societies alike: in the lives of free individuals and free societies.

# 7 Chartism and 'real socialism'*

## Miroslav Kusý

'There were two kinds of early Christians, did you know?
Open and secret. The open ones let themselves be thrown to
the wild animals. The secret ones made their sacrifices to the
Roman gods during the day and at night they went to
communion in the catacombs. The Church recognizes both
kinds. The ones who were devoured became saints. The secret
ones survived, and in the fullness of time, they spread the
teachings of Christ throughout the world.' *Josef
Škvorecký*, Miracle

The Charter movement is the natural child of Czechoslovak real
socialism. Unfortunately, that forced alliance between the powers
that be and the powerless did not produce a child conceived in love:
it is the product of a rape. The regime refused to acknowledge its
paternity and branded 'failures and self-appointees' on the unloved
child's forehead. This mark, however, cannot hide the obvious
family resemblance; it merely reveals the conditions under which the
child was produced.

Those conditions are genuinely absurd. Charter 77 was born out
of the degeneracy of post-August normalization and consolidation,
a process that has no future because it is reactionary and represents a
return to a former point of departure, which in this case is sometime
long before January 1968. This lack of future was obvious to both
the representatives of power and the representatives of the powerless. The former expressed this realization in the concept of real
socialism; the latter in the Chartist movement.

When I say conditions are absurd, I refer to the absurdity of what
is termed 'real socialism' in this country. The Chartist movement
is a particular (and in its own way, an absurd) reaction to these

---

* Translated by Paul Wilson.

conditions. It cannot be understood or explained either by external factors and influences such as the familiar International Convenants or Carter's human rights campaign, nor by general and abstract political and moral principles such as Freedom, Truth, Equality. We must instead begin with an analysis of the specific conditions.

## Real socialism

Real socialism is not a Czechoslovak invention. Our politicians and ideologists merely took it over and applied it. Originally it defined membership in the Soviet bloc: outside the bloc there is no real socialism. The Chinese reality is not socialism; Euro-communist socialism is not a reality. Yugoslavian reality is a source of embarrassment and Romanian socialism is even more suspect. The definition, however, is flexible. The bloc may expand or contract according to the willingness of its members to submit, and according to its tactical needs and strategic aims.

At home, the dominant quality of real socialism is considerably more stable. Originally it was defined in negative terms: real socialism is *not* democratic socialism, it is *not* socialism with a human face. Attempts to humanize socialism were called 'naïve, political romanticism' (Husak in Moscow, 11 June 1969). Realists at home first opposed these attempts with the 'harsh reality' of the post August status quo, which they gradually consolidated and normalized until it became in fact their own version of real socialism. Real socialism, then, is the petrification of the harsh post August reality.

Its limits are set by the *etatist* model of socialism of the Stalinist type, a model that was abandoned in its own time with loud declarations and 'overcome', to the extent that it became impolite to talk of it any more in polite company. It was replaced by successive stages of socialism: there was the socialism that formed the basis of socialism, socialism in the process of building an advanced socialist society and the socialism of the already developed socialist society. To this very day, theoreticians and ideologists have scholastic controversies over what the characteristics of a given stage are, and when a given country is ready to declare its transition from one stage to the next. Regardless of what stage they are in, however, they always remain within the sphere of real socialism, which stands and falls on the *etatist* model. And so by now, even in polite company, this *etatist* model is again beginning to be defended publically.

One indication of this was given at the highest real-socialistic theoretical forum, the International Scientific Conference on the Questions of Real Socialism, held in Sofia in December 1978. According to the Czechoslovak press, the important theoretical contribution to this conference was a paper by Vasil Bilak, which was liberally quoted and reproduced in the other socialist countries as well. The basic theory of real socialism it presents is positively *etatist*.

The classic Marxist authors, Stalin included, treated the *etatist* conception of the socialist state *negatively*. Marx said that the state was a necessary evil. As such, it will wither away under socialism, said Lenin, and therefore must be gradually cut back and excluded from the life of socialist society. Stalin fully underwrote this negative conception of the socialist state, but he introduced his notorious dialectical pivot-word '*but*': the state is a necessary evil and it must wither away, *but* for the moment we will only achieve this by strengthening it as much as possible. There is sophistry in this concept, but it does recognize the conditional and provisional nature of the *etatist* model of socialism. Bilak, however, rejects even Stalin's deference to the classics and, dropping Stalin's dialectical *but*, he goes directly to the higher stage of dialectics and negates the classics' negation: 'The socialist state is the main achievement of the working class', he declared bravely in Sofia (*Pravda*, 18 December 1978).

There is no longer any talk of necessary evil, nor of the withering away of the state: a main achievement cannot be evil, nor can it wither away. Entire generations of Marxists and socialists supposed naïvely that the main achievement of the working class under socialism would be the elimination of exploitation, the creation of a classless society and social equality, and that the state's sole function – a temporary, secondary, and servicing function at that – would be to secure these main achievements. From Bilak's thesis, however, it follows that these notions belong to an unreal, naïve, and romantic socialism. The main achievement under real socialism is the socialist state itself. Everything else, therefore, must be subordinated to this main achievement, must serve it. The servant of the classics becomes the real-socialistic lord and master, the instrument becomes the goal, purposefulness becomes an end in itself.

That this is not an accidental slip of the tongue but a deliberate policy follows from the fact that its author develops the notion very creatively, applying his positive *etatism* even to socialist man. Not surprisingly, he dialectically negates Marx's original idea. Socialism is a movement from civil (*etatist*) society to a society that is genuinely human, says Marx. Unlike civil society (which is a product of the bourgeois revolution), where one can only fulfil oneself as a citizen, the aim under socialism is now the *self-fulfilment of the citizen as a human being*. Not so, concludes Bilak. Real 'socialism contributes a new quality – the self-fulfilment of man as the citizen of a state'.

Just as Marx's socialism is a negation of civil society, Bilak's real socialism is a negation of that negation, a return to *etatism*. Just as the highest value in Marx's socialism is humanity, the greatest value in real socialism is once again the citizen. In Marx's socialism human beings overcome their civil being; under real socialism the citizen is once more superior to the human aspect of humanity's being. Gorky's romantic old saw has been replaced by the new slogan of real socialism: '*Citizen – how proud it sounds!*'

But why *real* socialism? Marx and Engels did not need this adjective to describe their notion of socialism, and they even wrote a very sarcastic book against a movement calling itself 'true socialism'. ('True socialists', they wrote in *The German Ideology*, 'always tend to treat the petty bourgeoisie as the public, and impotent and washed out writers as the representatives of that public.') Lenin began to realize socialism without the epithet and not even Stalin dared apply it to his brand of socialism. Only a decade ago, today's real socialists were shouting in unison: 'We recognize only socialism without modifiers.' Why, despite all that, did they decide to apply this word 'real', of all adjectives, to their brand of socialism?

With the advent of real socialism, a certain well-known part of the communist movement sharply divided itself off from the rest and declared the state it had reached as the *realized ideal*, as the achievement of this movement's aim. True, this realized ideal is still only incomplete, imperfect; there is much work yet to be done to bring it to fulfillment, the real socialists admit, but that is now fully within our powers; it is now a reality that merely needs the finishing touches. This split in the communist movement remarkably recalls the schism that took place in Judaism 2000 years ago. The Jews were waiting for their Messiah, who was to lead them into the kingdom of God on this earth. Some of them gave up waiting, went off with one of the prophets and declared: 'The Messiah is here!' Christianity began as a realistic form of Judaism. 'And where is your kingdom of

God on earth?', the Christians were asked by sceptical Jews who considered Christ a false prophet and continued to await the true Messiah. '*This* is the real kingdom of God on earth', the realists replied, 'we merely have to work on it a little!'

'Communism for us is neither a *state* to be established, nor an ideal to which reality must conform', said Marx. But for real-socialists, communism is an ideal that has become a reality on the way towards that ideal. This is precisely why real socialism has no future. That which is real no longer has any historical prospects; only that which is not yet real has any future. What is real can only keep itself alive, struggle for its own petrification. It can realistically reproduce, grow and flourish, it can grow in strength, but by itself it represents historical boredom. Historical movement takes place where that which is not yet real becomes real, and where the real becomes unreal. The petrification of the real is the conservative resistance on the part of given reality against that historical movement, against evolution.

Real socialism replaces historical movement with feverish pseudo-evolution. It creates the appearance of intensive, qualitative development by continuously enumerating enormous political, cultural and economic achievements: We won the election by a majority of 99.9 per cent; we've renovated a Renaissance castle that we let go to ruin for thirty years; in the second year of the sixth Five-Year Plan we far surpassed the targets set for heavy industry. Compared with such achievements, all shortcomings are insignificant – they merely require a little effort to be put right. The energy crisis is a minor detail; the fact that not even 25 per cent of our manufactured products measure up to standard is simply a growing pain; the fact that suddenly there is no salt, or nails or toilet paper is the result of poor attitudes or lack of consumer discipline. Present historical events are displaced by pompous celebrations of former historical events: someone's hundredth birthday, the thirty-second anniversary of the beginning of . . ., the sixtieth anniversary of the death of . . ., the twenty-eighth anniversary of the founding of. . . . Real socialism noisily proclaims the transition from one historical era to another – from the stage of building an advanced socialist society to the stage of an already built and advanced socialist society, from the stage of the dictatorship of the proletariat to the stage of the people's state – and yet, except for celebrations and formal declarations, nothing at all has happened. If there were no celebrations, no one would be aware of the transition at all; no one could sense an actual change. The state, the organs of power, the repressive apparatus, the same electoral system, the same compulsory military service – it all remains intact. When the Iranian Premier Bachtiar, before his fall, wanted to indicate nothing more than a simple change of direction, he at least disbanded the hated Iranian secret police. Real socialism, however, goes from one era to another without even doing that much.

Obviously, the pseudo-historical events of real socialism have no future. Real socialism still swears verbal allegiance to the final goal of the communist movement, but in fact it has deferred it indefinitely and anchored itself in the reality of what it has already achieved. 'Communism is the name we give to a *genuine* movement that overcomes the present state of things', said Marx, and by this he certainly did not mean only the state of things in 1845. This movement was to overcome *every* present state of things. Real socialism, however, has constructed a positional defence around its own present state of things. For this it has given up the movement in favour of improving the given state through both a simple proliferation of what it has already achieved and repairing the cracks.


**Idealized reality**

'Real socialism is what we have here now!' is how Vasil Bilak defined the present reality. But what do we have here? To answer this question we must consult harsh reality. For some, harsh reality means putting the prices up in stores for the plebs and maintaining low prices in special shops for the élite; it means Soviet soldiers and horrible sums spent on armaments, honorary doctorates and decorations for the Shah of Iran, the same prepared for Khomeini, an energy crisis and an antiquated industrial base, discrimination against large social groups and a movement for human rights. This, however, is not the proper real-socialist approach, which instead of applying Marxist criticism to the given state of things, apotheosizes it. The realized ideal can only be an *idealized reality*.

The greater the contradiction between the ideal and reality, the more the ideal must be pruned and cut back (a job for the real-socialist theory of socialism and communism), and the more reality must be idealized (the area of real-socialist ideology). The role of this ideology is to bridge the gap between the ideal and the reality by holding up a false mirror, in which reality is seen only as it wants to be seen, in which it is shown to be as close as possible to the ideal: it is the mirror of false self-awareness.

In this kind of idealization, real socialism employs the familiar tried and true method of *socialist realism*, according to which only the typical is real, and only what corresponds to the given ideal is typical, that is, whatever has the potential to grow towards the ideal. There is, for example, the ideal of socialist man. In our harsh reality, anyone who does not correspond to that ideal is atypical. Anyone who is atypical, and yet exists, is an 'evil' reality and has no place in real socialism. Anyone who is not a socialist man, therefore, can only be a residuum of the past, an agent of imperialism, a dissident. In any case, he or she is a foreign element. Because this foreign element is by definition outside real socialism, however, there are only proper socialist people in real socialism. What does it matter that we have to invent them and that the overwhelming majority of the nation is still foreign to real socialism? The essential thing is that the socialist man is typical of real socialism. Another of our ideals is that of free and creative work as one of the vital needs of socialist man. What does it matter that we guarantee this free work by making work compulsory, that its creative aspect, as far as most of the nation is concerned, is manifested in seeking ways to shirk it, that this foremost vital need is not pleasurable, but a necessary evil to earn a livelihood? The only typical and real work is socialist work.

And so a real socialist man necessarily becomes a schizophrenic. As a practical politician he fights against the total pervasiveness of indifference, bribery, passivity, absenteeism, theft on the job and lack of principles, but as an ideologist he oozes enthusiasm over the typical aspects of socialist work, socialist commitment, socialist unselfishness and socialist integrity. As an ideologist, he is a socialist man, but as a practical politician he is given special treatment in the government hospital, and he does his shopping in special shops, lives in a special residential district and has his children chauffeured to school in official limousines.

As an ideologist he has taken over and almost perfected an Orwellian language designed to cloud over the negative reality of real socialism and make it positive. Price rises are called 'adjustments in price relations', legal discrimination against equal citizens is called 'the class approach to law', the energy crisis is called an 'objective difficulty of intensive growth', the monopoly on information is called 'freedom of information', the attempt to practice freedom of religion is called religious backwardness, freedom of political opinion is called anticommunist, freedom of criticism is called a destructive attitude, freedom of association is called anti-state activity. It is an all-embracing language that reaches into the most banal areas of everyday life: firemen are called conflagration engineers, policemen are members of the Public Security Corps, prisons are correctional–educational institutes, the secret police is the State Security, an accident in a nuclear generating station is called a work stoppage, and when the district party secretary drinks himself to death, he is said to have laid down his life in the cause of socialism.

Thus, real socialism has politicized and ideologized the totality of life. It is total politics and total ideology. True, this totality enfeebles politics and ideology because every possible ideological and political expression has been made to interrelate. Thus, anything may become politically dangerous or ideologically damaging: Shakespeare's *Macbeth* must be banned for its mention of allied armies and Gogol's *Government Inspector* must be interpreted exclusively as a portrait of Czarist Russia; conversations over beer are just as dangerous as organized anti-state activity; musicians who play their own music and lads who read and copy out texts by unpublished authors are tried and imprisoned for incitement or for circulating anti-state material. Such an approach leads the regime to believe that every citizen is a potential enemy, and it leads every citizen to feel that, at any time, something incriminating can be found about him or her for, after all, which of us has not thought or talked in a way that could be described as slandering and deprecating our statesmen, including the highest representatives of the land and its allies?

On the other hand, this leads to the ultra-formalization of every positive political and ideological expression: that extra ton of coal only weighs the proper amount if it was mined in honour of the Nth anniversary of the Great Victory. This formalized manifestation of the ideological can go so far that it may appear to have lost any factual connection with reality. Look at the example of Václav Havel's greengrocer who sells carrots and onions with the slogan 'Workers of the World, Unite!' in his shop window. Havel has exposed very graphically the deeper significance of the greengrocer's behaviour, which has nothing to do with the proletariat, nor with vegetables, but rather with the formal manifestation of the greengrocer's socialist consciousness, which for him is related directly to his livelihood. The greengrocer who refused to display the assigned slogan, or who replaced it with a more relevant one, such as 'Workers of the World, Eat Vegetables!' or 'Vegetarians of the World, Unite!', might stand a chance of increasing his turnover, were he not prevented from doing so by immediate dismissal for loss of confidence according to Section 53, paragraphs 1 and 2 of the Labour Code. Real socialism does not rely on spontaneous manifestations of socialist consciousness by the citizen, but rather extracts such manifestations by tight monitoring and heavy legal sanctions.

What is the source of this total politicization of real-socialist life? Unquestionably, it has to do with the very essence of the totalitarian regime. For what is specific about real socialism is that once it has started that kind of idealization of reality, it cannot stop halfway, it cannot limit itself to only some aspects or spheres of life, for that would undermine the entire result. Potemkin's method can only be complex and comprehensive.

Real socialism is handicapped because it must somehow link the harsh reality of life under it with the 150-year-old theory of classical Marxism, to which it is bound by virtue of its historical connection with the socialist and communist movement. The ideological arch stretching between the reality and the theory is thus too highly vaulted, the ideological tension between them is of great intensity, the ideological wages that reality has to pay to theory are too high. But that, too, is not unique in history: most of the first Christians were circumcized.

From this point of view, totalitarian regimes that arise on an *ad hoc* basis have an easier time. The Nazi movement was not bound by any classics but rather chose them as required during its victorious march to power, cribbing from Nietzsche, Schopenhauer and others, and then installing its own classics when it was ready. The result was a deliberately utilitarian theory of the Germanic superman and his right to rule the world, a theory justifying the *Drang nach Osten*, the theory of enslaving and exterminating inferior nations and races. The ideological connection between Nazi theory and harsh Nazi reality was thus short, direct and impelling: the ideology did not need to veil itself in humanistic phrases; it could be openly cynical and ruthless. The lies it told did not concern its principles, but only the way they were realized; they neither veiled nor distorted the theoretical axioms or their interpretation, but merely what was achieved in their practical realization.

Real socialism is bound by the Old Testament, the stone tablets of Marx's Commandments. *Litera scripta manet* (the written word remains), which has its advantages and its disadvantages. Among the advantages is the fact that Marx's commandments are too general and too provisionary, leaving the field open for any and all authoritative exegeses of the One True Doctrine. The disadvantage is that somehow, through an oversight, the Song of Solomon – those frivolous works by the young Marx, as well as many of his explications and interpolations on the margins of the future organization of communist society – found their way into the Marxian Old Testament.

Real socialist ideology cannot simply renounce the Old Testament of communism. It cannot replace its doctrine with an openly cynical theory of real socialism that would be more adequate to its present reality, aims and goals. It would be a public betrayal of the movement from which real socialism emerged, a movement which it still formally declares itself to be not merely a part of, but its most faithful representative. What can be done in such a situation? Selections can be made from the old classics; a list can be made of suitable quotations, along with a list of quotations that should not be mentioned in decent real-socialist society; it can be shown that the 'young' Marx was not yet the 'mature' Marx, and that therefore the work of the former must be taken with reserve and the work of the latter must be interpreted in the only proper way. Despite these cosmetic alterations, however, the explosive revolutionary ideas continue to stick out their devilish horns, and, in their disrespect for authority and the status quo necessarily strike fear into the hearts of ideologues in real-socialist society, which is based primarily on authority and the petrifaction of the status quo.

So, because cosmetic alterations to the Old Testament of Marxism are inadequate, they are completed by the New Testament of communism, which is supposed to be the application of the Old Testament to new historical conditions, its dialectical development and completion. The New Testament of communism enters history as Leninism and gradually evolves into its Stalinist variations, which make it the ultimate in pragmatism and utilitarianism: it may now be applied *ad hoc* in any situation.

As we know very well, Marx himself did not write holy books and prophesies; his work was transformed into something very much like that much later on, through no fault of his own. Even Lenin had no aspirations to write a New Testament of communism: he simply regarded Marx as a teacher, and though he accepted him with the necessary respect, he was not pedantic about it. He was not concerned with the letter of Marxism, but its spirit, and therefore he did not hesitate to take issue with his teacher where his analysis of the new reality led him to do so. It was Stalin who raised Leninism to the status of a New Testament of communism. Stalin took Lenin's pragmatism and used and abused it both as a theory and as a method of utilitarian justification of the given reality. Using the notorious dialectic he transformed the original theses into their exact opposite.

All of this is the theoretical heritage of real socialism. Because it is sanctified by the classics, it cannot be questioned. It can only be applied in utilitarian ways, to sanctify and idealize reality in its own image. With the establishment of real socialism, the existing contradiction between theory and reality, between the ideal and reality has become even more blatant.

What is real socialism doing to lessen and gradually eliminate this contradiction? In practice, that is realistically, nothing. If something were done, it would have to be the transformation of reality in the direction of the given ideal. But every post-Stalinist attempt to do this has been stopped by force: real socialism took root with a return to the Stalinist model of power. Real socialism is the application of this model to consumer socialism, where the advantages of the consumer society are undermined by *etatism* and its shortcomings are made total. Only one of the goals of communism – and a secondary one at that – is emphasized, and the pretence is maintained that by achieving this goal, all the other ones are automatically achieved as well. Concessions to the principles of consumerism in real socialism are declared to be socialist achievements, although in fact they represent a retreat from those achievements. The socialist order entered Czechoslovakian life on a platform of progressive social policies, but gradually and quietly it began to back away from those principles. How else are we to understand the continually increasing differentiation in pensions, or changes in the way the housing problem is being resolved?

In the construction and distribution of state housing, the social policies declared by the regime were more or less adhered to. Co-operative housing represented a retreat from such policies, while preserving the right of the state to intervene on behalf of those policies. The new law on transferring state housing into private ownership has now eliminated even that intervention: with this 'achievement' of socialism, the real-socialist state abandons the right to apply its social policies to those who have enough money. On the grounds of consumerism it is undoubtedly a logical step, but it is a step away from the achievements of socialism. For those who today have the money, there are almost no limits upon where they can travel with Čedok; they can build a luxury villa worthy of a millionaire, buy the most luxurious western articles in Tuzex shops, and be content with 'what we have here now'. But who, under real socialism, really has that kind of money? Certainly not the worker who has stayed with his lathe or his shovel, certainly not the celebrated 'builder of socialism'. Far more frequently it is the one who preaches socialism, and most frequently of all, the one who neither builds nor preaches socialism, but simply lives in it for himself alone. Who will dare remind the present representatives of real socialism of Lenin's strict demand that they should all be given only an average worker's pay?

**The ideology of 'as if'**

Nowhere is any serious attempt being made to bring 'what we have here now' closer to communist goals. The entire burden of this delicate problem rests on the shoulders of real-socialist ideology. According to Bilak's speech at Sofia, 'working people in Czechoslovakia live genuinely freely and are the genuine masters in their own country. They are educated, have a high level of culture, are highly conscious patriots and internationalists'. Although real socialists, he goes on, 'cannot accept an abstract, non-class conception of human rights, freedoms and democracy', the fact is that 'socialism has introduced a new quality into democracy, the life of the state and political freedoms. . .'. What more could we want, what more is there to struggle for? 'We have solved the problem of nationalities. We have no more backward regions.' 'In our country, the people genuinely rule themselves'. (All quotes are from Bilak's paper.) Marx and Lenin must pale with envy and admiration at such a fantastic, brilliantly simple realization of those most complex and difficult tasks set by that most heroic of all programmes through which humanity challenged its own destiny. All that need be added is the apodictic judgement: 'The party and the people can be proud of their work, and of the fact that in our country, they have built a just, democratic, progressive, highly human social order, for which whole generations of warriors for a happy life for our people have dreamed and struggled.'* *La comedia e finita*, the dream has been realized: can any future communism add anything to such perfection?

And so, as real socialism in theory denies its own, immanent interpretation of its own reality, and since in practice it deepens the contradictions between this reality and the permanent communist programme, it makes up for it all in the sphere of ideology. In its entire spirit and thrust, real socialism is an ideology *als ob*, an ideology of *as if*: those who preach it behave *as if* the ideological kingdom of real socialism existed in 'what we have here now', *as if* they had, in all earnestness, convinced the nation of its existence; the nation behaves *as if* it believed it, *as if* it were convinced that it lived in accordance with this ideologically real socialism. This *as if* is a silent agreement between the two partners. Since one partner is powerful and the other is powerless, both sides break the agreement whenever possible. Occasionally, the regime threatens to take the unpleasant aspects of this agreeement seriously. It threatens, for example, to insist on a socialist relationship to work, on socialist discipline in work, on a socialist system of rewards for work performed, on a socialist relationship to the customer, the petitioner, or the bureaucrat, on socialist mass culture in discos, book stores and television programmes, on socialist football and hockey, and so on. Here and there they even turn to their own ranks and reprimand district potentates for accepting, on fiftieth birthdays, a half million crown gift from the state enterprises under their jurisdiction, renovating cottages that they had inherited at community expense through Project 'Z',† building a private asphalt road to their villa or raiding a girls' residence at midnight in the company of jolly drinking mates. But even threats such as these are meant only *as if*, for the regime does not usually mean them seriously.

If those in power occasionally break the agreement by treating seriously what is only meant *as if*, the powerless break it by making light of it and unmasking it. The *as if* game, however, can only be effective if both sides consistently avoid such extremes. The real-socialist regime is well aware of this fundamental weakness in its

---

* From the Report on the XV Congress of the Communist Party of Czechoslovakia.
† *Editor's note*: Initiated during the 1950s, 'Project "Z" ' required all Czechoslovak citizens to join brigades for the officially declared purpose of 'community development' work, such as the repair of roads and the tending of parks and gardens.

ideology and therefore it is very strict about prosecuting every breach of the agreement, every disruption of the game by its partner. When such things happen outside the ideological forum, off the playing field, in other words, privately or only partially in public, the regime essentially tolerates it. It cannot prosecute everyone who tells an anti-state joke, or everyone who laughs at it. Such disrespect for the *as if* is ultimately still within the norms; after all, anti-state jokes are popular even in the corridors of ideological power. Today the important thing is not to be a fanatical adherent of ideology, but to play the *as if* game: and that game always demands an adequate degree of detachedness.

A different situation arises, however, when the ideology of *as if* is ridiculed and unmasked publically. Those who do so flagrantly break the rules and must be punished and made to see reason. If they do so continually as a matter of principle, they exclude themselves from the game. Unfortunately, because they are involuntary partners, they cannot leave the field on their own and thereby hinder those who are still playing; this would be to ruin the game far more completely than any external observer or prejudiced onlooker could ever do. This is essentially the situation of the dissident in real socialism. The only way the regime can save the game is to compel the dissidents to leave the field, to silence them. There is too much at stake to tolerate their disruptions.

In most cases the nation is aware of what is going on, or at least it suspects the truth. Beyond that, it is inherently sceptical about real-socialist ideology and suspects it of impure motives and objectives. Yet people continue to play the game of *as if* and keep their reservations to themselves. They have grown accustomed to the confusion of concepts and the relativity of moral values. Not only that, they have been able to turn this weapon of real-socialist ideology to their own advantage. With its help, they ideologize their own behaviour *vis-à-vis* the regime and justify their way of life within the context of the harsh reality. People do not steal from the co-operatives, they merely take what belongs to everyone; they do not steal from the state sector, but merely bring their living standard up to the mark; they do not exploit patronage, but merely make use of their socialist acquaintances; they do not spread slander but rather criticize mistakes, and they are not criticized for mistakes but rather slandered; they do not take bribes, but merely receive small tokens of gratitude; they do not proffer bribes, but merely express their gratitude for positive assistance; they do not slack off during working hours, but merely participate in a social gathering to honour the Great Anniversary of someone's birthday. The ideology of *as if* is demoralizing, and not only on the ideological level. It affects the entire life of the nation in an inverted, caricatured form. Everybody who knows the ropes can do rather well for themselves. All they need is a thick skin and the willingness to pay their taxes in loyalty and conformity and not concern themselves with the regime's business. People expect no change for the better in the foreseeable future, and consider any effort to bring about change as vain and dangerous. Like the regime, therefore, the nation becomes defensive about what it already has. It is not much, but it could be worse. The *as if* game, therefore, demoralizes not only the regime, it acts equally destructively on both partners, on the nation as a whole.

**Charter 77**

The Charter movement appeared on the political scene at a time of ideological resignation, political apathy and moral nihilism. Nothing in particular was happening, certainly nothing that would attract the attention of the local public. Some young musicians, whom no one, apart from a narrow circle of young fans, was especially interested in, were arrested. After all, such things had happened before and would continue to do so, and at the beginning of the normalization and consolidation process, such things happened far more frequently and in far harsher forms. Somewhere, some international convenants were ratified and became law in our country, but by this time the nation was either utterly indifferent or was ignorant of the fact that it had happened. Somewhere in Helsinki we took part in a kind of summit conference and there was a lot of strident publicity surrounding it, but it failed to cause a stir, because the nation had long since become immune to press campaigns of this type. In general, then, 1976 was a normal year, in which consolidation and normalization were reaching a peak on the home ground. Internationally, too, it was an exceptionally 'successful' year. The world had begun to take us seriously again and the propagandists waxed enthusiastic: never before had we enjoyed such international prestige; never before had we had so many diplomatic contacts; no minister of foreign affairs had ever travelled so many kilometres.

It was into this idyll that Charter 77 exploded like a bomb. It damaged the regime's new-found renown and knocked down the façade of socialist consolidation it had worked so hard to erect. Consequently, the regime reacted against it with a campaign of hysterical vilification. This was no longer a sporadic expression of discontent by individuals who could be dealt with quickly and relatively quietly; this was a collective, public protest that enjoyed considerable publicity throughout the world. That, at least, was how it appeared on the surface.

The nation, however, reacted to the Charter somewhat hesitantly. At the official level, compulsory ideological meetings which were quickly convened, a new round in the game of *as if* began; and generally, people voted unanimously for a resolution against the Charter, against its 'failures and self-appointees', against the disinherited and the sell-outs. They compensated for being forced to participate in a disgusting campaign by harbouring private feelings of malicious satisfaction: at last someone has told the regime openly for us, at last they have flung the naked truth in their faces. In addition, people expressed their private sympathy to the Chartists by a covert handshake or by giving material aid to families in dire economic straits caused by existential persecution. There was a feeling that the nation appreciated the positive moral value of the Chartists' civic courage.

Nevertheless there was an obvious hesitancy, deriving from an intuitive sense of caution, an antipathy towards any declaration of high social ideals or Messianic missions, so often used in the past to rally people behind causes for which they ultimately suffered. Indeed, for the past thirty years the official ideology had also presented them with a grand, beautiful and flawless programme which, had they realized it by the work of their hands, would have meant paradise on earth. In the name of this programme, people were both executed and rehabilitated. Can any grand and flawless programme be believed? What exactly was the Charter offering them? Another grand and flawless programme?

No, it was simply saying that in this country socialist legality is bypassed. The constitution is violated, the international pacts ignored. But, came the reply, we've known all that for a long time and have felt the consequences personally and our everyday experiences clearly confirm this, even though we have not been able to describe it as precisely and expertly as you have. Have you just discovered this? What you are saying is meritorious, and courageous, but we know it already. You demand respect for the law, the constitution and the international pacts and that is certainly welcome, but who are you talking to? To the very same regime that shamelessly dishonours all these things when it is in their interests to do so. What are you going to do about it? Sign and distribute more appeals and protests that expose more wrongs, more abuses of power, more economic, political and ideological duplicity? Don't be ridiculous: you can't seriously believe that this will move anyone, that the conscience of the regime will be aroused. All it can do is arouse greater hatred towards yourselves. You are tormenting a wild beast with a feather and you forget that it is not he but you who are in the cage. Your effort is a noble folly, the brave act of a David armed with a sling going up against a Goliath armed with an iron club.

These misgivings of the nation towards the Charter increase where the Charter affects people's consciences indirectly. Look at it this way: this exclusive association of Chartists has decided to live from now on in truth, to struggle against evil and wrong doing. Some may have what it takes, but we, the vast majority of the nation, cannot afford such a luxury. We have children, we are building houses and cottages, we've applied for permission to go on a trip to the West, we're paying off a debt, we want a peaceful old age, we'd lose our half-price passes and our company vacations in the Tatras. We're willing to cheer you on and keep our fingers crossed for you. But with this appeal of yours you are demystifying the *as if* game, forgetting that it is a game between the regime and ourselves. True, we are not playing it voluntarily, but we're in the game and we've grown used to it. Moreover, you tell us that it is dishonourable and craven to vote for resolutions we don't believe in, to clap for speeches that leave us cold, to manifest our agreement with measures that gall us, to accept silently all the injustice going on around us, and which sometimes afflicts some of us as well. But that, after all, is the price we pay for not having to exert ourselves at work, for being able to chase down everything we need using the *catch as catch can* method, for playing our own private version of the game. By demanding that the regime consistently obey its own laws, you necessarily interfere in our private sphere as well. If the state organs began to function as they ought, then we too would have to work as we ought; if they stopped stealing wholesale from the nation, they would stop us from doing it retail; if they stopped pretending that the plans were being fulfilled, then it would be up to us to fulfil them in fact. If they started taking seriously those ideals of socialist man, socialist work relations, socialist competition – the whole real-socialist ideology – we, and we alone would be the ones to suffer. Is not the Charter, in this sense, a form of betrayal as far as we are concerned? Why should we accept its unbending principles and uncompromising stand? For a noble feeling of satisfaction because we have been brave? Or for the moral satisfaction of having clean hands and a clean conscience? But these are illusions in this rotten and corrupt world of harsh reality in which we must live. Moreover, the regime can offer us almost the same thing, and at a far more acceptable price, because it provides it to us in the sphere of its ideology. After all, everything is already *as if* it were really accomplished, and *as if* no one is asking us to change: it is enough to agree that it is *as if* we had everything.

Would that I were wrong in my assessment, but I have had the opportunity to observe and feel this attitude during my two years as a worker, among workers. Abstract moral values do not count for very much here. At the very most, moral indignation at the ills of society is a topic of light conversation, and not a starting point for amelioration. People have long ceased to think of improvement as their own business. That, if it can happen at all, is the exclusive business of the leadership. We have no say in the matter. And in fact, the Charter's declaration itself is based on the same assumption. It is addressed to the regime; it merely asks us to take note. It has tried to establish a dialogue with the regime on our behalf without our participation and therefore we have duly taken note.

Let us be frank: from the practical point of view, the Charter has done no more than that. Let us accept harsh reality for what it is, says the Charter, and merely call things by their real names. We accept the system, its political structure, its organs of power, and all the formal principles of the exercise of that power as well, and because we are deadly serious about it, we solemnly declare that we wish to change nothing in all this. We do not demand a change of rulers, we do not offer an alternative political programme, we are not, nor do we wish to be, a political opposition. We only make the most minimal of demands in the spirit of moderate progress within the law. We demand that the law be obeyed.

As a political programme, it is inadequate. It would be inadequate even for the most loyal of loyal oppositions in any constitutional monarchy. Why then did the regime react with such venom? Why did it beat the Chartists over the head with the very law they modestly appealed to in their declaration? Why did they reach for sections of the Criminal Code on incitement, illegal dissemination, subversion and many more?

I think the regime understood perfectly well that the Charter was far from being the innocent thing it appeared to be. The Chartists wish *only* to call things by their real names. Behind this touching effort to achieve ethical and semantic purity in political language is hidden the first pitfall: consistently calling things by their proper names means pulling away the entire ideological façade of real socialism, taking down the scenery and then removing the masks in this pantomime about the achievement of paradise on earth. It destroys the game of *as if*. If we deny ideology *that*, what does it have left? All that remains is the unbridgeable chasm between the harsh reality of real socialism and the nobility of the classical communist programme. *So the real issue is not proper names, or truth, but the ideological destruction of real socialism, the undermining of its ideological foundations*: this is how the regime interprets the first demand of the Charter.

Its second demand is no less destructive from the regime's point of view. The Chartists merely want a strict adherence to socialist legality, one that derives from the constitution and the international agreements ratified by the government. They demand that the legal order in socialist democracy occupy the same place it occupies in a bourgeois pluralist democracy, on the assumption that such an order would be generally good in itself if we really lived by it. That, however, is a dangerous demand because it threatens the very power base of real socialism. A pluralist democracy must treat its legal order as the highest constant, because that is what establishes the rules for the play of political forces and keeps it in place, though political programmes and governing parties may change. But the highest constant of the totalitarian regime is the political programme itself, which is guaranteed (and, if need be, altered) by the unchangeable leading political force. The legal order in real socialism is thus nothing more than a pragmatic instrument.

Although the law is formally constant (and even this is not always the case: in Czechoslovakia we have had three different constitutions in the past thirty years), the interpretation of the law changes according to the actual needs of the regime. It becomes strict or more liberal, and can be modified in this direction or that on the basis of political resolutions or directives issued by the regime. Independent justice becomes class justice and the judiciary is regularly instructed on how the law is to be interpreted so as to correspond with the particular requirements of power. A socialist constitution, socialist legality, cannot, after all, stand above the leading power in society, above its political power. They are an element of its ideological superstructure and in real socialism, therefore, they are an inseparable aspect of the ideology of *as if*.

To demand consistent adherence to socialist legality means that the law be set above political programmes established by the ruling power clique, above everything it does. Yet there is no other guarantor of this legality than those who hold the power. Accepting this demand would thus mean voluntarily undermining the foundations of their personal power, abdicating their privileged positions as creators and holders of power, and as interpreters and enforcers of the law.

Here, then, is concealed the enormous risk of the Charter's second fundamental demand. To observe the letter of socialist legality, to give the legal order of real socialism real substance, would mean renewing state sovereignty, rejuvenating and electing organs of state power, reviving the National Front, holding free democratic elections, radically restricting unwritten privileges for the aristocrats of power and eliminating their unwritten right to rule arbitrarily outside the law, and strictly subordinating the executive branches of government to the elected organs – and all of this in the sphere of harsh reality itself. Does not this modest, innocent demand almost too obviously recall other, similarly innocent and modest demands made during the Prague Spring? We all know what happened when the regime began to give in to those demands: to this day, that traumatic experience still gives the representatives of power nightmares. *So the real issue is not respect for the law, but the destruction of real socialism, the undermining of the foundations of its power* – this is how the regime interprets the second demand of the Charter.

Here is the essence of my introductory remark about the Chartist movement being an absurd reaction to absurd conditions. The absurdity of this reaction is distinguished by a certain degree of unalloyed Švejkism. The Good Soldier began to take the Dual Monarchy seriously at a time when that attitude had gone out of fashion once and for all. This caused suspicion on both sides. When he took to the streets with his historic cry 'To Belgrade!', those in power took him for a subversive and the powerless thought he was a provocateur. Nevertheless, both sides agreed on one thing: he was, if nothing else, a madman. We know, of course, that he was not and the manner in which he fought for the Dual Monarchy contributed in a very special way to its ultimate collapse.

## A disrespectful comparison

But what is Švejkian about the Charter? The Charter takes the regime's declarations and proclamations seriously, something that neither the regime nor the nation does. The Charter's demand that the regime take its own proclamations seriously is subversive, for the regime simply cannot afford to do so. If the Charter means this seriously, it is being naïvely and insanely utopian; if it is aware of what this would mean for the regime, then its demand constitutes a political provocation. In either case the regime is in trouble: it cannot retract its proclamations or permit them to be treated lightly, nor can it breathe some life into them. The Charter tolerates the regime and good naturedly encourages it to do both – and in this lies its Švejkian nature.

Though such a comparison may be disrespectful, my purpose is not to dishonour the Chartist movement, but to bring it down to earth. Even from the point of view of the Charter, the real issue is not Truth and Justice as such, but a decent and dignified life. The Chartist movement is fighting for this through a struggle for truth and justice because it is convinced that without such attributes a decent life is impossible. The movement, then, is aimed at people, and not an abstract ideal. Likewise the real issue is not Legality as such, but conditions in which a decent, dignified and humane life are possible. The Chartist movement is fighting for such conditions by struggling for the socialist legality proclaimed by the regime, because it is convinced that otherwise conditions are intolerable.

Here is both the source of one of the movement's main strengths and one of its fundamental weaknesses. The Charter proclaimed itself a moral, not a political programme, and it is working to realize this programme not as a political, but as a moral movement. In the kingdom of real socialism, the first Christians have emerged once more from the darkness of history. Those who were in the open have signed the Charter, sent the State Security forces their names and addresses, and allowed themselves to be thrown to the wild animals. The secret ones among them make their sacrifices to the gods of real socialism during the day and at night they go into the Chartist catacombs for communion. Those who are devoured may end up in the textbooks; the latter, however, have the thankless task of keeping the movement alive anonymously and carrying it forward until its objectives are reached.

The Charter's openness is undoubtedly the source of its great moral power. But it has a powerful political aspect as well. The Charter openly criticizes the reality of real socialism by holding up the moral and political principles publicly acknowledged by the regime itself, by demanding that the regime practice what it preaches. Truth and justice are not Charter inventions but ancient moral values and political principles that even the communist movement has emblazoned on its escutcheon. It is in their name that real socialism operates. Such a regime, therefore, cannot oppose the Charter frontally. It cannot publish the Charter and its documents, it cannot polemicize openly with it, nor publically attack it and refute its arguments; it cannot harass and lock up Chartists openly for their association with the Charter. The strength of this political aspect of the Charter leads to a paradoxical reversal of roles: the powerless Charter appeals to the law while the legitimate regime struggles against it using Mafia techniques, by breaking and abusing the law.

### A test of faith

The moral strength of the Charter, however, carries within it a fundamental political weakness. A moral programme cannot inspire the public to mass protests, to mass actions. It is a commitment taken by individuals upon themselves not to betray their own consciences and to remain faithful to their own principles in the face of opposition. It is an aspect of their personal philosophy. Therefore Chartism, as originally declared, is neither an organized political movement nor an organized mass movement, but no more than a free association of individuals, an exclusive community of personalities in which each person represents only himself or herself. Each person's faith is put to the test by the power of the state and its security organs, by the hardships of the dissident life in the real-socialist cage, while the rest of society can only wish it luck.

That, as far as it goes, is what the Charter has proclaimed as a programme and a movement. We have already seen, however, that as soon as it got underway, it entered the realm of politics and became a political phenomenon. Both the regime and the nation

have interpreted Chartism politically and drawn conclusions from
that interpretation: for the regime, it is a potentially dangerous
opponent; for the nation, it is a weak ally, at least for the time being.
Both sides are right. Jan Hus, with his moral programme for
reforming the Holy Church, did not inspire the Czech nation to
follow him. The nation – though it had tears in its eyes – waited to
see how he fared in Konstanz. The rulers, understanding almost as
the nation did the political implications and the subversive
substance of his moral programme, sent Hus to the stake. And
though the nation cheered his programme, the 'reform' offered was
not so close to its heart that it was willing to burn for it. The Hussite
movement was able to move the nation to action only when it
derived from Hus's heritage a broader social and political
programme involving a complete reform of the conditions of life.

The Charter has faced a dilemma from the outset. It can continue
to insist on its fidelity to its origins as a moral programme and a
moral movement involving an exclusive Community of the Just.
This leaves its political interpretation and, should it come to that, its
realization, in the hands of the regime, and perhaps of the public to
whom the Charter turns with its opinions, appeals and protests. All
that remains is for it to defend itself at its Konstanz, while relying on
the mercy of the rulers and the sympathy of the rest of us to ensure
that its moral heritage will not vanish from memory when the last
Chartist is burned.

But there is a second possibility: the Charter's moral position may
be developed into a political programme and movement appropriate
to the Charter's objectives. This potential is what the regime fears
most in the Charter and, in fact, it is increasingly pushing the
Charter in that direction. Moreover, the nation, too, judges the
Charter through this prism. The immanently political aspect of the
Charter has been there from the beginning in that it presented a
moral critique of politics and enunciated the moral principles by
which politics might be revitalized. Each Charter document, therefore, is in fact a political document, and everything it does is a
political act. Nor has the Charter ever tried to hide or camouflage
that fact. This immanently political aspect of the Charter, however,
has so far been radically restricted because it presented itself as a
moral programme and a moral movement. A moral programme can
do no more than state its principles and a moral movement can only
give public expression to the voice of conscience, in the ethos of its
appeal.

As we have already shown, the regime was first to interpret the Charter politically: the Charter is not concerned with truth, it said, but with the ideological destruction of real socialism; it is not concerned with observing the law, but with overthrowing the regime. The Charter is binding its own hands by rejecting this interpretation. Leave the ideology alone, the Charter is saying, and just make it possible for people to lead honest lives in truth and justice; leave the regime alone, just make decency and legality possible within its framework. If we understand this defence as an exclusively moral appeal, it is utopian; if we take it to be a tactical confrontation with the powers that be, it is Švejkian; if we see it as a political programme, it is inconsistent, half-hearted and toothless.

**From moral appeals to political activity**

By leaving the interpretation of its own political significance and the misinterpretation of its objectives to the regime, the Charter has put itself on the defensive. It must continually protest that it is *not* anti-socialist and anti-communist, that it is *not* run from espionage centres in the West, that it is *not* a product of the notion that socialism is eroding, that it is *not* all the things the regime imputes to it. For this very reason, however, it must not leave it up to the regime to make such political interpretations and misinterpretations; rather, it must integrate them into its own political programme. This implies discontinuing its talk about not wishing to be political and starting to articulate the positive objectives of its conception of politics. In other words, the issue here is an alternative political programme that implicitly and explicitly thinks through the political implications of its moral appeal. This means that if a decent life in truth is genuinely impossible under the real-socialist ideology of *as if*, a moral appeal for this ideology to rectify itself will not be enough: an alternative, positive ideological conception must be offered in its place, one that will correspond to the moral aims of the Charter. If the regime is *genuinely* incapable of providing decent and dignified legal conditions for people to live in, encouraging it to change will be a waste of time. To bring about such conditions, we will have to work out an appropriate political programme. All of this is implicit throughout the Charter, but the point now is to make it explicit. The powers that be, by interpreting and misinterpreting the Charter politically, have made such intensive efforts to force the Charter into a corner that the open expression of an immanent political programme could scarcely make its relations with the regime any worse. On the contrary, it could only clarify the real political essence of their mutual conflict.

A political programme would be still-born, however, were it not backed up by a responsible political movement. A free association of like-minded people, an exclusive community of individual Chartists, has from the beginning been forced, by the repressive measures of the regime, to act in solidarity, to co-ordinate its self-defence, to create at least the elementary organizational forms without which concentrated repression cannot be resisted. Intensive repression requires intensive defence – and this is already an embryonic form of a passive political movement. The regime treats the Charter as a political movement, thus compelling it actually to become such a movement. By this time, it has nothing to lose but the faint hope that exists in the heart of every hunted rabbit: that it may somehow escape from the narrowing circle of hunters and beaters.

In terms of self-defence, then, even a passive political movement is incomparably more resourceful and viable than the best free association of individuals. In terms of an alternative political programme, however, only an active political movement – one that has shifted from self-defence to a conscious, active attempt to carry out this programme, from moral appeals to a whole range of different, focused political activities, from the humanistic attempt to enlighten the regime, to actual political confrontations with it – can carry it and stand behind it. The basic stumbling block to this open transition is the fact that the totalitarian regime will not permit an alternative political programme and movement to exist. And even though it continually qualifies the Charter in those terms, it still does so, for the time being, only within the framework of its ideology of *as if*. If the Charter were actually to become what the regime *pretends* it is, it would have to be requalified as something even worse (a criminal conspiracy, a subversive centre, etc.) or else be recognized as a *fait accompli*. The public expression of an alternative political programme would make it no easier for the regime to extend the repressions, because this would create a far clearer, less ambiguous confrontation with the Charter and its real political programme. For the original moral appeal of the Charter had the potential of forcing the regime back on its own proclaimed principles. If the regime were to refuse these principles, the Charter would still have the option of adopting those principles itself by forming an alternative socialist programme, an alternative socialist movement. This would be a logical development for, from its inception, socialism was accepted as a given framework for Charter activity, even though it was understood as a socialism deformed by real socialism. In other words, this would lead to a confrontation not between an existing socialist programme and anti-socialism, but between the pseudo-socialism of the regime and an alternative socialist programme that embodies the moral and political aims of the Charter.

## A controversial subject

There is another alternative: the Charter, despite everything, could retreat to its original point of departure, and shut itself off within it. Despite all the opposition it offers, it would remain an exclusive Community of the Just, cultivating its own blamelessness and working for the moral regeneration of the regime and the nation. This would not be insignificant. History has shown many times already just how important is moral strength, the example of human bravery, the courage to stand up against untruthfulness, evil and injustice, even though it amounts only to raising the voice of conscience in public. Unfortunately, history has also shown that these moral values usually only gain such importance when sacrifices are made in their name.

# 8    Who really is isolated?*

## Jiří Ruml

In a society run by directive, power is based on a set of rules so numerous as to encompass and immunize citizens' lives totally from the cradle to the grave – and, in those cases of posthumous rehabilitation of innocent people who were executed, even *beyond* the grave. Despite this attention (or is it because of it?), the majority of citizens in 'existing socialism' stand in opposition to their own governments while putting up passively with all this bossing about. Why? The easiest answer would be: from fear. But this is neither an accurate nor a convincing answer.

While it may be true that citizens do fear brushes with authority, this is precisely why they seek to avoid them by feigning loyalty or even collaborating with the regime, and the only time they are frightened is when their feigned loyalty fails to convince and they stand at risk of dropping out of the game. Citizens know fear but they also engender it and help sow it, depending on the extent to which they have integrated themselves into the power structure. The name of the game is 'survive at all costs', and the citizens' contribution consists in seeing nothing and hearing nothing, while at the same time believing. Or at least looking as if they believe. The 'existing socialism' regime rewards citizens for their obedience by letting them enjoy the illusion of power-sharing (and guilt-sharing), while not only permitting them to raise their living standards within moderate bounds, but also by turning a blind eye to the manner in which citizens do in fact improve their living standards. Those in power do not even require any longer the degrading fawning behaviour of the past with its customary slogans of 'We thank our Party and Government!' So long as citizens set no great store by honour, conscience, truth and dignity, they have consumer socialism at an 'acceptable' price. Furthermore, this situation helps foster a general conviction that it is individual citizens' own fault if they forego these

---

* Translated by A.G. Brain.

'advantages' through their lack of discretion or failure to adapt and subordinate in time their 'individualism' to changes in official opinion (which is presented as the opinion of the 'overwhelming' majority).

People who deny themselves such 'advantages' instantly attract the suspicion of the regime (and often of their fellow-citizens as well). They are regarded as either mad or devious. Why otherwise should they want to harm themselves and their families? Citizens hanker after security, even if it is only the 'security' they have gained by adapting to the rules of a game to which they have become accustomed. Anything else is risky and untested. What is more, nobody can be sure that nothing will happen to them if they try something that runs counter to the long-established rules. The only time that citizens are known to stick up for themselves and start to protest is when, in contravention of those rules, they are deprived of those things they were wont to take for granted. This is the sign for them to protest and complain, and they turn into dissidents or drop-outs. Throughout the entire period of socialist construction, there have been 'drop-outs' as a direct by-product of running society by directive. Their numbers have tended to grow in proportion to the number and ferocity of the various purges in 'crisis' periods, when such individuals begin to voice their dissatisfaction and non-conformist views out loud. This happens occasionally in meetings, but more frequently in the company of those similarly afflicted, and most frequently in written complaints to various institutions or in proclamations circulated in *samizdat* form. This is the last straw. The regime is not too worried about 'dissenting' citizens, so long as they do not proclaim their dissent. But since it regards 'dissidents' as synonymous with 'enemies', it unleashes a relentless struggle against them.

Even within socialist countries, there is a differentiated scale of pressure on citizens, starting with occupational disqualification which combines both economic and social pressure and involves entire families, even extending to the third generation. It most severely affects children and descendants in general, unless the 'sinner' repents in time. Those 'incorrigible' sinners who fail to do so incur personal victimization and interference in their lives engineered by the authorities with the help of the police, both public and secret, and carried out with the collusion of the courts and other sections of the official machinery. Here, also, surveillance takes a variety of forms and is of different degrees of severity, ranging from stopping mail deliveries, failing to deal with complaints, cutting off phones, confiscating driving licences, summonses to interrogations, fines, holding on remand, enforced detention, the seizure of people's flats, public surveillance of homes, permanent visible tailing in the street, the cinema and on the train, attacks by 'persons unknown', intimidation of friends and acquaintances, ejection from public places, threats to employers, dismissal from employment, blacklisting from all jobs, etc., etc. All of this calls for the employment of huge numbers in the service of repression. (At a seminar in Oslo, Zdeněk Mlynář* declared that 'the number of secret police officers in Czechoslovakia is some 20,000 and they are assisted by 150,000 agents and informers among the population'. Yet the actual number of collaborators, who are not necessarily on the payroll of the Ministry of the Interior, is far higher than that when you take into account potential collaborators among managerial personnel in various institutions – such as personnel chiefs in industry – or among other committed officials, not to mention 'helpers' from the ranks of concierges, taxi-drivers and publicans, as well as prostitutes and the underworld in general. The number certainly exceeds his 1 per cent of the population, although it is unlikely to be higher than five times that figure.)

Concerted pressure on citizens can go as far as enforced exile or it can lead to imprisonment, though such 'incorrigible individuals' are generally jailed for something they did not actually do. This is not so much 'punishment' for avowing dissenting ideas. Rather, it is intended as a 'warning' to other 'dissenters' not to indulge in similar 'exhibitionism' – as the regime designates any public attempt to assert human rights publicly. Other citizens therefore sympathize with 'victims' solely in the privacy of their own hearts, for secretly they applaud anyone who does anything to annoy the regime for which they have no love and which they serve totally on the grounds that 'someone's got to do the job', justifying it in addition as a means of 'diluting the rule of still greater swine'. For this reason, they do not regard themselves as 'dissidents', although they are just

* *Editor's note*: Zdeněk Mlynar was a Secretary to the Central Committee of the Communist Party of Czechoslovakia, and a close associate of Alexander Dubček in Moscow after the Soviet invasion, and later became a Charter 77 signatory. He emigrated from Czechoslovakia in 1977, and is the author (in English) of *Night Frost in Prague* and, most recently, *Relative Stabilization of the Soviet Systems in the 1970s* (Koln 1983).

as much 'dissenters', and they make do with the crumbs of civil rights which are awarded to them at others' expense as a reward for not rebelling openly. This dissenting section of the populace actually constitutes the strongest allies of the human rights movement, even though the word 'dissident' terrifies them or, at the very least, frightens them.

Even I am not particularly happy about being described as a 'dissident', but objectively I have become one, whether I like it or not. Subjectively, I can dress up the motives of my actions in any honourable garb I choose, but objectively speaking I have dropped out of that 'majority' who, overtly out of loyalty, though actually out of indifference, accept things as they are. I have no idea as to the social origin of dissidents in other socialist countries. Unhappily, such information is not available to us and, to our detriment, we do not do enough to seek it out. In our society, however, dissidents are recruited chiefly from among those whom the regime has harmed, under-rated or persecuted in some way, and who have been denied the opportunity to lead full lives for reasons of their origins or unconventional views. Let me not be misunderstood however. The term 'origins' is not employed in this instance in the vulgar sense of class: there are no descendants of industrialists or other entrepreneurs. There are a minimal number of such cases among our dissidents, if any at all. 'Origins' here describes those cases where fate has decreed that offspring with 'healthy class backgrounds' are victimized because their parents – say, peasants or industrial workers – once defended non-conformist views or 'misbehaved' in some other way, or merely fell foul of sectarians of the 1950s or their descendants in the subsequent years.

Confirmation of my claim about the 'origins' of dissidents can be found, for example, in the list of more than 1000 people who signed Charter 77. They include former politicians or public figures, dismissed journalists, actors banned from acting, singers and musicians condemned to silence, clergy without pulpits, writers and academics forbidden to publish and carry out research, professors banned from lecturing, economists, philosophers, mathematicians, lawyers and psychologists obliged to fire boilers or clean shop windows, artists with no opportunity to exhibit, doctors without patients, and so on. And then there are a whole lot of young people who failed to finish their education because of their parents' transgressions, or who were thrown out of college because of their views. And even those manual workers who abound among the signatories, especially the younger ones, are frequently manual workers from obligation or as a punishment, and if discrimination were abolished it is unlikely they would remain in manual employment much longer. Thus, the absolute majority of those who either voiced their agreement with the proclamation of Charter 77 or in other ways expressed their disagreement with current official policies desire, on the one hand, a change in policies pursued hitherto and, on the other, they want to change their own personal situation in society. They would not necessarily end up better off as a result of such a change, since some of them are earning more nowadays with much less effort and risk than they did in their former occupations; indeed, they could be worse off financially in the situations to which they aspire. It is unlikely that poets would ever enjoy the economic security they now have as skilled crane-drivers; it is just that they would sooner 'raise spirits' than raise heavy loads.

From an enumeration of the causes, one might get the impression that people who signed Charter 77, or otherwise expressed their discontent with the development of society so far, were concerned chiefly about getting back their old posts, returning to their former workplaces and regaining their original social status. It could be that that is the overriding motive in a few cases, and evidence for this assumption is provided by the fact that some of them served the system for years as members of the élite, not to mention the suspicion that the mere illusion of a come-back would be enough to win their silence. On the other hand, if any of them really wanted to adapt they could achieve this aim much sooner merely by displaying a willingness to do so, just as was done by their colleagues, fellow employees and friends who are content with things as they are, or at least behave as if they were.

For this reason I maintain that, for the most part, our dissidents are chiefly concerned about being able to lead full lives, but not at the cost of concessions, self-abasement, tolerance of injustice to themselves or others, or denial of their convictions. The sort of self-fulfilment they seek is not that which is bought at the expense of something or someone. As I see it, creating the optimal conditions for every member of society to lead a full life marks the first stage of the struggle for human rights and is also a gauge of that effort. But I do not delude myself that this is the ideal way of going about it, that we are all clean and sterile inside. Far from it, for the motives for our actions are not, nor can they be, free from infectious germs. We do not live in a laboratory cabinet but are part of an organism which is full of malice and spite, envy and arrogance, cynicism and stupidity. It therefore cannot be ruled out that some of our number do what they do out of 'bravado', because they are so eaten up with hatred that all they want is to annoy and damage a regime that has caused them harm. It is possible that some of them have been persuaded by their thwarted ambitions that society has been going to wrack and ruin ever since they were forced out of it, and that it would recover fully, or at least partly, were they to be reinstated. On the other hand, there are those whose excessive self-flagellation prevents them realizing the futility of blaming themselves for all the ills caused by the system, for which reason they are loath to accept the idea that the system needs changing from its very foundations. They might be content to see one or two 'cosmetic' reforms but no more, for fear of discovering that all they had helped to create over the years, all they had believed in for so long and sacrificed so much to, had all been in vain. And then there are the 'rebels' for whom nothing is 'holy'.

Broadly speaking, there are only two basic solutions put forward for the future development of society: reforms or radical transformations. In our society protagonists of the one or the other solution would appear to be in the majority; and though the difference between the two currents would seem to lie chiefly in the time-scale and the manner of change, one cannot ignore the considerable role exercised by the generation gap in deciding to which camp people belong. The partisans of each approach virtually ignore the other possible currents, or at least do not treat them seriously enough. There is a large part of society, the one that wields the greatest power, which does not want any change at all, but would rather conserve and consume what we have now. But there are also other, what we might describe as extreme positions. For instance, there is a small group which would like to see society sink even further into the mire of dogmatism, who would like to see still greater centralization until the total domination of the citizen is achieved and the individually virtually eliminated. The other 'minority', though more numerous than the preceding one, considers that the liberation of people and life in general can only be achieved by way of the total abolition of all society and convention. Thus, in total, we are faced with five approaches, out of which I consider only the first two to be tenable: reform or revolution. However, one cannot rule out the eventuality that antagonism between them could, temporarily at least, strengthen the hand of one of the other three.

The whole situation appears to be very complicated, and while I have likely failed to cover all the various ideological currents, it most probably accounts for much of the fragmentation in dissident ranks. Heterogeneity may well ensure an unprecedented breath of choice, but the resultant motley character of the movement can, at the same time, conceal the 'danger' of eccentric tendencies. This is why the human rights movement has so far spent so much time trying to find a way to weld together incompatible elements, in a possibly mistaken pursuit of unanimity. Many within it have apparently not yet broken old habits of 'united fronts', so that they still confuse personal responsibility with military discipline. Not everyone has yet learnt patient tolerance, nor the ability to listen to others' opinions fairly, attentively and with respect, even when these are at variance with what they have been used to. My feeling is that these restricted concerns are holding back the development of the human rights movement. I fear that they needlessly fragment and erode its strength. On the other hand, it might be that this in fact is a guarantee of a broader spectrum in future, after thirty years of removing one shade after another until only one colour remained.

Experience indicates that the persecutors of Charter 77 have also begun to grasp this possibility, albeit late in the day. In place of the frontal attack by which they sought to wipe it out in the first week, they are starting to employ another tactic: a sort of differentiated approach, whereby varying degrees of repression are employed, aimed at trying to break up the 'drove' of supporters which its repressive methods had cemented together, and then picking them off one by one. Both factors, i.e., the structure of the citizens' movement and the victimization of it, have created a situation in which Charter 77's activity has been excessively introspective and displayed an exaggerated concern with its own cares, sufferings and minor problems, and occasionally indulged in obsessive complaining and a sort of self-pity. In short, it is defensive. Often it does no more than parry attacks from outside, and it even differs on the best means of defence, wasting effort seeking a universal panacea. This also explains why many Charter documents tackle problems which seemingly are not of general concern, and however disturbing these may be, other people do not find them so and nor do they regard them as particularly urgent. Occasionally, the topics are of such narrow interest as to be incapable of winning 'allies' among the wider public. Our fellow citizens are prepared to keep their fingers crossed for us, but that is all, since the threat of losing their 'advantages' discourages them from supporting us publicly – even though our aim is not to transform the Charter into a mass association, but instead to awaken an awareness among people that their rights are in jeopardy and that the time has come to stand up for themselves and demand remedies. Surely this is the purpose of the human rights movement. If hitherto the activity of Charter 77 has been inadequate to fulfil its role as an initiator of the campaign, it is because the document has yet to arouse an echo throughout our society. All we are doing thereby is to isolate ourselves, since there are plenty of problems which the centralized bureaucratic regime, hemmed in by its own 'unchanging' rules, is incapable of solving. There are problems which confront people every day of their lives, problems which vex and exasperate every citizen. This is the crux of the matter. The key to the future development of the human rights movement is, I believe, to be found in our ability to break down the barriers between narrow and general concerns.

Everything I have written so far may look superficially like an opposition political platform, even though the Charter Proclamation did not conceive of such an alternative and, indeed, specifically ruled it out; instead, the Proclamation offers the present regime a dialogue. However, the precondition for any dialogue is an exposition of one's own views, and if we seek to conduct a dialogue about human rights, we must necessarily contrast the existing situation with that which the regime has claimed it to be in the international arena and indeed, what its ideology insists it must be. The liberation of humanity from exploitation and the guarantee of the right to work are the touchstones, so to speak, of the respect of human rights. On that point we no doubt concur with our opponents. Where we will undoubtedly differ is over what we understand by those terms, and this should provide substance for dialogue.

Another issue I would suggest is international solidarity or, as Marxist-Leninists are wont to call it, proletarian internationalism. In the course of constructing existing socialism, this cliché always meant in practice the imposition of something that required a centre of faith, whether it involved a hollow proclamation or actual operations of one state against another. Usually it has entailed the unity of the entire 'camp' and the use of verbal and material arsenals to crush and silence a given 'sinner'. This is termed 'fraternal assistance' within the framework of proletarian internationalism, although in fact it was never anything but support for hegemonistic chauvinism. This is because, for a long time now, Marxism-Leninism has had far

186 The Power of the Powerless

less to do with ideas than with supporting superpower interests. It has also been used as a vehicle for a deliberate policy of establishing 'gendarmeries' around the world as bastions of order and obedience, and as bases for sowing disorder and insubordination in neighbouring countries. There you have a prime example of 'dialectics' – speaking of disarmament while arming oneself, calling for peace while inciting war (of a 'just' variety, naturally, in which foreign troops on another's territory are suddenly not aggressors, but 'liberators').

In the face of this alliance of the mighty who hold frequent and regular consultations on how to wipe out grassroots movements in one country or another of the bloc, the best defence for those movements must be to organize co-operation across frontiers. They should keep themselves mutually abreast of the situation and even exchange visits whenever possible, as well as share experiences, exchange books and *samizdat* magazines, hold joint seminars and other events, and so on. In short, it is necessary to establish international solidarity on a firm footing for the benefit of our peoples, as Charter 77 has been seeking to do with the Polish *KSS–KOR*. We do not have the capacity to do more at present, since we are hermetically sealed from each other. But we are not alone after all. Every human rights movement in every country of the 'socialist camp' has its exiles who have chosen or been forced to live abroad, and not all of them, by any means, have given up all ideas of returning home. No doubt, each of them views the possibility of return in different terms; after all, they left at different epochs and for the most varied reasons; they share a wide variety of political viewpoints, and are even known to voice contradictory demands. But if they want to return with the hope that the society they come back to will be different from the one they were expelled from or left, then they ought to work towards cementing international solidarity among the human rights movements. After all, unlike us, they do not have the police breathing down their necks all the time. If, in repressive conditions, it is possible to talk about parallel structures and, indeed, to begin establishing them, then what is there to prevent the setting up of a parallel international movement – a sort of advisory board – made up of exiles, in conditions which are much more relaxed then ours? This would enable them to engage more effectively in dialogue with governments and parliaments, to co-ordinate the activities of human rights activists in their present home countries, and to submit demands on their behalf at international conferences.

A dream, you might say. But it is far better than sitting back and giving the impression that nothing can be done. I recall a newspaper leader written by Karel Čapek in the immediate post-Munich period when he was dreaming of the reconstruction of Europe at a time when Nazi armies were already on the march. He wrote then: 'In a period of months or years – and this is no prophecy but a statement of fact – the whole of Europe will have to be reconstructed. By that I do not merely refer to boundaries, but to internal reconstruction as well, since the moral foundations and power structures of the whole of Europe have been shaken.' And further on: 'This process must necessarily go on evolving; elsewhere maybe, but never without us.'

Our strivings are complicated by the creation of artificial antagonisms between the defence of human rights, on the one hand, and international *détente*, on the other. The person who thought up that supposed contradiction had to be paranoid. Without peace, human rights are not worth a pin. So peace and human rights cannot be contradictory. The one depends on the other. It is true, of course, that it is difficult to accept as sincere partisans of *détente* those who oppress their fellow citizens and deny them their fundamental rights. Sooner or later – exactly when is immaterial – they will eventually discover who really is isolated.

# 9 The alternative community as revolutionary avant-garde*

## Petr Uhl

The social system in which I live can, from the economic point of view, be described as bureaucratic centralism and, from the political point of view, a bureaucratic dictatorship. The system developed as a revolutionary rejection of the capitalist mode of production and the bourgeois political system. The social revolution was inconsistent, however, and from the outset was distorted by Stalinism. Both politically and economically it led to an even greater subjugation of workers than had been the case under capitalism and bourgeois democracy. Both capitalism and Stalinism, in fact, display common features: the reification of labour, the manipulation of those who carry out that labour and of the entire society, the political and economic expropriation of workers and the feeling of alienation. Even so, the essence of capitalism and bureaucratic centralism is different.

In the latter, the central class contradiction is the conflict between the ruling bureaucratic centre supported by a hierarchical bureaucracy and the working people of various social classes and strata. The fundamental social conflict is between the nature of work, on the one hand, and the disposition of the means of production, the forces of production, commodities and non-productive property on the other. A narrow segment of society decides centrally on the means and forces of production, and on commodities and non-productive property, whereas the workers, who create these values, are entirely excluded from the decision-making process.

The two focal characteristics of the system of bureaucratic dictatorship are its totality and its centralism. The confusion of totalitarianism of the Stalinist-bureaucratic type with dictatorships developing out of other social and production relations is superficial

---

* Translated by Paul Wilson.

and harmful. Stalinist bureaucratic dictatorship and bureaucratic centralism in Czechoslovakia were established according to the Soviet model. As in the other countries in the Soviet bloc, Czechoslovak bureaucratic centralism is subordinated to the Moscow centre, which expresses the interests not only of the Soviet bureaucracy, but also of the individual national bureaucracies. The actions of the Czechoslovak bureaucracy and its centre are not, therefore, entirely imposed upon them by dictatorial fiat. The relationship between Moscow and its subject states is better described as one of co-operation, despite disagreement and controversy. The Soviet troops in Czechoslovakia are only a reserve force and have no direct influence on internal developments in Czechoslovakia.

Historically, the central European nations are going through a period of transition between a stage of overcoming the capitalist mode of production and the future socialist development, which is the first phase of communism. Stalinism, which represents one of the most bestial periods in history, is a blind alley.

A dilemma facing the bureaucracy is the contradiction between its attempt to preserve the status quo and therefore to survive as a bureaucracy, and the need for social changes, particularly in the fields of culture and economics. The institutions of bureaucratic centralism are unreformable, but minor improvements within the framework of the system are important because they encourage the development of a critical spirit, a mood of opposition, and embryonic structures independent of the state. Reforms in themselves have limitations that are well-known: they always stop – or are repressed by terror – when they touch on fundamental solutions to social contradictions. In this sense every attempt at reform has a revolutionary aspect to it, for it reveals the illusory nature of reform and strengthens the growth of a revolutionary consciousness.

At a certain stage of development, the societies of eastern Europe are going to have to face up to the necessity of eliminating the bureaucratic dictatorship. This social change, even were it to disrupt bureaucratic power over a period of several months, will radically affect all the present institutions of power, disrupt the relationships between them and, ultimately, destroy them. Therefore it is correct to term this overthrowing of bureaucratic power a revolutionary process.

The anti-bureaucratic revolution will be chiefly a political revolution. By removing bureaucratic obstacles to economic development, it will transform considerably the relations of production by, in a

sense, completing the revolutionary process that was going on
between 1945 and 1948. In other words, it will begin to socialize the
means of production. It will not destroy any social class (the bureaucracy must be considered a strata, not a class) and therefore it cannot be called a social revolution. It will also be – chiefly in terms of
its consequences – a cultural revolution that will alter interpersonal
relationships and relations between people and things.

The revolution will necessarily be accompanied by violence, but if
it is well organized, this need not degenerate into brutality nor, even
less, into terror. Revolutions do not happen because revolutionaries
call for them, nor are they a result of indoctrinating the masses.
They happen when people choose violence and use it to take power
away from those who hold it. They happen when the broadest strata
of people can no longer bear their oppression, when the incompe-
tence of the rulers goes hand in hand with brutality and terror. The
role of the revolutionaries is to indicate to the masses in revolt the
best way to go which means, among other things, trying to limit
revolutionary violence to the smallest necessary degree and consistently opposing brutality and terror, which even when it is a
necessary factor in the revolution's survival, damages the revolutionary process because it tends to degenerate it.

There are many conceivable varieties of the revolutionary
process, both internally and internationally. The anti-bureaucratic
revolution in Czechoslovakia, however, can only hope to succeed if
it does not limit itself to this country, but becomes part of an
international revolutionary process.

History has shown that anti-capitalist and anti-bureaucratic revolution has always favoured self-management, frequently posing
self-management as the only possible framework for the new organization of life. This was so in the pre-revolutionary ferment among
Czechoslovak workers in 1968–9, and it will be so in the Czechoslovak anti-bureaucratic revolution, where of course a parliamentary or other representative system may emerge parallel to it and
even dominate it for a time.

Parliamentary government means government by the leadership
(i.e. of representatives, a presidium or a politbureau) of one or more
political parties. At the same time, parliamentary government does
nothing to develop forms of direct democracy which can help
emancipate society and individuals and overcome alienation. Social
(not merely economic) self-management is, on the other hand, a
combination of direct and indirect forms of democracy. Indirect

(representative) democracy means a system of workers (and other) councils, horizontally co-ordinated, which would invest authority in a general council to replace today's legislative and executive state organs. It would be a democracy of the productive forces complemented by the territorial principle. The indirect democracy would be complemented by elements of direct democracy: referenda, even at the local level, public opinion polls whose results are binding, the direct administration of things by groups of people, and so on. Social self-management is not a panacea: it is only worthy of support if it guarantees the continual expansion of direct democracy in favour of the gradual dismantling of representative democracy. The self-management system is consistently pluralistic: political parties, which would function more as political clubs or movements, would present proposals but would not actually run society, as they do in the bourgeois democratic system.

In the crisis that will precede the revolutionary process, organs of self-management will appear in the workplaces: strike committees, revived trade unions, workers' councils. Their activities will have to be co-ordinated with that of workers in other enterprises so that a workers' council with society-wide authority can be created as rapidly as possible. The workers – and eventually other citizens as well – must be able to take over the military and reconstruct it to fall in line with the economic structure of the country. The permanent standing army and the police will also be abolished. And, finally, it is important that self-management be not limited to the economic sphere but that workers' councils become centres of political power, causing a further decentralization of power and the creation of many different foci of popular initiative.

The driving force in the revolutionary society will be its contradictions: the political antagonism, already material, between the parliamentary system and self-management and, in the economic sphere, between the technocratic and democratic production tendencies. There will also be conflicts between nationalist and internationalist concepts, between different notions of consumerism and ecology, conflicts over competence and problems of the emergent particularism of confederated producers, and so on.

The future course of events depends not only on the degree to which living conditions remain bearable and on the international situation, but also on the daily activity of each of us. And that, in turn, depends not only on our abilities, education and vision, but on our determination and will to transform the social conditions in which we live.

Václav Benda, a Catholic intellectual and revolutionary demo-crat, has written an essay, *Parallel Polis*,* in which he essentially calls for organized, parallel activities independent of the state, in which the various currents gradually form a broad, unlimited asso-ciation of people, a community, a *polis*. Benda's essay met with a positive response from the Czechoslovak opposition. His project was based on his experiences in Charter 77 and on the experiences of the Czech cultural underground and other movements and initia-tives, though he was certainly looking at the Polish experience as well. Benda's project is reminiscent of 'alternative' social activities in capitalist societies. There, however, they have an ambivalent character. Under a bureaucratic dictatorship the 'parallel polis' is different in many ways.

In capitalist society, alternative life-styles and communities are created without regard for 'the establishment', that is, for the rest of society and its organizations. They simply exist alongside society and in no way try to disturb it. The political establishment leaves these groups alone: they are a welcome safety valve that drains away some of the general discontent with social conditions. The hall-marks of alternative communities in the capitalist world are political and social passivity, the exclusivity of the voluntary ghetto and escape from the real world. It would be wrong, however, to see the notion of 'alternatives' as a reactionary utopia. Alternative commu-nities provide the soil in which is nurtured the critical spirit that can influence the whole of society. They have a potential in the future anti-capitalist revolutionary process, for they are ultimately a potential corrective to the future revolution and represent the hope that it will not be crippled by bureaucratic degeneration.

In its liberal and bourgeois-democratic forms, capitalism can coexist with these alternative ghettos. Bureaucratic dictatorships of the Stalinist type cannot. Here any form of expression that is not under bureaucratic control is necessarily disruptive. Every indepen-dent act, both individual and, even more, collective, consequently provokes conflict with bureaucratic power, regardless of whether it is deliberately aimed against the system or whether it merely desires to exist *an sich*, 'outside', without provoking conflicts. Constant

---

* *Editor's note*: Václav Benda's highly influential *Parallel Polis* was written in May, 1978, and thereafter circulated in *samizdat* form in Czechoslovakia. An English translation is published in *Palach Press Bulletin* (London, 1979).

effort at achieving independent (critical) expression or independent forms of living means constant conflict with state power, and that in turn broadens and deepens people's awareness. The associations which thus arise – like Charter 77, the Czech cultural underground, the Committee for the Defence of the Unjustly Prosecuted, the Charter working groups and other semi-official and unofficial associations of friends – create internal relationships, rather like a club, movement or organization, which offer a genuine alternative to the forms of social life that have been fettered and deformed by bureacratic power and the middle-class conventions it supports. Benda's 'parallel structures' should therefore really be called *alternative* structures or an *alternative* polis, just as communities in the western sense may frequently, with more accuracy, be termed *parallel* organisms.

The capacity to evoke conflict and social awareness is the primary justification for alternative forms of living or, if you like, of the 'parallel *polis*'. The second condition is openness, both in principle and in practice, in the sense that more and more people should be able to participate. Moreover, the alternative society should have an influence on people who do not participate directly in its work. This openness is not merely a consequence of conscious will; it is also a result of the balance of power between the alternative movement and the state that is trying to shut it away in a ghetto.

The Czech cultural underground is an association or movement that seeks an alternative to consumerism, middle-class attitudes and hypocritical morality. It attempts to fulfill itself through independent cultural expressions. In this it is closer to alternative communities of the western type than Charter 77, which has no equivalent in the bourgeois democracies. Nevertheless, the condition of 'automatic' conflict holds true and it would seem that the underground is, in many ways, more open than Charter 77, which though professing openness, has so far been kept in relative isolation by the repressive apparatus. However, there are negative expressions of the 'western type' to be found in the Czech cultural underground as well: its mere existence seems to be a reason for self-congratulation, and there is an exclusiveness about it, an escape from its inability to solve practical problems into the world of dreams. The underground, however, is aware of the danger in these tendencies, and this promises further development.

Negative 'ghetto' qualities have affected Charter 77 as well. The stress on Chartist morality and the explanation of Charter 77, incorrectly, as the consequence of a sudden decision to 'live within the truth' (both vulgarizations of Jan Patočka's intellectual heritage), create the feeling of moral exclusivity among the Chartists. As Václav Havel points out, the signatories of Charter 77 are just like the rest of the population; the only difference is that they say out loud what the rest only think. The conditions of life are compelling people to say what they think more and more frequently and loudly.

It would be wrong to claim that the idea of a parallel *polis* is accepted by all signatories of Charter 77. There are still powerful reformist currents inside the Charter and the Czechoslovak opposition. Interestingly, young people in the Czech cultural underground criticize these reform efforts as 'political' while, in fact, they are the ones making the real politics, or at least anticipating it, if we understand politics as an effort to emancipate the oppressed and the manipulated, and do not confuse politics with a desire for power. Although a critique of this reformist trend does not fall within the scope of my essay, it is worth noting that a spirit of conspiracy, sectarianism and 'moral' exclusivity is a feature of the reformist environment. Conspiratorial methods, often the only possible way to get things done given the conditions in Czechoslovakia, considerably slow down the evolution of alternative projects like the parallel *polis*. The principle of operating in the open, which Charter 77 established to a broader extent, must be strengthened and extended.

Self-organization is one essential condition for the further development of alternative communities. The approaches taken in Poland between 1976 and 1979 cannot be imported mechanically to Czechoslovakia because it is technically impossible, although there is nothing to prevent us trying to apply the Polish experience to a far more modest extent everywhere possible.

In any community, democracy is created through democratic rules. Such rules will only work, however, if the community is organized. Thus, if alternative communities are to be the embryos of a future society, democracy *and* self-organization are utterly essential. Self-organization must gradually push out spontaneity.

Should the alternative movement limit its sphere of interest to human rights? Charter 77 is so limited while the Czech cultural underground has already directly realized some democratic freedoms. The Charter is limited because under the existing social conditions, it cannot force the regime to recognize some of the rights enshrined in international covenants. Yet it can achieve minor successes in the area of human rights. Its main significance, however, lies in the fact that it is helping to bring closer a gradual recognition of all the natural rights of human beings, which I consider to be the real point of such a revolution. It is also becoming more and more an alternative community that anticipates the future. The Czech underground has a role similar to that of Charter 77 but, even more than the Charter, it is a school of independence even thöugh it will never achieve the emancipation for which it strives. As the creation of Solidarity in Poland indicates, the parallel *polis* can potentially expand to include the trade union movement, the Church, the student movement, the school system, and even include local government and agricultural production. It would seem, however, that as soon as it touches economic questions, a showdown with the bureaucratic power takes place. Thus, I do not see alternative modes of production, transportation, trade and even an educational system as practicable. It would be more natural to bring the economy under the control of democratic organizations that have been established and tested during the parallel *polis* phase. An alliance of producers would provide an alternative to bureaucratic centralism. The relationship between an official (state) economy and its alternative, however, cannot be a parallel one: they will be separated by revolutionary transformation.

It is wrong to imagine that under a bureaucratic dictatorship alternative associations will continue to grow until they affect practically the whole of society. It is utopian to assume that society will 'merge' with the parallel *polis*, thus causing the withering away of the state and its bureaucratic machinery. On the contrary, the parallel *polis* will always be a minority phenomenon. It is only during the revolutionary process that it will rapidly 'absorb' society, which will create, on the islands of alternative associations and activities, a *polis* which is no longer parallel, but an authentic *polis* of free people. Therefore both the quality of the alternative associations of today (their inner *democratic* and anti-authoritarian structure) and their orientation towards creative work and working relationships, are immensely important, for working relationships stand to be changed most by the anti-bureaucratic revolution, and this will happen in the way suggested by pre-revolutionary, alternative activity.

Except for the field of economics, where we will have to be content with preparatory work (activity in independent unions, demands for workers' control), and except for alternative activities of a peripheral nature (particularly in the cultural field, in the production of books and magazines, but also in common work, construction, etc.), alternative activity will thus affect all areas of social life. This is even true of foreign policy: an alternative foreign policy is an essential condition in any parallel *polis* that tries to be a genuine alternative. Relationships between Charter 77 and the Polish democratic opposition have immensely strengthened Charter 77. It makes us feel good to know that Polish workers, students and Catholics are on our side. And that feeling comes after the first handshakes, the first hours of conversation, the first months of thinking about Polish and other common problems. These contacts should result in concrete common ideas about future relations and modes of co-operation between the populations of Poland and Czechoslovakia, about the future elements of an international *polis*. An alliance of individual national alternative communities, which must not remain limited to Poland and Czechoslovakia, is today a powerful anti-bureaucratic factor, and is an essential condition for any future revolutionary process.

The use of the term 'citizens' initiative' for the theme of this collection of essays has different shades of meaning. The word 'initiative' usually refers to an impulse, an action or a campaign, and is not very appropriate for an unorganized, spontaneous movement such as the Czech cultural underground, for an institutionalized association of people with a limited range of activities such as Charter 77, or even for an organization with specific aims like the Committee for the Defence of the Unjustly Prosecuted. For the future, we must also be thinking about 'initiatives' like independent trade unions, political discussion clubs and parties. The term 'citizens' initiative', which unfortunately does not express the lasting nature of the alternative associations, is used in Czechoslovakia to stress that a given association is not an organization. At the same time, it is precisely the lack of such organization that is the Czechoslovak human rights movement's greatest weakness. The word 'citizen' is equally inappropriate: today, a citizen is understood more as the subject of a state than as the member of a community (the Czech language preserves that original sense of the word: citizen – *občan*; community – *obec*); civil rights are only an aspect of human rights. This is why I use the expression 'alternative community' rather than 'citizens' initiative'.

History suggests that the revolutionary process which is awaiting Czechoslovakian society will be more peaceful and orderly to the extent that it is organized, that is, if the people who bring it about can agree on the most acceptable forms of revolution (which, among other things, will limit violence to a minimum), and if they can create structures that will make such an agreement possible. In the past, the avant-garde, usually a revolutionary party, has assumed the role of organizer. However, in all independent or independent proletarian revolutions (Russia, China, Yugoslavia, Cuba) this party always became the cradle of a bureaucracy. It seems that in eastern Europe this lesson has been learned. Only a community consisting of both informal and institutionalized groups with experience in action and practice can become the new type of avant-garde that can genuinely express the main interests of oppressed society. In such a revolutionary avant-garde, various alternative associations can join forces informally. Such revolutionary associations do not exclude the organizing of various groups, and perhaps even of political parties. On the contrary, such groups, often in connection with other groups, may play an important role in the anti-bureaucratic struggle. In the conditions in which we live, they will frequently regroup and divide, unite and separate once again. This will not harm the cause. Most of those changes need not be institutionalized at all, for their influence will spread among representatives of groups or trends. Public opinion itself will judge which of the points of view it will accept, whom it will support, from whom it will accept advice, in other words, who in the given situation best fulfils the role of the revolutionary avant-garde. The question should not be who this avant-garde is, but which problems are being dealt with, by which alternative association (or community), and in what way? These questions are asked by the revolutionary avant-garde itself, particularly when its component parts – the individual alternative associations – work closely together and accept the need for a certain institutional expression. In Charter 77 each group, circle, current or more or less accidental grouping of friends is revolutionary in its own way, whether it realizes this or not.

In a bureaucratic dictatorship, therefore, the revolutionary avant-garde of society is located in the independent alternative associations, in their national and international alliances, in their improvement and expansion, in their rapid proliferation, and in their impact on society as a whole. This is the beginning of the revolutionary process.

# 10  Thoughts inside a tightly-corked bottle*

## Josef Vohryzek

In Czechoslovakia, the conditions of life are in some respects very peculiar. Sometimes we encourage each other so effectively that it seems, even to us, that we live in the best of all possible worlds. This is because our misery is artificial. It is not caused by famine or war, but by a deliberate regression, an artificial reduction of the vital functions, an entirely new and unprecedented form of retrogression that expends unheard of amounts of energy in compelling people to be passive.

Charter 77 is an act of self-defence. It came into being solely because the laws in Czechoslovakia are not observed. All the other faults, wrongs and inadequacies that cannot be considered direct results of this illegality could never have inspired unity among people whose opinions and attitudes differ so widely as those who are grouped around the Charter. The illegalities that the Charter highlights form a logically unified entity. They are not a result of carelessness on the part of the state machinery, nor of confusion arising from negligence. They form a purposefully constructed system: they *are* the 'order'.

Nevertheless, Charter 77 is merely a legal expression of the will to demand proper citizens' rights; it is *not* an appeal to eliminate the power structures without which these systematic illegalities would be no more than anomalous abuses which, lacking deeper roots in Czechoslovakia, could therefore never have lasted so long.

This legalism does not merely make a virtue of necessity; its background lies deep in the national experience. A violent *coup d'état*, which could never be achieved spontaneously by enraged citizens but only by the actions of armed units, could just as easily replace the mass discrimination of today with a new wave of discrimination

---

* Translated by Paul Wilson.

that would only deepen the social degeneration. The purpose of Charter 77 is to oppose this degeneration, which is a result of the apathy of those who do not demand their rights.

Czechoslovakia – as do other states in the Soviet bloc – has the most powerful machinery of violence that ever existed to protect those in power. This is because those who created this machinery have learned more from historical revolts, *coups d'état* and revolutions than any other power élite in the past. Their 'historical solidarity' with all ruling groups who have ever been swept from power goes deeper than any ideological differences, because it is consistent with the principle of self-preservation. Moreover, the machinery of violence is continually expanding because, among other things, the group in power feels no reliable support from the population. The movement from which the ideology of the present regime derived originally has been marked from the outset by a traumatic awareness of an incongruity between its 'historical mission' and the possibility of ever gaining a sufficiently broad and spontaneous support to carry that mission out. Various forms of police activity, therefore, have always appeared in utter secrecy even before power was seized, and subsequently, the police apparatus has expanded to such an unprecedented degree, partly because the official ideology contains nothing to inhibit such a development. The material, and ultimately the moral, burden that this places on society has no precedent in history. To make this burden bearable, the totalitarian state has had to raise the policing function to one of the greatest virtues. In television films and propaganda programmes, it is no longer a worker or a party secretary who embodies all the finest human qualities, but a cop. The vast amounts of energy spent on maintaining 'order', however, contribute nothing to the development of society because its sole purpose is to prevent change. This is also the regime's main concern, and in recent decades it has been ostentatiously stressing those aspects of the ideology. Life without change is unattainable, of course, but it is possible to permit only unavoidable changes, changes that can be approved of and 'vindicated' after they have already happened on their own and can no longer be kept a secret. And, to the contrary, it is possible to eliminate changes brought about by human will, even though it is immensely difficult and expensive.

The meaningful activity of a citizen as a member of the *polis*, however, consists exclusively in creating change. The civic will to create change has, in the past, achieved its purposes in a variety of ways, but the choice as to whether peaceful or violent means were used was always made on the basis of what those purposes were, and how great was the arrogance of those who wanted to prevent the changes from taking place. Progress in the technology of violence, however, has kept pace with progress in the field of production, and the ancient fear of retribution in the other world has meanwhile been replaced by fear of outright non-existence. Today, the violence of the Parisians who stormed the Bastille seems almost as innocent as a knife in the hands of a cook in a kitchen.

*Effective* violence as a form of civilian resistance has lost its human dimensions. The rhetorical arguments of terrorist groups who operate today in various corners of the world are frequently no more demagogic than the slogans of those who fought on the barricades in the nineteenth century. Yet all such groups, without exception, use fascist methods because they put all their energy into a confrontation with institutional violence, and therefore they degenerate morally.

The pre-1968 totalitarian regime in Czechoslovakia demanded that everyone act in conformity with aims it laid down itself. Non-participation was an expression of disagreement that weakened the totality because it prevented it from achieving its mission, which was to embrace everything, bring everyone together, represent a single will, in short, to be total. The totalitarianism of today has given up its former goal, and now demands precisely the opposite: a total vacuum of civic will, a *perpetuum silentium*, passivity and quiescence. Quiet disagreement is no longer considered an act of civic resistance and has come to be generally accepted by the regime. There is no forum in which to express one's discontent, and silent disagreement is one of the pillars of totalitarian power.

Charter 77 is a response to this development. It encourages people to act legally and, at the same time, appeals to the legal code already in force, refusing to acknowledge the fact that the regime treats it only as a stage prop à la Potemkin.

The activities of the different groups associated with Charter 77 are varied in the extreme, but they have one remarkable feature in common. In most cases Charter activity consists in people practising their original professions. The fact that simply doing what one was originally trained to do constitutes an expression of resistance to totalitarianism throws a sharp light on the character of the entire social system. There was a time when the bloc of states to which Czechoslovakia belongs could boast of a great innovation:

legislating the right of every citizen to work. But from the start this legal guarantee was used, to an enormous extent, in a way quite opposite from the way in which it was presented to the world. In the developed countries, where the right to work is not enshrined in law, there is nevertheless a general and effective notion as to what constitutes such a right. This notion is expressed in how unemployment statistics are kept, in how unemployment benefits are distributed, in how the problem of unemployment is treated by governments and oppositions, and so on. From all these positions and practical measures, we may conclude that, although the right to work does not legally exist, it is in fact understood as the right to a real job opportunity in one's own profession and according to one's own choice. Unemployed people are understood to be those who have not found a job in their own field, or those who were offered such work but who rejected it for good reasons, the range of generally acceptable reasons being very liberal.

In Czechoslovakia the right to work means that renowned surgeons or violinists may be forced to make a living at manual labour and still count themselves fortunate that they can at least earn their keep that way. If surgeons or violinists do practise their real professions, they are not exercising a right, but enjoying a privilege that can be denied them at any time. In the course of the 1960s, only those against whom this elementary rule of totalitarianism was used were aware of its full extent, whereas in the 1970s everyone knows it, including children.

Working at one's real profession was very probably made a privilege that can be denied the disobedient because otherwise there would be nothing left to take away from people. The levelling of the living standard has gone so far that everyone is in the same boat and the totalitarian power must therefore endow even the most natural social functions with the qualities of privilege.

In the early 1960s, when even the leadership of the state began to feel the effects of that levelling, they initiated what they called 'de-levelling', which, of course, attacked the problem from the silliest possible end, that of wages. The real essence of levelling, in fact, does not lie in reducing the differences in people's ability to consume, but in making sure that everyone is equally without rights, that there is an equally small area for everyone to exercise their initiative or realize their ideas – even the most insignificant ideas – and that the pressure of the system, compelling everyone to behave like everyone else and to desire what everyone else desires, bears down upon everyone with equal force, on dish washers and company managers alike, on poets and officers of the State Security police.

The principle of the closed society, however, requires not only that everyone be in the same boat, but also that no one be able to confer with anyone else or even – perish the thought – form associations. Therefore a levelling process that rejects equality while demanding uniformity can be maintained only by the continuous renewal of particularization. The highest expression of this is the so-called *nomenklatura* system. At the beginning, it only involved those who held leading positions of great importance, but in the past decade, in the field of culture at least, it has been expanded to include a vast number of subordinate employees who have no powers of decision whatsoever, but whose work, given the regime's insensate fear of culture, is considered particularly sensitive. It is surprising that independent political scientists do not study this utterly unique institution more closely, and that so far no one has attempted a thorough description of it. This creature of purely feudal imagination is said to have been introduced by Peter the Great, but whoever it was, he displayed unquestioned genius, for the *nomenklatura* system functions to this day even in industrially advanced Czechoslovakia. It functions destructively, of course, but it combines destruction with self-preservation and thus, despite being an anachronism, it persists in a way that other feudal institutions have not.

Particularization, however, does not consist merely in separating the populace into closed 'estates', in which movement from one 'estate' to another – for instance, the promotion of an 'unvetted' person to a 'nomenclatured' position – is far more difficult than it ever was in the age of feudalistic class society. The most obvious consequence of particularization is the sundering of spontaneously appearing networks of relationships which are the essence of social being based on the constant appearance of new forms of co-operation.

The artificial isolation of individual categories of people from each other strengthens the sense of mutual support in natural associations such as professional groups. In this way, too, co-operation of a type that is threatening to those in power is created. But professions cannot be broken up or banned the way associations and magazines can. The totalitarian state is in constant organizational conflict with some professions because by their very nature they are too closely involved in the gathering of undesirable information, so that neither monitoring nor purges, nor even the conformism of the professionals themselves can prevent this from happening for long. Oddly enough, however, totalitarian power does not try to disband such professions, although in fact it has no need for them at all.

The citizens of a totalitarian state who have had the good fortune to land an interesting or advantageous job cling to it because it represents the only thing they can ever achieve in society. If, moreover, their job allows them to do creative work and thus to function in an area where they can make independent decisions and so partially escape the barrack-like atmosphere of the closed society, then their work becomes a substitute for a whole number of vital functions and rights, the loss of which they would otherwise find it hard to come to terms with.

Belonging to a professional group, therefore, is a far more important part of a person's identity than it is in open societies where, by contrast, one's personal identity is often reinforced by the ease with which one can change roles, professions, areas of work and milieu, and so on. In a closed society, people do not go out of their way to seek a change in roles or fields, not even when their present profession provides them with no particular advantages, because they lack a basic emotional fund of self-confidence and security which such a desire for change assumes.

Denying people the right to practice their own profession is, it turns out, disadvantageous, because then there is nothing left to deny them and, therefore, there are certain things they cannot be compelled to do.

Practising one's original profession in the various activities within the circles of Charter 77 therefore means maintaining a right that has been usurped by the state. It is an expression of civic resistance, but at the same time it reproduces some of the retrograde elements that the totalitarian state has imposed upon society. Human beings are certainly more than just a product of the system or the conditions in which they live, yet they realize their potential in a game with an opponent not of their own choosing; even in their triumphs, they do not cease to relate to what they have transcended. In freer conditions, the feeling of civic responsibility for what happens in one's own country and in the world at large is expressed in the effort to overcome the limitations of membership in a professional group. The education required in certain professions is then genuinely considered a privilege, chiefly by those who benefit from that privilege. In societies freed of poverty and class barriers, it has become generally accepted that gaining the kind of qualifications that allow one to work creatively in a given field is less a matter of personality and primarily one of motivation, which is a socially determined factor. In a totalitarian state, the road to education is encumbered by artificial barriers and to overcome them, one is dependent on anonymous forces. Applicants for any type of education whatsoever beyond the official school-leaving age are subjected to an unmonitorable selection process that goes against common sense and human dignity.

The callousness with which totalitarian power takes revenge on the least expression of disobedience by educated people is, of course, natural in its own way. Let us not deny totalitarian power human feelings! In a sense the apparatus is a living organism consisting of a number of people. It is well known that such groups sometimes behave according to rules similar to those governing human behaviour. Totalitarian power delights in paternalism. Let us imagine it for the moment in the role of an old-fashioned, authoritative patriarch who is deeply convinced that he only wants the best for his children and even provides them with higher education, which costs money, after all. When all he gets in return is ingratitude, what does he do in his righteous wrath? He disinherits them. But how can those who are disinherited conclude – or insist – that the job of which they have been robbed can be done by anyone when this, along with a lot of slander, is precisely what is being broadcast by the one who took the job away in the first place? The realization that a free intellectual comes to awareness by reflecting on his or her position and on the equality of people, is turned against the unfree intellectual in a caricatured form. The ability of totalitarian power to transform any insight of free people into an indictment and use it against those who were meant to make fruitful use of it has been demonstrated many times over, and it always throws society backwards through a whole state of evolution.

Among the signatories of Charter 77 and those who take part in its activities, workers' professions are represented very modestly. This is because workers are cut off far more effectively from information, and the repression of their right of assembly cripples them far more as citizens than it does other groups. Their profession can usually be practised only in large plants where they cannot escape surveillance, and in the form of small-scale free enterprise, which evades all government control but which can only serve customer ends. The absence of civil rights and the disarray of the shortage economy are two ends of the same stick, which is used against those who are holding it in the middle. Industrial workers have become small businessmen without ceasing to be workers. They cannot formulate a position, and the only way they can respond to their lack of rights is by trying to sell their labour as dearly as possible. Without the slightest support from the unions, they have brought pressure on wages and prices – which under the circumstances is economically quite considerable, and definitely bears comparison with the pressure brought to bear by trade union organizations in countries where union rights are respected. As producers and consumers, they have created a situation in which there is a double market, of which the second, i.e., the shadow labour market – chiefly in the area of services – has become so significant that society could not function without it.

Independent political scientists are sometimes critical of the conformity of people who have fully adjusted to the consumer society. However, they overlook the fact that when people like this are cut off from coherent information and stop listening to government appeals, the regime is confronted with several unalterable realities, none of which can be changed with the instruments of control at its disposal. This means, effectively, that a considerable portion of the economy, which the regime would like to govern absolutely, has effectively escaped its control. For this reason, moral critiques of consumerism in Czechoslovakia usually have very limited appeal. Today, no one can say with certainty that this ignoble form of resistance may not, every day and every hour, damage the apparatus of total power far more effectively than the efforts of those who think of their positions in ethical terms, and whose civic dissent is expressed through non-conformist cultural activities.

The combination of a consumer society, a shortage economy and totalitarian centralism, however, provides rather horrifying prospects for the future. A consumer who has no rights is in many ways more objectionable than one who does. Yet when people's social function, under the threat of repression, has been reduced to earning money and spending it, the way the rulers treat them has an effect on their behaviour. Consumers may not appear to be the embodiment of courage but, at the same time, they do not accept all the humiliation as apathetically as it would seem. They behave according to a norm that approximately reproduces the moral foundation of totalitarian power, based on the principle of taking maximum advantage of a momentary superiority; at the same time, however, they live in a constant state of provisionality, and they do not accept what fills their daily lives as a new code, but as an undesirable digression from the norm. In any case, 1968 showed how superficial the norms of totalitarian behaviour were, and how easily and 'naturally' quite opposite norms took hold. Society did not have to make these norms on its own; they merely had to be 'recalled'.

These attitudes of people who are utterly immersed in the consumer society, on the one hand, and of Charter 77 on the other, represent two quite contradictory ways of dealing with the pressures of totalitarian power. There are certainly many more such ways. For the time being at least, all the others represent only a wide range of possibilities stretching between these two outer limits. Official 'culture' has nothing to say to these pure consumers, who are one of the largest elements in society. Yet I think it is worth remembering that Charter 77 has nothing to say to them either. The barrier separating the two groups from each other has been hardened by totalitarian conditions to the point where it is almost impenetrable, and activities of quite a different sort will be necessary to overcome such an obstacle. Charter 77 has neither anticipated nor prepared for such a struggle, because in doing so it would abandon the aim it set itself, thus leaving a vacuum behind it. The Charter must nevertheless reflect on the situation I have indicated here and be aware that its role, and its determination to maintain this role, is all the more important because it is not a universal role, but a partial one – and that, therefore, nothing can take its place.

# 11 On not living in hatred*

## Josef Zvěřina

*To my friends and enemies*

In its diagnosis of our situation, Charter 77 revealed the pathological symptoms of the diseases of power and lying. It is possible
that in the midst of tribulations and struggles, the symptoms of
another malady to which the Charter pointed indirectly have
receded in our awareness: I refer to the disease of hate. By virtue of
its creation and survival, as well as its entire meaning and mission,
the Charter was an act which indicated a cure for this disease, and by
actually having overcome hatred itself, the Charter showed the path
to unity. This aspect of the Charter has not been stressed sufficiently. Nevertheless, I believe it to be fundamental, and an indication of how we may identify the deeper roots of our poverty, with a
view to transforming ourselves individually and collectively, and
providing a remedy to society's ills. This is a matter which falls
outside the scope of the Charter, but is one of humanity's fundamental problems: the quest for inner unity.

It is because of this character of the Charter that, in accordance
with my Christian beliefs, I signed it and why I take the Charter as
my launching pad for a campaign against hate. Charter 77 is a
statement of belief in humanity which, for a Christian, naturally
entails a belief in God. 'How can a man who does not love the
brother he can see, love God whom he has never seen?' (1 John: 4,
20b). However, the Charter is not, significantly, a compromise
between world outlooks, between atheists and believers, between
rival political parties, or between inner-party cliques. Nor, for that
matter, is it the 'historical compromise' of which Pope Paul VI and
the Italian Communist Party used to speak. The expression
'historical compromise' can, after all, have three meanings: a
compromise which is a definite historical event; a compromise as a
mutual agreement at a given moment in time; or a compromise

---

* Translated by A. G. Brain.

which is the natural outcome of historical developments. By none of these criteria is Charter 77 a compromise.

It was created in a spirit of *partnership* and supra-party unity, as the outcome of an incorruptible quest for truth. Thus it goes much further than any compromise, since it expresses what is truly common along the broad spectrum of views represented by the signatories. The very fact that Charter 77 was the child of joint reflection and courage, of a love of freedom, truth and justice – seen as an expression of unity and human community – is an historic event in this fragmented world. Thus, in a sense, the Charter is a sign of the times. But sceptics voice doubts in the form of the 'political' question: 'What support does it enjoy here and abroad?' And here and abroad both friends and opponents give the same reply: a handful of intellectuals. Regardless of the fact that this is just not so, and recalling that one of our traditional watchwords has been the Hussites' 'The numbers matter naught!', the greatest support the Charter enjoys is something called Truth. This factor has united an extremely mixed group of signatories with the incalculable numbers of those, i.e., the *de facto* majority of the nation, who overtly or covertly agree with it and support it.

At the same time, it has received the unwitting support of those who unleashed the infamous campaign against it. They placed at its disposal all the mass media under their absolute control: a facility that the 250 or so signatories would never normally enjoy. They publicized the Charter with the assistance of the entire bureaucracy, something that even the most optimistic signatories never dreamt was possible. Indeed, what the signatories had expected was a deathly silence or silencing by force. By every crude act on their part, the opponents of the Charter helped raise a wave of sympathy both here and abroad. Imprisonment, surveillance and other imaginative expressions of police diligence only served to create new links for us: so intimate that the police will try in vain to detect and destroy them; so lively that they are managing to arouse young people from the lethargy of normalization. In opposition to the Charter, then, there is an 'unqualified' majority of the nation. How numerous it is is hard to say. We must include in this 'unqualified' majority the timid and careful – their reactions are quite understandable – but also, and above all, the apathetic and indifferent. The latter are a very dangerous and even apocalyptic phenomenon: 'because you are lukewarm, neither cold nor hot, I will spit you out of my mouth' (Rev.: 3, 16).

The sceptical ask: What has the Charter achieved? Hasn't it in fact made matters worse? Couldn't we have waited to find another way? There is no easy answer to these questions, above all because they tend to be framed in the conditional (What would have happened if. . .?). What ought to be or ought not to be, our dear Hamlets do not know, however. Therefore, it makes more sense to ask what *has* been done by those whom the Charter roused; or similarly, what has *not* been done by those who agreed with the Charter, but have yet to take the plunge. Thus, it is not so important who are the *actual* supporters of the Charter, but who are its *potential* supporters.

The Charter has become a sounding board for people's hidden aspirations for freedom, truth and unity, and not only for our people here but also for people throughout the world. The Charter not only listed the misdeeds of our regime. It also provided a warning and an example which transcends national frontiers and whose significance is not restricted to the moment in time when it was written. And I suspect that that is how it was understood by people abroad. But Charter 77 has also aroused scandal and protest. Pharisees of various denominations are scandalized. They are scandalized by the unity of communists and non-communists, atheists and Christians. One would have expected that it would have been the Communist Party rather than the Christians who would be scandalized. (Although it is the case that leading representatives of Christianity around the world have welcomed the Charter and defended its signatories.)

So as to atone for those Christians who were scandalized, I would like to say a few words here about the 'ex-communists' and atheists in the ranks of the Charter. I am not acquainted with all the twenty schools of Marxism identified by Guenther Bartsch in 1970. I have to stick to communism as we have observed and experienced it here ourselves.

In the Nazi concentration camps, suffering and resistance to the monstrous ideology of Nazism united communists and non-communists alike. The communists constituted well-organized groups with clear ideas but which were often cruelly exclusive, I am afraid to say. When the Second World War was over, a section of those former inmates started to construct in this country, according to an old blueprint, a form of totalitarian regime foreign to us, together with a new generation of concentration camps destined initially for the non-communists but, in the end, for communists as well. As I was to see with my own eyes, the communists of the 'Slánský gang' were treated very badly.* Those who escaped the gallows were worse off than the rest of us, both outwardly and inwardly. They were even beaten up by the criminal elements among whom they found themselves, because the concept of political prisoner had been abolished (thanks partly to them), and so we were all just 'common criminals'.

At that time in our prisons, dialogue with the communists was no longer as easy as it had been in the Nazi camps, and their dialogues among themselves were vengeful and bitter. The communists could be divided into three categories: conformists (those faithful to the Stalinist model); reformists (who recognized 'deformations' and the need for redressment); and non-conformists (those who had despaired at communism as such). Nowadays, there is a new version: 'ex-communists'. I am not sure to what extent this description expresses a reality; my intention here is to demonstrate what it was that united and unites them with the non-communists, that is, the Charter. The Charter was not exclusively their achievement, but they are partners in it. They signed what they signed, and not any of the other things slanderously attributed to them.

The unity which was thereby created and which has aroused all the scandal, is built on a simple reality. The discovery was made that people are people whether they belong to the Party or not; that there is more that unites human beings than divides them because of party affiliation or ideological conviction; further, that people are not just an *animal producens et consumens*; that *homo faber* has the right to be a *homo ludens* who is creative in terms of responsible freedom; that *homo sapiens* does exist and therefore always has the right to the truth; that *homo religiosus* is automatically one sort of *homo sapiens*; that religious freedom determined by the needs of state atheism is an absurdity, as absurd as atheism in the form of state directives, state systems, state machinery and state constitutions; and, last but not least, that half-truths, violence and hatred are no

---

* *Editor's note:* Rudolf Slánský was Secretary-General of the Communist Party of Czechoslovakia from 1945-51, and was demoted to Deputy Prime Minister in 1951. In 1952, he was imprisoned and executed, with ten others, on charges of treason. The Slánský trial, together with the Ana Pauker affair in Rumania and the Rajk trial in Hungary, formed part of a wider campaign of Stalinist terror aimed at high Party officials accused of Zionism, 'Jewish bourgeois' origins, collaboration with 'American Imperialism' and 'Titoism'.

basis for any socialist society – nor any society at all, for that matter. That is why I trust these 'communists'.

I do not regard distrust as a solution. I consider it to be deeply un-Christian. There are some who think it wise and courageous to wait in the wings, and who ask me: 'What would these "communists" do if they came to power?' I have no idea. What I do know is what they are doing now, namely, suffering for their 'sins', as well as for the wise and cautious who never thought for one moment to join the struggle against injustice and lies. I would be ashamed to slander these atheists as some Christians do. On the contrary, I thank them for the depth of their conscience and their courage which has frequently given me strength. It is painful for me to admit that seldom have I encountered 'such faith in Israel'.

If we are to understand the *pathology of hate*, which is what I am seeking to do here, it is necessary to trace the genesis of this spiritual malady, identify its forms and symptoms, and search for a 'cure'. It is possibly true to say that throughout the course of our history as a small and vulnerable nation, real hatred was never part of our experience in war or in peace. We have known stormy events, anger, passion and fury; until recently, however, we did not fail, I believe, to show respect for human dignity. After all, a love for the truth has tended to dominate our national character, along with a feeling for the underdog, humour in our dealings with the mighty, coupled with generosity towards the vanquished. What we *do* have, as has been frequently noted, is a tendency towards a mediocrity complex at one extreme and megalomania at the other; either spiritual sloth or shallow fanaticism; either coarseness or a martyr-complex; either slavish, uncritical behaviour or arrogant hyper-criticism.

But until recently, hate in an extreme or pathological form was foreign to us. Until recently, that is. It erupted first of all in the bestial treatment meted out to the Germans, and then to their collaborators. Then the hate was redirected at ideological opponents; then political opponents; then to a fraction of the Czechoslovak Communist Party, and so on. Where did it come from? There was, of course, the terrifying school of Nazism and the cruelty of war. But these cannot be used to excuse all the cruelty, barbarity and hate that followed. The guilt for that lies with everybody – though to varying degrees, of course – and not only with those who actually carried out vile deeds of revenge. The guilt must be shared by those who were then in leading posts in government, the church, the media, the universities and other institutions: they must bear much greater responsibility than those less endowed and worse informed. It could well be that there was a greater proportion of the latter who, in specific cases, opposed the fury.

Unhappily, when the post-war psychosis and passion had died down, hate was once more whipped up and fostered by the socialist governments. It was not of the frenzied variety, but instead was more cold-blooded, premeditated and thorough. Hate became an instrument of political power – particularly after 1948. A whole *ideology of hate* came into being. This ideology justified everything it required; everything was permitted to achieve its success; it encouraged hatred and even required it on occasions. There can be no worse threat than this to human morality and life. While, unhappily, we find hate in various guises all over the world, hate here has its specific features. The education of people into a single permitted ideology creates a much more extensive basis for such hatred. Hate is thereby 'nationalized', as it were. It assumes the most varied forms at every level: regional, district, local, federal and international. In this way, lies, violence and hate become an indissoluble trinity. Each needs the others. Half-truth hates because it is afraid and, because it is afraid, it employs violence. Violence in turn is a power which serves and coexists with hate – and lies are used to excuse it, and so on.

Is there a cure for this pathological hate? Seeing that scepticism and defeatism are no use at all, we have to find one! Violence is no solution to violence, since it merely breeds hate. The only real and lasting power is 'the power of the powerless'. The powerless have no power, either because they have lost it or because their internal 'make-up' has never allowed them to serve it. Or there are those who have never striven for it, or never wanted it. But they are strong. Their strength has a different source than power, but it exists in the world. For Christians, this 'make-up' is the highest moral 'qualification' – Jesus' beatitudes of the Sermon on the Mount: 'Happy are the poor in spirit' (Matt.: 5,3). It is they who have renounced immediate means, preferring a deeper teleology, a broader eschatology and more substantial goals. 'Happy are the gentle, for they shall have the earth for their heritage' (Matt.: 5,5). The gentle will implement the most thoroughgoing, generalized and lasting revolution. They do not conquer the earth, nor dominate it, but instead shall transform it into a heritage for humanity and shall answer for it to God and to the planet's peoples.

Such a universal, holistic, 'planetary' way of thinking, as was

implied philosophically by Heidegger and developed here by
Patočka, is undoubtedly a therapy for hate. Others have found
valuable solutions in other areas. There are philosophical solutions,
in the re-evaluation of values; personal ones, such as concern for the
spiritual, new ways of thinking, and for the details of everyday life;
spiritual/cultural solutions, such as attempts to develop a parallel
culture, parallel structures, and a parallel polis; and there are even
political solutions, evident in new basic concepts of politics in
general, conscious opposition, new types of democracy, and so on.
These solutions also serve as remedies to hate because, as we have
pointed out, lies, violence and hate are interdependent. But the
specific malice of hate, which represents a profound threat to the
world, generates concern and the pursuit of a more specific solution.
This is because hate represents the most absolute division of people
and the most total destruction of unity. Therefore the only way to
counter hate is through a patient and earnest *quest for unity*.

As a citizen of this country, I fully appreciate people's allergic
reaction to this word unity. So it will be necessary for me first to
define the term. Basically speaking, it is impossible to accept the sort
of outward unity which is no more than the unification and
manipulation of people by means of half-truths and lies, in order to
create a uniformity of personal and public expression. This is the
unity of the mass; uniformity of the herd; the fictive 'unity of the
Party and the people'; a unity of fanaticism and passion. It is a type
of unity that provides all the more reason for rejecting the unity
promoted by regimes, under police supervision, with the help of the
administrative bureaucracy, emergy powers, the iron curtain, and
all the other technical innovations of the Golem monster.

The only acceptable unity is internal unity, the free unity of truth,
the unity of the powerless, of the 'poor in heart', who refuse every
injustice and lawlessness, and hate in every form. But how does one
*achieve* such unity? It will be necessary to seek an answer for each of
the different levels I have so far mentioned.

As far as *ideas* are concerned, the remedy will undoubtedly be
pluralism: serious, responsible pluralism, of course, not the sort
that leads to nihilism. The latter has no power to overcome hate,
even when it is itself devoid of hatred. It will entail belief in the
possibility of truth, freedom and justice combined with the courage
to achieve them – under the constant gaze of one's opponents.

In the field of *morality*, there will be a need for respecting
humanity and people's inalienable dignity; believing in humankind

and the meaning of life; making a virtue of hope, spiritual energy and the eschatological striving for a higher good.

*Everyday life* will require the assertion of tolerance. Pluralism and tolerance are both paths or methods – a unity of means and ends, which could even eventually provide a basis for a new concept of politics.

Lastly, there is the need for a sort of 'international conspiracy' against hate and violence. This ought to pervade all our human dealings and thinking. What is required is a universal purge, a radical conversion of hearts.

What is the real guiding principle of unity, though? For that question I have only a Christian answer. To begin with, I would quote S. Averintsev who, in the fifth volume of the *Filosofskaya entsiklopedia* (Moscow 1970), and under the heading 'Christianity', writes: 'Love, which is regarded ontologically in Christianity as the essence of the godhead, is advanced from the ethical point of view as the supreme commandment. It forms the basis of the Christian social utopia. . . . The idea is that each member of society should, out of love, assume the burden of social disharmony on themselves individually and thereby alter it – "redeem" it.' However this requires the Christian *agape*, which does not separate people into friends and enemies, 'which vaunteth not itself' (I Cor.:13,5), and which combines extreme selflessness and extreme unworldliness. (Compare Matt.: 5,34). Hence it calls for the rejection of 'love' in the sense of personal interest (Luke: 14,26); it is a demand for one to overcome self. In place of belonging to some national, ethnic, family or other body, Christianity proposes the ideal of 'universal openness'.

Christianity does indeed know about the supreme principle of all being and has faith in its power to unite humanity, and has a name for it: it calls it *agape*. This is the very 'substance' of God, and thus of humanity too; it is not just an 'ethical characteristic'. Christianity owes its greatness to it – as well as to its shame on those occasions when it has betrayed it. Although it may have been profaned on many an occasion, it is necessary to reiterate that word again and again. This is already happening, even outside Christian theology. But it is not so much the word, as the reality that counts! It is necessary to elevate this principle and highlight it once more, to dust it off and reinstate it to the place always known to, and still acknowledged by, the great thinkers who conceivably are familiar with every religion on earth. It must be made a foundation stone of the future world we are to create. It is our task to seek to enact it at every level of existence if we are not to build in vain.

Truth must be integrated with love; morality is not whole without it. Love is the greatest strength of the powerless. Unity founded on love will never be coercion; power guided by love will never be violence. Love is all-powerful and will even overcome hatred. And only love can do this! The people of the future will be *homo dilectionis*, 'people of love'. Love has always been part of our make-up but, until now, we have never realized it. 'My military commanders never understood the meaning of love', said the 'strategist' of the modern spirit, Antoine de Saint-Exupery. The highest throne is destined not for 'pure reason' but 'pure love'.

Scepticism and defeatism will not help us. They are the fifth column of violence, and an internal ally of hate. The fact that I attribute the principle of the new human being to the biblical *agape* should not provoke doubt in others, for this principle is not solely a biblical expression but a universal idea. Those who cannot accept it will have to find another expression; the task and goals are none the less identical. Solzhenitsyn's 'not living a lie' and Havel's 'living in truth', not to mention 'the power of the powerless', are just as much biblical expressions. Naturally, there are other exponents of *agape* and powerful opponents of hate. The same terms are employed by the Russian orthodox priest Dudkov in Moscow. Pastor Wurmbrand, the martyr of the Romanian jailors, heroically warns against hating the communists. Then there is Archbishop Helder Camara, a fighter against fascist dictators in Latin America and elsewhere. We need a 'crusade against violence' as Prior Roger Schuetz of Taize puts it in other words. And, as Pope John Paul II proclaimed on 1st November, 1979:

By expressing everything in terms of power, group interests and class struggle, as well as in terms of the friend – enemy concept, we pave the way for social exclusiveness, disrespect, hatred and terrorism and their covert or overt supporters. On the other hand, there is readiness to listen and understand, respect for others, consideration which in reality means strength, and trust, all of which flow from hearts which have been won for the greatest good of peace.

The words of these people are substantiated in deeds and blood, so our struggle against hate is not lost. We recall in this connection Maksymilian Kolbe, who willingly laid down his life to save the father of a family. He was just one of the victims of Nazi hate. I add to their names my memory of Father Josef Šterberk who, of his own free will, asked to be shot along with his parishioners at Lidice, as well as the victims of the absurd, anti-religious hate propaganda in Czechoslovakia in the 1950s: the martyred Father Toufar, Bishop Gojdič, the Jesuit Father Kajpr, the priest Antonín Mandl, and many other priests and lay people. Drops in the ocean? That doubt has been answered by that 'specialist' of active love and non-bureaucratic aid, Mother Teresa – who has saved thousands of people from dying in India – when she said: 'But without that drop, the ocean would not be full.'

Such people are a light in the darkness of hate. Without them, we are lost. With them, we all know what is the right course. There is a need not only for greater or lesser deeds but, above all, for a radical 'change of course', for a new direction. Hate is capable of cruel bravery. We must display still greater courage and still greater love. 'Anyone who is afraid has not attained to love in its perfection' (I John: 4,18).

# Appendix

## Charter 77 Declaration*

In the Czechoslovak Register of Laws No. 120 of 13 October 1976, texts were published of the International Covenant on Civil and Political Rights, and of the International Covenant on Economic, Social and Cultural Rights, which were signed on behalf of our republic in 1968, reiterated at Helsinki in 1975 and came into force in our country on 23 March 1976. From that date our citizens have enjoyed the rights, and our state the duties, ensuing from them.

The human rights and freedoms underwritten by these Covenants constitute features of civilized life for which many progressive movements have striven throughout history, and whose codifiction could greatly assist humane developments in our society.

We accordingly welcome the Czechoslovak Socialist Republic's accession to those agreements.

Their publication, however, serves as a powerful reminder of the extent to which basic human rights in our country exist, regrettably, on paper alone.

The right to freedom of expression, for example, guaranteed by article 19 of the first-mentioned Covenant, is in our case purely illusory. Tens of thousands of our citizens are prevented from working in their own fields for the sole reason that they hold views differing from official ones, and are discriminated against and harassed in all kinds of ways by the authorities and public organizations. Deprived as they are of any means to defend themselves, they become victims of a virtual apartheid.

Hundreds of thousands of other citizens are denied that 'freedom from fear' mentioned in the preamble to the first Covenant, being condemned to the constant risk of unemployment or other penalties if they voice their own opinions.

---

* *Editor's note:* On 7 January 1977, a call for civil and human rights to be respected in Czechoslovakia was issued in Prague. Published on 1 January 1977, the declaration and the informal association of its supporters were titled Charter 77. The text of the Declaration is reproduced here in full.

In violation of article 13 of the second-mentioned Covenant, guaranteeing everyone the right to education, countless young people are prevented from studying because of their own views or even their parents'. Innumerable citizens live in fear of their own, or their children's right to education being withdrawn if they should ever speak up in accordance with their convictions.

Any exercise of the right to 'seek, receive and impart information and ideas of all kinds, regardless of frontiers, either orally, in writing or in print' or 'in the form of art' specified in Article 19, clause 2 of the first Covenant is followed by extra-judicial and even judicial sanctions, often in the form of criminal charges as in the recent trial of young musicians.

Freedom of public expression is inhibited by the centralized control of all the communication media and of publishing and cultural institutions. No philosophical, political or scientific view or artistic activity that departs ever so slightly from the narrow bounds of official ideology or aesthetics is allowed to be published; no open criticism can be made of abnormal social phenomena; no public defence is possible against false and insulting charges made in official propaganda; the legal protection against 'attacks on honour and reputation' clearly guaranteed by article 17 of the first Covenant is in practice non-existent; false accusations cannot be rebutted and any attempt to secure compensation or correction through the courts is futile; no open debate is allowed in the domain of thought and art. Many scholars, writers, artists and others are penalized for having legally published or expressed, years ago, opinions which are condemned by those who hold political power today.

Freedom of religious confession, emphatically guaranteed by article 18 of the first Covenant, is continually curtailed by arbitrary official action; by interference with the activity of churchmen, who are constantly threatened by the refusal of the state to permit them the exercise of their functions, or by the withdrawal of such permission; by financial or other transactions against those who express their religious faith in word or action; by constraints on religious training, and so forth.

One instrument for the curtailment or, in many cases, complete elimination of many civic rights is the system by which all national institutions and organizations are in effect subject to political directives from the machinery of the ruling party and to decisions made by powerful individuals.

The Constitution of the Republic, its laws and legal norms do not regulate the form or content, the issuing or application of such decisions; they are often only given out verbally, unknown to the public at large and beyond its powers to check; their originators are responsible to no one but themselves and their own hierarchy; yet they have a decisive impact on the decision-making and executive organs of government, justice, trade unions, interest groups and all other organizations, of the other political parties, enterprises, factories, institutions, offices and so on, for whom these instructions have precedence even before the law.

Where organizations or individuals, in the interpretation of their rights and duties, come into conflict with such directives, they cannot have recourse to any non-party authority, since none such exists. This constitutes, of course, a serious limitation of the right ensuing from articles 21 and 22 of the first-mentioned Covenant, which provides for freedom of association and forbids any restriction on its exercise; from article 25 on the right to take part in the conduct of public affairs, and from article 26 stipulating equal protection by the law without discrimination.

This state of affairs likewise prevents workers and others from exercising the unrestricted right to establish trade unions and other organizations to protect their economic and social interests, and from freely enjoying the right to strike provided for in clause 1 of article 8 in the second-mentioned Covenant.

Further civil rights, including the explicit prohibition of 'arbitrary interference with privacy, family, home or correspondence' (article 17 of the first Covenant), are seriously vitiated by the various forms of interference in the private life of citizens exercised by the Ministry of the Interior, for example, by bugging telephones and houses, opening mail, following personal movements, searching homes, setting up networks of neighbourhood informers (often recruited by illicit threats or promises), and in other ways.

The Ministry frequently interferes in employers' decisions, instigates acts of discrimination by authorities and organizations, brings weight to bear on the organs of justice and even orchestrates propaganda campaigns in the media. This activity is governed by no law and, being clandestine, affords citizens no chance of defending themselves.

In cases of prosecution on political grounds the investigative and judicial organs violate the rights of those charged and of those defending them, as guaranteed by article 14 of the first Covenant and, indeed, by Czechoslovak law. The prison treatment of those sentenced in such cases is an affront to their human dignity and a menace to their health, being aimed at breaking their morale.

Clause 2, article 12 of the first Covenant, guaranteeing every citizen the right to leave the country, is consistently violated, or under the pretence of 'defence of national security' is subjected to various unjustifiable conditions (clause 3). The granting of entry visas to foreigners is also treated arbitrarily, and many are unable to visit Czechoslovakia merely because of professional or personal contacts with those of our citizens who are subject to discrimination.

Some of our people – either in private, at their places of work or by the only feasible public channel, the foreign media – have drawn attention to the systematic violation of human rights and democratic freedoms and demanded amends in specific cases. But their pleas have remained largely ignored or been made grounds for police investigation.

Responsibility for the maintenance of civil rights in our country naturally devolves in the first place on the political and state authorities. Yet not only on them: everyone bears his or her share of responsibility for the conditions that prevail and accordingly also for the observance of legally enshrined agreements, binding upon all individuals as well as upon governments.

It is this sense of co-responsibility, our belief in the importance of its conscious public acceptance and the general need to give it new and more effective expression, that led us to the idea of creating Charter 77, whose inception we today publicly announce.

Charter 77 is a loose, informal and open association of people of various shades of opinions, faiths and professions united by the will to strive individually and collectively for the respecting of civil and human rights in our own country and throughout the world – rights accorded to all people by the two mentioned international Covenants, by the Final Act of the Helsinki conference and by numerous other international documents opposing war, violence and social or spiritual oppression, and which are comprehensively laid down in the United Nations Universal Declaration of Human Rights.

Charter 77 springs from a background of friendship and solidarity among people who share our concern for those ideals that have inspired, and continue to inspire, their lives and their work.

Charter 77 is not an organization; it has no rules, permanent bodies or formal membership. It embraces everyone who agrees with its ideas and participates in its work. It does not form the basis for any oppositional political activity. Like many similar citizen initiatives in various countries, West and East, it seeks to promote the general public interest.

It does not aim, then, to set out its own platform of political or social reform or change, but within its own field of impact to conduct a constructive dialogue with the political and state authorities, particularly by drawing attention to individual cases where human and civil rights are violated, to document such grievances and suggest remedies, to make proposals of a more general character calculated to reinforce such rights and machinery for protecting them, to act as intermediary in situations of conflict which may lead to violation of rights, and so forth.

By its symbolic name, Charter 77 denotes that it has come into being at the start of a year proclaimed as Political Prisoners' Year – a year in which a conference in Belgrade is due to review the implementation of the obligations assumed at Helsinki.

As signatories, we hereby authorize Professor Dr Jan Patoçka, Václav Havel and Professor Jiţí Hájek to act as the spokespersons for the Charter. These spokespersons are endowed with full authority to represent it *vis-à-vis* state and other bodies, and the public at home and abroad, and their signatures attest the authenticity of documents issued by the Charter. They will have us and others who join us as their colleagues, taking part in any necessary negotiations, shouldering particular tasks and sharing every responsibility.

We believe that Charter 77 will help to enable all the citizens of Czechoslovakia to work and live as free human beings.

# Notes on
# Czechoslovak contributors

**Rudolf Battěk** is a leading representative of the democratic socialist opposition and human rights movement in Czechoslovakia. He was born in 1924 in Bratislava. During the war he was trained as a fitter mechanic, and after the war he worked briefly as an office employee. After graduating from university he held various economic posts and again worked as a manual labourer. Between 1965–9 he was employed at the Institute of Sociology of the Czechoslovak Academy of Sciences. There he published numerous sociological essays and four books. In 1968 he was one of the founders of the citizens' initiative, the Club of Committed Non-Party members (*KAN*) and became a deputy of the Czech National Council (the parliament of Bohemia and Moravia). In 1969, after petitioning the authorities on the first anniversary of the Soviet invasion of Czechoslovakia, he was deprived of parliamentary immunity, arrested and charged with subversion of the Republic. He was released in October 1970. He was again arrested in 1971 and sentenced to three-and-a-half years' imprisonment for participating in a leaflet campaign urging the public not to vote in the 1971 elections. After completing his term of imprisonment he worked briefly as a lathe operator and as a cleaner of shop windows. He has never been a member of any political party; in 1978 he co-founded the Charter 77 'Independent Socialists' group, which supports the programme of the Socialist International. He was a Charter 77 spokesperson in 1980 and a founding member of the Committee for the Defence of the Unjustly Prosecuted (*VONS*). His *Essays From an Island* (a collection of political and philosophical treatises written from Ruzyně prison) was published in *samizdat* in 1977. In June 1980, he was again arrested and imprisoned. After more than a year in detention, he was convicted of subversion of the Republic and sentenced, after an appeal, to five-and-a-half years' imprisonment, which he is still serving. According to the state authorities, his criminal act consisted of his correspondence with Willi Brandt, Olof Palme, Bruno Kreisky, and others within the Socialist International, his participation in the activities of Charter 77 and *VONS*, and his contribution to the Czechoslovak original of this volume. On the occasion of his sixtieth birthday in November 1984, and following a European-wide Charter 77 appeal, the socialist parties of Italy and France demanded his early release from prison; he was also offered political asylum in France by the Mitterand government.

**Václav Benda** was born in Prague in 1946. He graduated from the Philosophical Faculty of Charles University where, in 1968, he was chairperson of the Academic Council of Students. After obtaining his doctorate in 1974 for a study of Ladislav Klíma, he worked briefly as an assistant university lecturer. He was dismissed from that post for political reasons, and after a short period of unemployment, he enrolled in the Faculty of Mathematics and Physics. After graduation, he worked as a mathematician and computer programmer. He signed Charter 77 following a virulent press campaign against its signatories. Because of this action, he again lost his job, and was forced to work as a stoker in the Hotel Meteor in Prague. He is a member of *VONS*. He was a Charter 77 spokesperson from February 1979 until his arrest in May of that year. During the 1960s, he occasionally published poems or literary reviews and, in the 1970s, he published theoretical articles on mathematics and applied logic. He has also published a novel in *samizdat, Black Girl*, as well as various political essays. He was arrested in May 1979 together with nine other members of *VONS*, charged with subversion of the Republic, and sentenced to four years' imprisonment. Since his release, he has had only occasional employment, and is still looking for a full-time job. Václav Benda is a Catholic and, during 1984, he was a Charter 77 spokesperson.

**Václav Černý** was born in 1905 in Jizbice, near Náchod. After studying at home and abroad, he qualified as a lecturer in comparative studies at the University of Geneva, where he taught until 1936. From 1930–4 he was also Secretary at the Institute of Slavic Studies in Geneva. He began lecturing at the Philosophical Faculty of Charles University in 1936, and during 1938-9 he was Professor at the University of Brno. As scholar and critic, and editor and publisher of the pre-1948 periodical *Critical Monthly*, he is among the most eminent living personalities in Czech cultural life. He has written a series of outstanding studies of classical Czech literature and its relationship to western literary traditions, and he also takes a keen interest in modern Czech literature. His unofficially published works on Kolar, Hrabal and Prochazka are regarded widely as an invaluable contribution to the understanding of Czech cultural life. His memoirs comprise several volumes; the section dealing with the war and the resistance movement has been published separately under the title, *The Tears of the Crown of Bohemia*. In 1945, he became a member of the first Czech National Council. On account of his critical approach to Czech cultural and political life, he was imprisoned towards the end of the Second World War, again in the early 1950s, and is today prevented by the state authorities from teaching or publishing freely. Václav Černy was among the very first signatories of Charter 77. He has been awarded honorary doctorates from several French universities, and is a member of the Royal Spanish Academy.

**Jiří Hájek** was born in 1913 in Krhanice near Prague. He graduated in the Faculty of Law in Prague in 1937. He was active in the progressive students' movement from 1932 and in the Social Democratic Youth movement from 1933. During the Nazi occupation of Czechoslovakia he was imprisoned for five years in a concentration camp. After the war, he participated in the establishment of the World Federation of Democratic Youth. He also spent a brief period as Secretary of the Central Council of the Workers' Academy. From 1947, he was a university lecturer; from 1949 until 1955 he was professor of the history of the international workers' movement and of international relations. He joined the Communist Party of Czechoslovakia in 1948 when the Czechoslovak Social Democrats merged with the Communists, and remained a member until his expulsion in 1969. He was in the diplomatic service from 1955 to 1965, and was ambassador to Britain between 1955 and 1958. He was Minister of Education from 1965 to 1968, and in 1968 was appointed Minister of Foreign Affairs. He resigned after the Soviet invasion, after which he was employed in the international relations section of the Czechoslovak Academy of Sciences. He was forced to retire and in 1976 was stripped of his membership of the Academy. He was among the first three spokespersons of Charter 77, a position he again held during 1979–80. His publications include *Between Yesterday and Today* (1947), *Munich* (1958) and numerous short articles and essays. His frequent *samizdat* articles, some of which are reprinted in the Rome-based émigré journal, *Listy*, concentrate mainly on questions of international relations and peace.

**Václav Havel** was born in Prague in 1936 and went to school there. After military service, he embarked on a career at the then renowned Theatre of the Balustrade in Prague, working as a stage hand, lighting person, administrative assistant, assistant director, play-reader, dramaturge and, finally, as resident playwright. He was already publishing essays in a theatre magazine in the 1950s, before the success of his first play, *The Garden Party* (1963). *The Memorandum* (1965) was staged all over the world, including in London and New York. Among several subsequent plays are *The Increased Difficulty of Concentration* (1968), an adaptation of *The Beggar's Opera* (1976), *The Mountain Hotel* (1976), and two short autobiographical plays, *Audience* and *Private View* (1976) shown on BBC television in 1978 as *Sorry. . . .* A third one-act play, *Protest*, was staged at the National Theatre in London in 1980. Since 1969 the Czechoslovak authorities have prohibited publication or performance of Havel's work. In 1977 he was arrested and jailed for four months for his Charter 77 activities. In 1979, together with nine fellow members of *VONS*, a group working for the protection of democratic rights, Havel was again convicted and sentenced to four-and-a-half years in prison. After an international protest campaign, and owing to his extreme ill health, his sentence was suspended in early 1983. He is presently under surveillance by the state authorities and he could, if the authorities so wished, be returned to prison at any time to serve the remaining ten months of his sentence. Václav Havel has received numerous literary awards, including the prestigious American Obie Prize (1968 and 1970), and he holds honorary doctorates from York University (Toronto, Canada) and the University of Toulouse, France. His most recent works include a play, *Largo desolato* (1984), and a book of letters written from prison.

**Ladislav Hejdánek** was born in Prague in 1927. He matriculated from a grammar school in the Vinohrady district of Prague, and later studied mathematics for two years at the Faculty of Natural Science at Charles University. He transferred to the Philosophical Faculty where he acquired his doctorate in 1952. After graduating, he worked as an unskilled labourer and then as a concreting specialist in the building industry. After completing his compulsory two years' military service in 1956, he started work in the documentation department of the Institute of Epidemiology and Microbiology. At that time he began to publish articles in journals and magazines such as *Vesmír, Křesťanská Revue, Plamen, Tvář* and *Slovenské Pohlady*. In the years 1968–9, he became a founding member of the Society for Human Rights, convenor of the preparatory committee of the Ecumenical Movement of Intellectuals and Students, and a member of several editorial boards. In mid 1968, he was the first non-Marxist to be offered employment at the Philosophical Institute of the Czechoslovak Academy of Sciences. He was dismissed from that post in March 1971. Since then he has worked as a nightwatchman, porter and a stoker. He is an active member of the Evangelical Church of the Czech Brethren. In 1972 he was arrested and sentenced for alleged incitement to 9 months' imprisonment; following an amnesty, the remainder of his sentence was suspended. He was one of the first signatories of Charter 77. Following the death of Professor Jan Patočka in March 1977, he became a Charter 77 spokesperson, a position he again held during 1979–80. Philosophically speaking, Ladislav Hejdánek belongs to the Masaryk-Radl school and is a pupil of J.B. Kozak and Jan Patočka. He currently runs an unofficial philosophical seminar in Prague. He presently suffers from a serious spinal illness. In 1984, his disability pension was suddenly withdrawn, and he has since that time been forced to work as an accounting clerk in a Prague warehouse.

**Miroslav Kusý** was born in Bratislava in 1931. He commenced his studies at the School of Political and Economic Sciences in Prague, then transferred to the Faculty of Philosophy at Charles University, from which he graduated in 1954; he gained the title Candidate of Science in 1964. Between 1957 and 1971, he was an Assistant Professor, and later a Professor in the

Faculty of Philosophy at the Comenius University in Bratislava. Owing to his unorthodox political stance, he was forced to leave the university. Thereafter, and until 1976, he was employed at the Institute of Journalism in that city. He was dismissed from that post for 'organizational' reasons. After signing Charter 77 (one of the few people in Bratislava to do so) he was promptly dismissed from his new employment in the Bratislava University Library. In recent years, he has had various manual jobs, and he presently works as an urban sociologist for the Architectural Office of Bratislava. Kusý was a member of the Czechoslovak Communist Party from 1952 to 1970; in 1968–9, he held the post of Director of the Ideological Department of the Party. In addition to academic papers, essays and reviews, he is the author of several books, including *The Marxist Theory of Knowledge* (1962), *Art and Cognition* (1963), *The Philosophy of Politics* (1967) and *Marxist Philosophy*. He is also a fine *feuilleton* writer, and his *samizdat* essays are reprinted regularly in such émigré journals as *Listy* and *Svedectvi*; one of his most recent and important contributions, 'Hostages of the Superpowers', is a penetrating critical commentary on the deployment of nuclear weapons in both halves of Europe.

**Jiří Ruml** was born in 1925 in Pilsen. He worked briefly as a clerk and then as an official of the regional Communist Party Secretariat responsible for administering culture. In 1946 he moved to Prague, working first as a proofreader and then on Czechoslovak radio and as a journalist at the Communist Party daily, *Rudé Právo*. Later he worked for two years as a reporter on the Prague evening newspaper, *Večerní Praha*, after which he resumed his work on Czechoslovak radio as a foreign correspondent in a number of posts, including Berlin. Following his return to Czechoslovakia, he became chief editor of political broadcasting. In 1963, he was dismissed for criticizing the slow pace of de-Stalinization in Czechoslovakia; he then did television work, but was dismissed for the same reasons. In 1966, he was one of the founding editors of the Union of Journalists' weekly, *Reportér*. In 1968, he was Chairman of the Prague branch of the Union of Journalists and was elected as a delegate to the extraordinary Party Congress which met in Prague-Vysočany during the Soviet occupation in August 1968. In late 1969 he was expelled from the Communist Party, deprived of his journalistic appointments, and banned from working in his profession. After signing Charter 77 in January 1977, he worked as a crane operator. He was detained in 1979 together with several other members of *VONS*, but was soon released. He was again arrested in May 1981 and charged with subversion of the Republic. He spent thirteen months in detention without trial in Ruzyně prison. Criminal proceedings against him have not been dropped. He writes a large number of topical *feuilletons*, and is also the author of several books based on his experiences as a journalist. Jiří Ruml was spokesperson for Charter 77 during 1984 and, despite a prolonged illness, works as an unskilled construction labourer in Prague.

**Petr Uhl** was born in 1941. After graduating from the Engineering Faculty of the Technical University in Prague, he taught at a secondary technical school. As a school teacher, he participated in student meetings and played a part in initiating the Movement of Revolutionary Youth, whose manifesto he also co-authored. He later founded the Revolutionary Socialist Party (Czechoslovakia). This led to his arrest at the end of 1969. He was sentenced in 1971 to four years in prison in one of the first political trials to be held after the 1968 Soviet invasion. After his release in 1973, he continued to be active politically. He was one of the first signatories of Charter 77, and participated actively in the drafting of its early documents and statements. In 1978, he helped found *VONS*. In May 1979 he was again arrested, together with other members of *VONS*, and sentenced to five years' imprisonment. He was released in May 1984. He presently works as a stoker and continues to be a civil rights activist. In the 1960s, Petr Uhl wrote *Czechoslovakia and Socialism* for his friends; later the book was published in West Germany under the pseudonym Vladimír Skalský. He has also published unofficially a number of political articles, letters and essays, and is the co-author of *Programme for Social Self-Management* (a revised version of which appeared in French as *Socialisme emprisoné*). He has also been an editor of the monthly periodical *Informace O Chartě* since 1978.

**Josef Vohryzek** was born in 1926 in Prague. During the Second World War and for some years after he lived in Sweden, where he worked at various jobs. On returning to Czechoslovakia, he became a student and graduated in 1956 from the Philosophy Faculty of Charles University. He has worked in publishing and in the Czechoslovak Academy of Sciences, and has contributed to many literary journals. In 1959 he was dubbed a revisionist and was banned from engaging in literary criticism; since that time he has devoted himself to translation and, in the 1970s, to publishing in Czech *samizdat* periodicals, especially *Kritický Sborník*. In 1964 he published a short novel, *The Walker*, which also appeared in Polish in a collection of works by Czech and Slovak writers. Since 1972 he has worked as a driver, storeman and nightwatchman, and today he works as a driller and water sampler in an agricultural construction team. He is a signatory of Charter 77.

**Josef Zvěřina** was born in 1913. He studied philosophy and theology in Rome, and archaeology and the history of art in Paris. He concluded his studies in 1948 with a doctorate in theology at Charles Univesity. During the Nazi occupation of Czechoslovakia he was interned by the Gestapo in Zásmuky. In 1952, in the period of Stalinist rule, he was sentenced to twenty-two years' imprisonment, fourteen years of which he served. After 1969 he was deprived of his post at the Faculty of Divinity in Litoměřice and, subsequently, he was also deprived of state consent to conduct pastoral duties. He nevertheless continues to be involved in private pastoral activity, and writes frequently for religious *samizdat* publications. He is a signatory of Charter 77. His published books include *Wall Paintings in Tavant* (in French), *Artistic Work as Device* (1971) and *The Christian in a Socialist State* (1969). He has written a number of articles on theology and on the theme of culture and public life. A collection of these writings has been published in Italian in two volumes: *L'esperienza della Chiessa* (1971) and *Corragio di essere Chiessa* (1978). His latest reflections on Catholic doctrine are presently being published in Italy, West Germany and France.